MUSTANG: The Racing Thoroughbred

MUSTANG:
The Racing Thoroughbred

This is what a typical air start looks like at Reno. Six racers streak for the course as Bob Hoover banks left after telling the pilots: "Gentlemen, you have a race!" Photo Credit: Jim Larsen

Dustin W. Carter & Birch J. Matthews

Schiffer Military History
West Chester, PA.

Acknowledgements

A great many people generously supported our research in ways great and small. Each bit of information, documentation, reminiscence, and photograph aided in weaving the fabric of this history. Each valuable contribution is deeply appreciated and made our task infinitely easier, challenging, and interesting. There is perhaps no way of adequately expressing our gratitude except to hope that each finds a measure of satisfaction in the written narrative which follows. In this context, we gratefully acknowledge the following individuals:

Oliver Aldrich, historian
Bill Ames, engineer
Chuck Aro, photographer
Roger Baggenstoss, engineer
Gerry Balzer, engineer
Roger Besecker, historian
Warren Bodie, historian
Bruce Boland, engineer
Pete Bowers, historian
Walt Boyne, author
Fred Buehl, engineer
Margaret Carter, an inspiration
Al Chute, historian
Diz Dean, engineer
Bill "Tiger" Destefani, race pilot
Carl Friend, engineer
Harry Gann, historian
Al Hansen, photographer
Al Heinike, engineer
Ed Horkey, engineer
Shirley House, manuscript typist
Roger Huntington, historian
Mike Kusenda, historian
Pete Law, engineer
Jim Larsen, engineer
Bob Lawson, photographer
Gerry Liang, photographer
Ed Maloney, historian

Bill Meixner, historian
Mike Nixon, engine rebuilder
Neil Nurmi, photographer
Sharyn Peet, manuscript typist
Dick Phillips, historian
Ray Poe, engineer
J.D. Reed, owner of "Beguine"
John Sandberg, owner of "Tsunami"
Russ Schleeh, race pilot
Lyle Shelton, race pilot
Chris Shih, engineer
Robert Smith, engineer
Emil Strasser, photographer
Jack Sweeney, engineer
Virgil Thompson, engineer
Bruce Treadway, photographer
John Tegler, historian
Tony Yusken, historian
Dave Zeuschel, engine rebuilder

A few final words are in order. First, the completion of this book would never have occurred except for the dedication, determination, and enthusiasm of Dusty's wife of many years, Margaret Carter. She was determined to see this project reach a successful conclusion after her husband died. She understood his love of air racing and in particular, North American's P-51 *Mustang*. Without her support, I would never have been able to attain the final objective.

A second element involved in the final product was Peter Schiffer, the driving force behind Schiffer Publishing. Peter was willing to accept this project in spite of the fact that neither author could point to a prior history of published books. We are both indebted to him for his interest and support.

Book Design by Robert Biondi.

FRONT COVER PHOTO:
E.D. Weiner entered two racing Mustangs in the late 1960s each powered by a Rolls-Royce Merlin. The traditional Rolls emblem is seen on the nose of both of E.D.'s checkerboard P-51s in this photograph. *Photo Credit: Dusty Carter*

REAR COVER PHOTO:
This racing Merlin is built from the rugged Merlin 620 transport engine heads and banks together with a dash 9 crankcase and supercharger. The polished large diameter tube inducts the fuel-air mixture from the supercharger into the engine. *Photo Credit: Jim Larsen*

Published by Schiffer Publishing Ltd.
1469 Morstein Rd.
West Chester, PA 19380
Please write for a free catalog.
This book may be purchased from the publisher.
Please include $2.00 postage.
Try your bookstore first.

Dedication

This book is dedicated to the memory of Dustin Carter, or as he was familiarly called by all of his many friends, "Dusty." It was his inspiration that inaugurated this project and his tireless research and enthusiasm which carried the effort to near conclusion. One imagines he may still be listening for the roar of a mighty Merlin.

Courage is the price that life extracts for granting peace.
The soul that knows it not, knows no release From little things;
Knows not the livid loneliness of fear,
Nor mountain heights where bitter joy can hear
The sound of wings.

– Amelia Earhart Putnam
Courage

Preface

The North American Aviation P-51 *Mustang*, originally developed during 1940 for the British Purchasing Commission, proved a remarkable – some would say the best – fighter aircraft in World War II. It was truly state-of-the-art technology in that era. Some ten years later, it soldiered on at the start of the Korean War. Perhaps even more remarkable is the fact that numerous examples still fly in the hands of sportsman pilots over fifty years after the design was conceived.

Design factors which made the *Mustang* a formidable adversary include adaptation of the Rolls-Royce *Merlin* engine, use of a laminar flow airfoil and a very aerodynamically clean, compact arrangement. The aircraft proved versatile in combat, performing long range escort missions, ground attack roles and, of course, its primary mission of air-to-air combat with opposing fighters.

In the euphoric post-war years of the late 1940s, some of these same qualities made the *Mustang* a prized racing machine for pylon events in the resurrected National Air Races which opened again in Cleveland, Ohio, in September, 1946. Fifteen years following the demise of "big bore" racing in 1949, a new era of pylon racing began near Reno, Nevada. Once again, *Mustangs* were in competition and indeed were the most numerous type to be seen. The same remains true at this writing. Few hearing the thunderous blend of engine noises emanating from a highly tuned *Merlin* in a fast moving *Mustang* ever forget this unique sound. As one unknown Reno race fan once observed, the sound of a flight of *Mustangs* at full bore coming down the straightaway is truly "awesome."

The purpose of this book is to document the evolution of the *Mustang* design from a superb fighter into a premier pylon racer. As noted in the dedication, the inspiration for this subject was derived from Dusty Carter's interest and knowledge of the *Mustang*. In 1986, I received a telephone call from Dusty wanting to know if I would be interested in collaborating on what was to essentially be a photo essay book depicting the racing *Mustang*. Descriptive text would be incorporated in expanded photographic captions. I accepted with enthusiasm. What neither of us anticipated was the amount of material our research would uncover and the degree of cooperation extended by so many people involved in modifying, crewing, and racing P-51s. The project rapidly took on a scope entirely different from what was first envisioned.

Numerous books have treated North American's P-51 *Mustang* as a design, combatant, and to a much lesser extent, that of a racing machine. None have sought to convey the comprehensive, detailed technical considerations behind preparation of the *Mustang* for pylon racing. Lest the reader take flight at this point from the thought of grinding through a sterile recitation of unending formulae and statistical compilations, be aware that this is not the case. Although the text has a technical flavor, it is presented in a manner that should intrigue the layman and technician alike. So come along and enjoy the history of the fastest motor sport in the world as flown with the P-51 *Mustang*.

Birch J. Matthews
Palos Verdes Peninsula, CA
July 1991

Low profile cockpit canopies are employed on many racing Mustangs. Shown here is Jimmy Leeward's interpretation on his semi-stock P-51, "Cloud Dancer." The wings on this Mustang are clipped at the production break and concave custom tips have been added. In addition to a racing engine, Jimmy uses spray bar cooling. Photo Credit: Birch Matthews

Contents

Introduction

There have been numerous books written about North American Aviation's P-51 *Mustang*, most dealing with design, development, and combat operations of this famous fighter. This book touches on *Mustang* design and development, giving the reader insight to the talented people who conceived this aircraft and perhaps why, after more than fifty years, it is still performing magnificently as a racing machine. The primary objective of this book is to describe the racing thoroughbred into which the *Mustang* evolved over the past four plus decades of unlimited air racing.

The sport of air racing started little more than five years after the Wright Brothers were successful at Kittyhawk, North Carolina, in December of 1903. The first international air meet was held in Rheims, France, in August of 1909, thus beginning a long legacy of pylon air racing. This very first meet in France consisted of demonstration flights, air show performances, and closed-course racing. Spectators in attendance had the convenience of viewing stands and all the accouterments and atmosphere of a carnival. A formula or pattern for air shows and races was established that indeed continues today.

The perpetuation and continuity of air racing events has been interrupted over the years by war. However, when fighting ceased, air race programs soon reappeared. After World War I, such events in the United States were dominated by military aircraft designs. In 1929, civilian race plane designers emerged to successfully challenge their military counterparts. This precedent continued through September of 1939, when World War II erupted in Europe. Ironically, it was the European conflict which ultimately led to the creation of the P-51 *Mustang*, a design which after the war would be fashioned into a superb racing machine.

Cleveland, Ohio, became the center of air racing in the pre-World War II era that some fondly remember as the "golden age" of this sport. That short ten year period during the 1930s saw a prolific number of single purpose aircraft designs suited for free-for-all racing. It was an era of individual designers such as Chester, Crosby, the Granville Brothers, Howard, Laird, Rider, the Wedell-Williams team and Wittman, all of whom created unique racing aircraft. After World War II, Cleveland was once again home to air racing, but what a change! Gone were the innovative, classic, one-of-a-kind racers of earlier years. In their place appeared surplus military fighters. In a brief seven years, airframe and engine technology advanced at an exponential rate driven by the urgencies of war. Pre-war racers were instantly obsolete, suitable only as museum pieces with respect to the free-for-all (unlimited) category of racing. The relatively low cost and ready availability of surplus military aircraft easily converted for racing meant the demise of the so-called golden age. Coming full circle, military planes once again dominated the racing scene. The trend continues today.

This book concentrates on one of those ex-World War II fighters: North America's P-51 *Mustang*. The objective here is to describe how the *Mustang* evolved into a thoroughbred racing machine. To accomplish this objective, the narrative first touches on design and development of the military fighter. This provides a foundation upon which the reader may appreciate how attributes of the original configuration built to meet a multitude of operational requirements facilitated design refinements to achieve a single purpose; namely, ground hugging, high-speed pylon racing. That both the original designers and later racing teams were eminently successful is testified to in historical records of World War II as well as racing chronicles from 1946 onward. This is why, after more than fifty years, the *Mustang* is still ever-popular and performing magnificently.

A description of the military P-51 conversion into a racer is presented in general terms, discussing typical modifications made to the airframe. Selected racers are described in more detail with regard to specific changes. Surfacing throughout the narrative is the feeling of the energy and focused dedication brought to bare in seeking the ultimate *Mustang* racer.

In addition to airframe modifications, two subjects seldom discussed except in superficial ways are engine modifications and racing fuels and their additives. Both are treated in detail. In this context, the reader is briefly introduced to the history of the famous Rolls-Royce *Merlin* engine of World War II fame that powered the military *Mustang*. Various engine modifications and operating practices devised to win races are reviewed. No racing powerplant will yield high performance without complimenting fuels and additives concocted to deliver maximum power. The technology of high performance fuels is recounted and major fuel system additives identified which when combined with a highly tuned *Merlin*, point the way toward victory on a racecourse.

Throughout the book, emphasis is placed on technical factors leading to a competitive *Mustang*, explaining what is done and why. Hopefully, this perspective is presented such that non-technical readers will comprehend the essence of these dedicated racing modifications. If this occurs, the authors will have achieved a personal objective and perhaps added to the excitement of your next air race. So read along and discover more about the fabulous *Mustang* and the fascinating history of air racing, the world's fastest motor sport.

Prototype AG345 undergoing weight and balance determination. Photo Credit: NAA via D.W. Carter Collection

PART I
Workhorse to Thoroughbred

MUSTANG! The word evokes different images depending upon one's heritage and passions. To students of the great American Southwest, it can only mean the wild scrub horse native to the Texas plains. To the World War II air combat veteran and aviation enthusiast, it is North American Aviation's P-51 fighter . . .

. . . And to the classic car buff it signifies the jaunty little sport car introduced by Ford Motor Company in March, 1964. All totally different images but, as we shall see, seemingly tied together by historical threads.

The Mustang horse certainly played a major role in the development of Texas, a vital part of the American Southwest. A large bronze statue depicting a herd of these magnificent creatures graces the grounds surrounding the Texas state capital in Austin. Ancestry of the Mustang horse traces back to the admirable steeds brought into Mexico by Spanish conquistadors. As the Spanish horses escaped or were turned out of their Mexican ramadas, they migrated north onto plains of the Southwest where they foraged on meager vegetation and little water. The wild Mustang became a wary and lean animal that Indians and early white settlers found indispensable as mounts for hunting, tracking and cattle herding. As ranchers developed larger spreads, cowboys sought new mounts by crossing Mustangs with other breeds to obtain agile cutting horses so necessary in herding cattle. From cutting horses came the quarter horse used in short quarter mile sprints, providing recreation and entertainment in the otherwise harsh environment in which the cowboy existed. Over the years, quarter horse racing became an important class in "the sport of kings." Its heritage traced to the early cowboy workhorse, the Mustang.

The P-51 fighter aircraft or "pursuit" as it was called during the war, was also a product of the great Southwest, but it owes its name and being to Great Britain. As the Nazi blitzkrieg began to overrun much of Europe, both the British and the French recognized their dire positions. The two countries eventually formed a joint Anglo-French Purchasing Commission chartered to procure war material in the United States. The Purchasing Commission bought nearly everything available even though the task was often encumbered by a need to move cautiously and hesitantly through American neutrality laws.

The French government purchased large numbers of Curtiss Hawk Model 75 fighters, export version of the Army Air Corps P-36. And the British soon procured Curtiss P-40 variants while simultaneously looking for a second production source to meet their ever growing defensive needs. North American Aviation at the time was building trainers for the British. However, the company still had capacity for more work. As a consequence, The British government and North American entered into a contract to build a new fighter that the English would subsequently name the Mustang. Selection of this name was propitious and perhaps demonstrated a British talent for choosing names that withstand the erosion of time. In any event the choice baptized a truly classic design. One wonders if the name was conceived by someone quite familiar with that magnificent horse of the American Southwest in hopes that North American, located in the same region of the country, would produce a product of similar value.

Ford's Mustang, introduced in 1964, was a new class of personal, sport car. It was the beginning of what became known as "pony cars." In marketing the car, Ford christened it Mustang, though ironically, not for the wild horse of Texas. In his autobiography, Lee Iacocca states that:

> *". . . Mustang had been the name of one of the car's prototypes. Curiously, it was not named for the horse but for the legendary World War II fighter plane."[1]*

The Mustang car, like its aeronautical counterpart, is still considered a desirable and classic design. Mustang - be it horse, automobile or airplane - is a name associated with American history. Recent years have added to the Mustang's lore when the aircraft was used to set new world speed records over three and fifteen kilometer courses as well as record speeds at the 1987 Reno National Championship Air Races.

Chapter One
THE WORKHORSE

When the British issued a letter of intent to buy a new design from North American Aviation, Inc. (NAA), no one could have foreseen that it would arguably be the most outstanding fighter aircraft of World War II. This would never have been predicted because North American at that point had produced a grand total of only thirteen fighter planes, the performance of which were inferior to existing first line Army Air Corps Seversky P-35 and Curtiss P-36 aircraft.

The company was well established in the trainer aircraft market, producing these products for both England and Canada as well as other countries. Their early fighter aircraft designs were produced using components from the trainer models. The modified designs utilized larger, more powerful radial engines and were equipped with offensive weapons. Known as model NA-50 series aircraft, seven of the fighters were sold to Peru in 1938. Six more export model NA-50A versions were built for Siam in 1939. With conflict stirring in Europe, the U.S. Army Air Corps appro-

priated these planes before they could be delivered. The machines were subsequently designated P-64s by the Army and used as training aircraft.

North American chief designer, Edgar Schmued, very much wanted to design and build a first rate fighter aircraft. Apparently, it was a feeling shared by James Howard "Dutch" Kindelberger, president of the company. Preliminary design, performance estimates, armament definition and weight estimates were prepared in March, 1940, in anticipation of Dutch Kindelberger's forthcoming sales trip to England. The British were definitely interested. After Kindelberger's return from Great Britain and as the war in Europe escalated, Sir Henry Self, head of the British Purchasing Commission in New York, signed a letter of intent to purchase a North American fighter design – at that time designated the NA-50B. The date was 11 April 1940. From an historical point of view, this was a seminal event as it foreshadowed design and development of what would be-

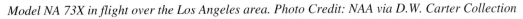

Model NA 73X in flight over the Los Angeles area. Photo Credit: NAA via D.W. Carter Collection

North American Aviation (NAA) Mustang prototype known as Model NA 73X. Photo Credit: NAA via D.W. Carter Collection

come the *Mustang*, a name conferred upon the airplane by the British.

This new design had a Model NA-50 heritage even carrying the NA-50B designation during the early conceptual stage. However, it was quite certainly a unique design, configured to accept the relatively new Allison V-1710 liquid-cooled, twelve-cylinder engine driving a three-blade propeller. The proposed fighter would also utilize an advanced technology laminar flow airfoil section for its wing. Predecessor NA-50 models used the well established National Advisory Committee on Aeronautics (NACA) 23000 series airfoil. This was a popular airfoil series used on the contemporary Lockheed P-38 *Lightning*. It was considered for the North American design as well, to the extent that a backup wing section incorporating this airfoil section was indeed built for wind tunnel testing.

As the new fighter evolved, the designation was changed to NA-73X to reflect the fact that it was a discreet, state-of-the-art design. The creator of the *Mustang* was North American's chief designer, Edgar Schmued. He was supported by a number of very talented people in the North American engineering group. Several key people who contributed heavily to the *Mustang* design and development effort came from the California Institute of Technology

(Caltech). One of the first to become involved was aerodynamicist Edward Horkey, Caltech class of 1937. Another was Irving Ashkenas who completed his masters degree at Caltech and joined the North American team one year later. He worked in aerodynamics with Ed Horkey. Harrison "Stormy" Storms would become another well known name associated with the *Mustang*. Storms, another Caltech graduate, joined the company in 1940. Although he was not with North American during the conceptual stage of the new fighter, he participated in most of the subsequent development work. There were others from this famous engineering institution, including Jack Daniels who specialized in performance determinations. Not only was the core team of specialists who conceived and developed the *Mustang* gifted, they were quite young. The latter proved not to be a hinderance.

Ed Horkey was given the task of defining an airfoil for the design project. During this period in time, NACA was in the throes of extensive theoretical and experimental work concerning high-speed airfoils.[2] This work involved a whole family of sections designed to preserve laminar flow boundary layer conditions much further aft on the wing chord. In so doing, aerodynamic drag is reduced and performance improved for a given amount of available engine

Model NA 73, prototype Royal Air Force Mustang I, RAF serial No. AG345. Photo Credit: NAA via D.W. Carter Collection

power. When design work commenced on the *Mustang*, little was available in the form of technical literature on NACA high-speed airfoil work.[3] However, aerodynamicist Russ Robinson and West Coast representative Ed Hartman, both of NACA, introduced North American's aerodynamics group to ongoing laminar flow development results.[4] In the absence of published data, Robinson provided the necessary link between NACA and North American which allowed the incorporation of a laminar flow airfoil on the *Mustang*. He described the type of pressure distribution required to achieve extended laminar boundary layer flow as well as the procedure to calculate the airfoil shape.[5]

This new technology was eagerly accepted by Ed Horkey and the members of his group. A mathematician working in the stress group at the time was familiar with the Theodorsen method of calculating airfoil shape. He was borrowed by Ed Horkey's aerodynamics team and, with a number of others, performed the lengthy calculations leading to the *Mustang's* airfoil design. Models of the airfoil were built and wind tunnel tested at the Guggenheim Aeronautical Laboratories of Caltech in Pasadena, California. Results were encouraging, but the tunnel was basically too small for the model wing. Tunnel wall affects compromised data near the wing tips. A large model of the wing was built and tested by Irv Ashkenas

in the University of Washington wind tunnel. Results from these tests appeared quite good and a decision was made to use the laminar airfoil design for the *Mustang* wing.

The North American airfoil section approximates the NACA 6 series airfoil; however, these airfoils had a maximum depth well aft of the leading edge. While this would have been satisfactory for high wing aircraft or one with a tricycle landing gear configuration, the relatively thin leading edge was inadequate to house the retracted landing gear of the *Mustang* design.[6] For this reason, Ed Horkey revised the NACA airfoil to provide sufficient volume ahead of the front spar to fully and cleanly accept the retracted gear, yet retain most of the high-speed laminar performance of the basic NACA section. This is why the leading edge of the *Mustang* wing projects forward near the wing-fuselage intersection. The resulting airfoil became known as the NAA-NACA High-Speed Airfoil, thus giving a measure of credit to both organizations.

As the Allison-powered *Mustang* entered service with the Royal Air Force, it became apparent that high altitude performance was lacking. To increase performance, changes were made internally to achieve better carburetion and to improve the engine cooling system. When the P-51 was conceived, not much design attention was paid to internal

Mustang I, serial AG346, in British camouflage and markings. This was the third airframe produced. Photo Credit: NAA via D.W. Carter Collection

U.S. Army Air Corps. P-51B-5-NA version of the Mustang taken at Mines Field (Los Angeles International). Photo Credit: NAA via D.W. Carter Collection

P-51D model on the ramp at Mines Field. Photo Credit: NAA via D.W. Carter Collection

duct airflow, sometimes referred to as "internal aerodynamics." For instance, carburetor inlets were usually scoops or tubes of constant cross sectional area that ran from the carburetor mounting flange to an external location on the forward section of the airplane. The inlet was placed to pick up relatively undisturbed air. Air entering the carburetor inlet is known as "ram air." The original NA-73X model had a very short carburetor scoop located atop the engine cowling. Following a few test flights, it was lengthened to improve the ram air condition delivered to the carburetor. Eventually, this inlet was extended forward to a point just aft of the propeller arc to insure more uniform and consistent inlet air pressure. In addition, the inlet design was also elevated slightly above the surface of the nose cowl, a design feature that allowed air to enter the inlet free of any boundary layer air disturbances.

During the same time period, improvements were also being made to the cooling system ducting located in the belly scoop. The original British *Mustang* and Army Air Corps P-51 fighters employed a variable area inlet duct arrangement. In these early models, the engine glycol coolant radiator and oil radiator were concentric cylinders with the oil unit in the center. Oil temperature had to be controlled within certain specified limits as did the glycol fluid cooling the engine. To obtain adequate temperature control, it was decided to control both the duct inlet *and* exit areas. This was done by hinging the inlet scoop so it could be lowered into undisturbed air below the wing and fuselage. The exit portion of the duct was also hinged to control the air leaving the radiators. When newer models of the airplane were designed–the Army Air Corps A-36A and P-51A–the hinged inlet duct geometry was abandoned in favor of a fixed-area inlet design. Air flow through the radiator cores was now controlled only by the variable position of the duct exit door. The upper lip of this fixed inlet duct was positioned perhaps an inch below the fuselage undersurface to permit slower moving "boundary layer" air to "bleed," or spill, around the sides of the underslung air scoop, thereby admitting undisturbed ram air to the oil and glycol radiators.[7] In addition to improved flow into the duct, mechanical aspects of the design became simplified with elimination of the hinged inlet.

When the *Merlin* engine was introduced to the *Mustang*, major changes were in order for the carburetor and engine cooling systems. The highly supercharged *Merlin* allowed the airplane to operate at greater altitudes than did the Allison powerplant. The difference was the degree of supercharging provided by the *Merlin*. Some cooling problems developed with the *Merlin* installation. This was coupled with a need to provide cooling for the aftercooler used in conjunction with the two-speed, two-stage *Merlin* supercharger.[8] Many hundreds of engineering, wind tunnel test, and flight test hours were expended perfecting internal and external aerodynamic and cooling system aspects of the distinctive *Mustang* belly scoop design.

Early belly scoop designs produced a noise characterized as a rumble in the inlet duct. The problem was identified as erratic high-speed air flow from the belly scoop inlet to the radiator face. This high-speed flow could become quite violent, even damaging the radiator structure. The critical condition arises when the velocity of the air into the inlet is low compared to flight speed of the aircraft. This can occur in a high-speed dive with the throttle closed. Cooling air requirements are then at a minimum and the exit door of the scoop is nearly closed. In this situation, air approaching the inlet acts as though it were approaching a solid wall, namely the face of the radiator. The air tries to go around the radiator to continue the flow pattern. As the air velocity slows, the boundary layer thickens and finally separates. The resulting separated turbulent flow goes down the inlet duct and vibrates the structure rather severely. The solution evolved by Irv Ashkenas was to move the inlet duct lip about two and one-half inches away from the fuselage surface and boundary layer. In effect, a gutter was provided to divert the boundary layer flow away from the duct inlet. It was a simple yet elegant solution to the problem.

The entrance and internal ducting of the *Mustang* constitute what is now known as a "pressure recovery" system. This simply means that high velocity air taken into the duct with the aircraft in flight is decelerated or slowed by expanding the cross-section area of the duct. Expansion of the duct cross-section continues very nearly to the front face of the radiators. As the air velocity decreases, static pressure increases across the radiator face. Properly designed, the resulting pressure across the radiator face will be nearly constant. Relatively low velocity, high pressure air then flows through the radiator core, improving heat transfer. Air passing through the radiator core rises in temperature due to heat transferred from high temperature engine oil and coolant fluid. Air leaving the radiator is accelerated due to its increased temperature from the waste engine heat and because the exit portion of the duct converges, forming a nozzle. Heated air is ejected into the outside air stream at a velocity near that of air flowing around the aircraft. The overall configuration can produce useful thrust, offsetting a portion of the aerodynamic drag due to the belly scoop. At first sight, the large belly scoop on a *Mustang* would appear to be a significant source of aerodynamic drag, resulting in a speed penalty. This is not the case. We shall see in subsequent sections of the book how several designers attempted to improve the original *Mustang* layout by re-

P-51D-5-NA in flight over the high desert north of Los Angeles. Photo Credit: NAA via D.W. Carter Collection

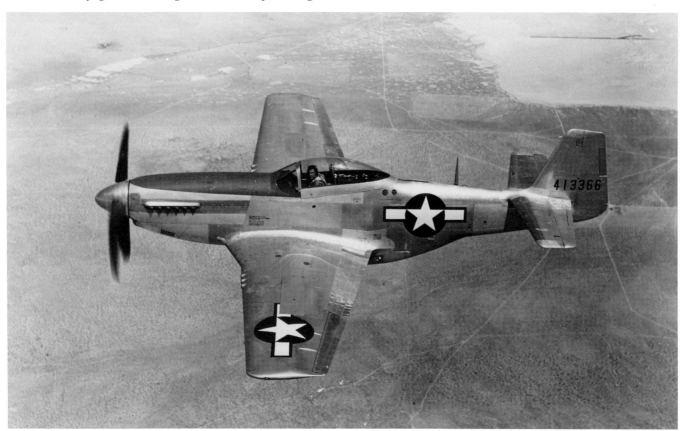

moving the belly scoop and relocating the radiators. In each instance, the results were questionable.

Principles of air pressure recovery were also applied to the carburetor inlet duct to provide more uniform air distribution at the carburetor inlet face. This minimizes a problem which can cause the engine to backfire and possibly result in damage. Another aspect of internal aerodynamics is prevention of internal air leakage into the slip stream moving over the outside surfaces of the aircraft. Each point of external leakage causes a disturbance in the boundary layer and induces more drag. While this is important to a fighter, it is even more important to a racing airplane.

The design team selected by Edgar Schmued was, by today's standards, small in number, but each was an experienced designer. Some, like race pilot and builder Art Chester, were already established designers. This group of experienced and talented men designed a fighter that stretched the existing state-of-the-art. Yet the *Mustang* was constructed in a manner that utilized available manufacturing equipment from the late 1930s. For this reason, the *Mustang* has a relatively simple structural design. This allowed the airplane to be rebuilt, repaired, and modified over the last several decades both as a racing machine and as a sport airplane.

Structural design of the original NA-73X was retained throughout the complete line of *Mustang*s except for the P-51H. The airplane consists of several major components: A powerplant section, which is everything forward of the fire wall; a forward fuselage section; an aft fuselage section; the empennage, or tail section; a lower forward fuselage comprised of the belly scoop and radiators; and a wing assembly including wing tips.

The powerplant section includes the engine, propeller, engine accessories, oil tank, carburetor inlet ducting, engine mount and cowling. The engine mount is the same type for an Allison or a *Merlin*, differing only in detail. The engine mount design differs from most in that it is made of aluminum sheet metal that conforms to the external lines of the engine compartment. Normally, engine mounts are constructed of welded steel tube. The sheet metal mount of the *Mustang* was designed for the Allison-powered NA-73X and remained essentially unchanged for all variants powered with this engine. The same concept was again employed when the *Merlin* was adapted to the airframe, beginning with the P-51B version.

The forward *Mustang* fuselage is a classic "skin and stringer" structure. Basic load carrying members are the four longerons, two upper and two lower, with attach points at the fire wall to mate with the engine mount. The aft end of these longerons have attach fittings to couple with the aft fuselage. Each lower longeron is bent or "cranked" to provide the four point attachment of the wing and the radiators located aft of the wing. The fuselage contour is formed by frames and stringers. When the wing was lowered three inches for the P-51B, lower longerons were revised to meet the new wing location and to accept new, larger coolant radiators. New frames were made for the area between the longerons, thus retaining frame stations and upper fuselage contours from the original design. When the bubble canopy was introduced, only the section above the upper longerons had to be changed. The remainder of the fuselage was untouched. Because of this simple design approach, it is still a relatively easy modification to revise the canopy and upper fuselage contours for racing.

The aft fuselage, tail wheel, and empennage of the *Mustang* have remained basically unchanged from the original prototype NA-73X model. Minor alterations include a stabilizer incidence change from plus two degrees to plus one-half degree on certain late model P-51D and P-51K aircraft. It is also understood the Australian-built P-51s had the option of plus two or plus one-half degree stabilizer incidence settings. At the time an incidence change was made on the P-51D and P-51K models, conversion to all-metal elevators was also effected. A final addition was the small dorsal fin extending from the fuselage break forward of the empennage to the vertical fin leading edge. But in reality, the original design of the aft fuselage was retained throughout.

Structural design of the wing departs from that found on some contemporary fighter aircraft. Often, the wing is designed around a center section with outer panels attached to complete the planform. Typically, the wing center section contains the landing gear and fuel tanks. The *Mustang* wing consists of two panels joined at the centerline of the airframe. Each wing panel has a wing tip assembly that is approximately three feet long. The wing assembly is comprised of a front and rear spar that terminate at the juncture of the wing tip assembly. The reason for this unusual spar termination may have been due to limitations of the fabrication capabilities available to North American manufacturing engineers when the design was first conceived. Because time was of the essence in getting the new fighter designed and built, a very simple structure was employed. Schedule did not permit development of new extruded shapes nor intricately machined spar caps. As a result, sheet aluminum was used for both spars and spar caps. These parts were formed on large power brake machines that apparently could accept parts no longer than fifteen to eighteen feet.

The wing is designed with a two degree wash out at the wing tip. The angle of incidence at the fuselage centerline is plus 1 degree and the tip is minus 1 degree. The airfoil is designed so the effective aerodynamic twist is nearly 3

Lineup of P-51 D model Mustangs undergoing final servicing prior to delivery to the Air Force. Photo Credit: NAA via D.W. Carter Collection

degrees. In most tapered wings the spars are located on percent elements of the wing chord. For instance, a spar might be placed at the 25 percent plane. This means that anywhere along the wing the spar is located at a position which is 25 percent of the chord length relative to the leading edge.[9] When spars are located on percent planes the upper and lower mold lines (the point where the spar plane intersects the outer shape of the airfoil curve) are straight. Both spars on the *Mustang* cut across the percent plane that would normally produce curved mold lines for the spar. Because the spars were made on a power brake it was necessary for the mold lines to be straight. To do this the airfoil was reshaped to provide straight spar caps. As a result, the airfoil changes in shape as well as length and thickness from root to tip.

The basic wing remained unchanged from the original NA73X design except for a break in the leading edge contour to provide space to cover the retracted main landing gear. On P-51s through the B and C models, this break occurred some fifty inches outboard of the airplane centerline. On P-51D and K models, the break was some sixty plus inches away from the centerline. Because of fuel and armament requirements, most of the wing bending and torsional loads are carried by the stringer reinforced skins. The wing fuel tank bay has a completely removable lower skin for access to the fuel cells. Armament bays have similar removable panels over the guns and ammunition trays. For these reasons, there are not many full depth ribs in a *Mustang* wing.

The entire structure is aluminum alloy using a clad-type material that was coming into general usage when the NA73X was designed. Prior to this clad material it was necessary to paint the aluminum to prevent corrosion. Aluminum suppliers developed techniques to roll a very thin layer of pure aluminum over the alloy during the milling process. Pure aluminum oxidizes slightly to provide a surface condition that resists further oxidization or corrosion. This clad material accounts for the chrome-like finish on some all-metal aircraft. Only the rudder and elevators were fabric covered. On later model P-51D and K aircraft, all metal elevators were installed.

A significant factor in the excellent performance of the P-51 is the method used to define the total shape of the aircraft. At the time the NA73X was designed, state-of-the-art production of airframe contours was known as "lofting." Lofting is a very old method of developing contours and body shapes, evolved by early boat builders to produce hull shapes for their sailing ships. Ship designers created the art of lofting and aircraft designers accepted and emulated that art even to the nomenclature of its elements, such as waterline, chines, butt plane (bulkheads) and keels. One of the designer's

drafting tools is still known as a "ship's curve."

The traditional procedure for developing lines was to produce full scale lines on huge plywood boards laid out on the floor of the "loft." Preparation of these "loft boards" took a great deal of time and designers were required to approximate these lines or wait until lofting was completed. The men in charge of the loft group at North American Aviation were Carter Hartley and Roy Liming. Liming developed a technique of establishing basic aircraft contours by using geometrical shapes that could be defined mathematically. When North American Aviation received a contract for the NA73X, it was decided to use the Liming method of lofting, called "conics." Conics involved the use of hyperbolas, parabolas, ellipses and circles, all defined by algebraic terms. When the designer required contours from a particular section of the airframe, the loft group provided him with dimensional data in a matter of hours rather than days, as required by the older lofting method. In addition, Liming developed methods whereby the designer could accurately determine his own contour data using a graphic drawing method. All contours on the P-51 were done in this manner resulting in an extremely smooth shape of minimum size to enclose engine, pilot, fuel, armament and subsystems.

Forward end of the NA73X showing the early carburetor air intake which had inferior ram air characteristics. Photo Credit: NAA via D.W. Carter Collection

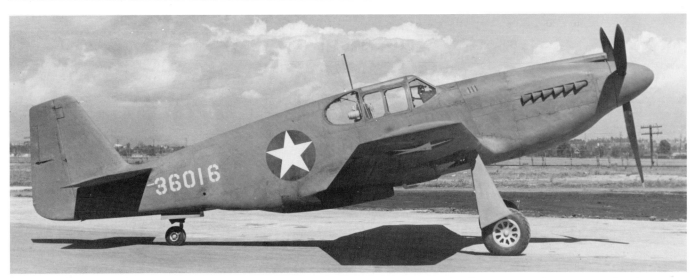

Profile view of the 14th Army Air Corps P-51A aircraft built. Clean lines of this early Allison-powered version are clearly evident. Photo Credit: NAA via D.W. Carter Collection

Development of the "conics" method by Liming and Hartley is one of the reasons the *Mustang* is still considered an aesthetically pleasing design. Today's aircraft contours are done in a similar manner but instead of using a Frieden calculator or slide rule as Liming did, they use sophisticated computer-aided technology. This newer concept, used by the auto industry as well as the aircraft industry, is called Computer Aided Design, or simply "CAD." The NA73X was the first aircraft to use CAD in its most primitive stage.

Landing gear for the P-51 is a simple design with a single inward retracting motion. The upper end of the gear strut is integral with the pivot shaft. A large aluminum alloy casting houses the pivot shaft bearings and provides a structural load path from the landing gear loads into the front spar and heavy wing rib. Retraction fittings are attached at the aft end of the pivot shaft. The wheels are 27 inch Goodyear tires with multiple disc brakes. The landing gear is faired over when retracted by a strut-supported, fixed fairing that covers the strut. A hydraulically operated, retractable door sequenced by the landing gear retracting mechanism completes the enclosure of the gear. The door covers the landing wheel.

The military P-51 had self-sealing fuel tanks, or cells made of rubberized fabric inner and outer shells with a soft synthetic, rubber-like core about a half inch thick. The core material would react with the aviation fuel so that a pronounced swelling or expansion occurred. Small punctures or bullet holes would be sealed by the swelling core material. The P-51 had three fuel cells: one in each wing and a third in the fuselage. Each wing tank carried 91 gallons. Some of the early P-51s carried no fuselage tank. As range requirements increased during the war, a fuselage fuel cell was added behind the pilot's seat. Radio and oxygen equipment were relocated to provide room for this 85 gallon fuselage tank. The fuselage tank affected airplane center of gravity and all aerobatics were prohibited when the fuselage tank contained more than 40 gallons of fuel.

To indicate just what kind of a workhorse the P-51 could be, long range missions of 2600 mile range were achieved with a takeoff weight of 11,500 pounds. This mission was bomber escort and the airplane was armed with 50 caliber machine guns. It carried 489 gallons of fuel of which 220 gallons were in combat drop tanks. Similar missions were flown with the addition of 5-inch rockets. With rockets, the gross weight was 11,800 pounds. In this configuration, range was shortened to 2400 miles. This was quite a feat for a little airplane that normally weighed in at about 6900 pounds. The *Mustang* proved to be a real workhorse!

Notes

1. Iacocca, Lee, *Iacocca, An Autobiography*, Bantam Books, New York, 1984.
2. Some of the earliest work reported by NACA on the subject of laminar flow airfoils was written by Eastman N. Jacobs in a report completed in April, 1939. Conclusions of this work focused on the NACA 27 series airfoil section.
3. The most comprehensive document on contemporary airfoils was not formally published by NACA until 1945. This compendium was prepared by Abbot, et al, under the guidance and initiative of Eastman Jacobs.
4. The decade of the 1930s saw a great amount of research by noted investigators dedicated to airfoil design and the reduction of aerodynamic drag in general. This work centered in England, Germany, and the United States. Investigators at NACA pioneered the organization and nomenclature associated with airfoil characteristics. It is believed they also led the field in the evolution of what became known as high-speed airfoil sections.
5. This was known as the Theodorsen method. T. Theodorsen was another NACA research specialist involved in airfoil development during the 1930s.
6. With a tricycle landing gear arrangement, the main wheels and struts would typically be located further aft from the wing leading edge, where the airfoil is thicker. For instance, note the placement of the main gear on the Bell P-63 fighter which utilized the NACA 6 series airfoil.
7. This design improvement is credited to Irving Ashkenas. It was a significant advancement in duct inlet configuration and is still employed to this day.
8. The Merlin supercharger used an aftercooler (heat exchanger) to reduce temperature of the compressed fuel-air mixture entering the engine induction system. When gas is compressed, its temperature rises.
9. The leading edge of the wing represents zero percent and the trailing edge is 100 percent of the wing chord.

Chapter Two
MAKING OF A THOROUGHBRED

Conversion of the sturdy, lean workhorse *Mustang* into a thoroughbred racer involves elimination of military equipment and related systems, reduction of airframe size and weight and improved performance of the engine and supporting systems. Most civilian *Mustangs* have the military equipment removed but retain some systems and components. When these machines are converted for racing, aircraft owners are often reluctant to change the exterior appearance of the aircraft, preferring to retain its original military appearance. In many cases, these aircraft will have highly tuned engines to provide improved performance over a stock *Merlin*. Although these stock appearing P-51s are raced, they are not in a championship class. The making of a thoroughbred *Mustang* racer is accomplished through modification of the airframe, both structurally and aerodynamically together with installation of a modified high performance racing engine with custom fuel and cooling systems to achieve peak engine performance.

Structural & Aerodynamic Modifications. One of the more frequent and notable changes to a racing *Mustang* airframe is removal of the P-51D bubble canopy. This is replaced with a low profile, low drag canopy suited for racing. In most cases the front fuselage is reworked by removing all structure above the upper longerons and replacing it with an all new structure designed and fabricated to mate with a new, smaller low-drag canopy. The fairing aft of the canopy terminates at the rear frame of the front fuselage so that mating with the rear fuselage is unchanged. Some racers have relocated the pilot's seat to a more aft position, requiring relocation of the rudder pedals, control stick, engine controls and instrument panel. The control stick location may be changed as much as twenty inches aft of its normal position without revising the elevator or aileron controls. This change is made to keep the airframe center of gravity in an acceptable range in context with the removal of non-essential equipment and other race alterations. The control stick is mounted on a tubular assembly attached to the top surface of the wing. Moving the control stick is done by simply shortening the forward end of the tubular assembly. The elevator and aileron controls attach to this assembly aft of the rear spar.

The lower front fuselage assembly, more commonly known as the "dog house" by those in the business of aircraft restoration, is a housing and fairing for the cooling system radiators. The radiator inlet assembly and the exit doors, with fairing, complete the structure of this distinctive belly scoop. The size of the inlet and shape of *Mustang* belly scoop, or doghouse, is the result of extensive wind tunnel and flight testing. Cooling requirements for military operations are not the same as those for pylon racing at low altitudes. Augmented cooling and improved heat exchangers (radiators) are now available for racing. These allow a reduction of the duct inlet area and a cleaner diminished profile for the doghouse. The result is a reduction in frontal area and improvement in aerodynamic drag.

Two important factors make this size reduction possible. One is removal of the standard P-51 oil cooler. This is replaced with a P-51H oil heat exchanger. The replacement heat exchanger is a completely enclosed unit that uses supercharger aftercooler fluid to cool the engine oil. The hot engine oil flows through tubes that are emersed in chilled liquid that eventually flows into the supercharger aftercooler. This system permits the heat exchanger to be located in a more convenient place other than the belly scoop, usually in the engine compartment next to the oil tank. The second factor is revision of the flow system in the engine coolant radiator. In a standard P-51D radiator, coolant flows into the top of the radiator, out the bottom and then into the engine coolant passages. Engine coolant return lines are connected to the bottom of the radiator. A relatively large space is required for fittings and lines with this configuration. For stock P-51 airplanes, this space was not costly because it was immediately behind the oil cooler and its exit door. But, with the standard oil cooler removed the belly scoop external contour may be raised several inches. A slimmer, cleaner belly scoop profile is the result.

The belly scoop inlet area may be reduced by as much as 25 percent and still permit satisfactory air flow through the radiators. With racing engines running at high speeds and manifold pressures, more waste heat is generated which must be dissipated by radiators originally sized for less demanding requirements. Photographs of P-51s racing at Cleveland after the war reveal that all ran with belly scoop exit doors wide open. *Mustangs* racing today run with the exit door nearly closed. The difference is augmented cooling from the installation of "spray bar" systems. Spray bars located just forward of the radiator face are designed to emit a fine spray of water droplets across the radiator face. Introduction of water to the air flow provides a medium to

Earl Ortman's 1946 Mustang sits on the ramp at Cleveland, preparing for an engine run up. This was the first P-51 to have the wing tips removed and the ailerons shortened correspondingly, a racing trend that continues to this day. Photo Credit: Warren Bodie

In outward appearance, Bill Destefani's contemporary Mustang racer, "Mangia Pane," is a replica of Ortman's 1946 P-51. The only visible modification are the clipped wings. This flight shot was taken at the 1985 Bakersfield Air Race. Photo Credit: Neal Nurmi

The effect of clipped wings on a racing Mustang is clearly seen here on Don Whittington's beautiful "Precious Metal" running up on the ramp at Reno. Photo Credit: Birch Matthews

remove additional heat from the coolant by turning the water mist into steam. A faint trail of water vapor can often be seen leaving the cooler exit door on *Mustangs* equipped with spray bar cooling.

Details of spray bar design varies somewhat. The Griffon-powered *Red Baron Mustang* using a P-51D oil radiator and stock coolant radiators had spray bars located in the air scoop, well ahead of the oil and glycol radiators. Three horizontal spray bars were used with one dedicated to the oil radiator. The latter had a flow rate of 1.6 gallons per minute. The other two spray bars covered the upper and lower halves of the engine glycol radiator with each emitting 4.2 gallons per minute. Spray water was carried in a 92 gallon tank in the right wing of the *Red Baron*. Spray bar systems designed for racing *Mustangs*, *Dago Red*, and *Strega* were somewhat different in detail. Because the oil cooler was removed and replaced by a heat exchanger located near the oil tank, only the glycol coolant radiator required water spray. In these two racers, four spray bars were arranged in a vertical pattern located just twelve inches ahead of the radiator face. The water-alcohol mixture was pumped through this system at a rate of 10 gallons per minute. The right wing carried about 92 gallons of water in the main fuel bay.

In the quest to minimize drag on a *Mustang*, aerodynamicists and engineers have tried a variety of designs for such things as the wing fillet. Although the stock wing fillet was a product of many engineering and flight test hours, experimentation continues in the field of air racing. At one extreme was Bob Abram's bright red P-51D, where the entire fillet was removed. This radical surgery is thought to have contributed to Abrams' fatal accident during the Los Vegas races. Removal of the fillets may have adversely altered the stall characteristics of the airplane and contrib-

uted to his fatal accident. At the other end of the spectrum is a Jim Larsen-designed aft sweeping fillet, seen on John Crocker's racing P-51. Jim Larsen's fillets were designed based upon tuft patterns photographed during flight tests. However, most racers retain stock P-51 wing fillets.

Reducing the wing span has been an accepted speed seeking modification since the invention of the aeroplane. The Baby Wright racer that appeared during the 1909 Rheims meet was a "clipped wing" Wright biplane. As racing progressed through the years it appeared possible to make an airplane go faster with smaller wings. When *Mustangs* appeared on the racing scene in 1946, the first thing done in the way of airframe modification was removal of the wing tip panels. The task is made easy by designers of the P-51 because the 33-inch-long wing tip assembly is simply bolted to the main panel wing structure. Removing the wing tips on a *Mustang* shortens the span by almost six feet. Because the airframe is considerably lighter compared to the military version, wing loading remains in an acceptable range. True, the ailerons must be reduced in span but the stock version incorporates three hinges and only two are needed with the shortened aileron span. The very first *Mustang* to race with clipped wings was Earl Ortman's P-51 in the 1946 Thompson Trophy Race. He set a trend that continues to this day.

In the 1946-1949 era, not much was done to improve wing tip design. Clipped wing tips were simply round in cross section and approximated the stock contour. No thought was given to the phenomenon of wing tip vortices. Vortices are caused by air flowing around the tip from the lower surface of the wing to the upper surface. This flow pattern occurs because the bottom of the wing is at a higher pressure than the top surface. This is known as lift. There is also some degree of spanwise flow that adds to the turbulence. This turbulence flows aft along the tip and leaves the trailing edge in the form of an expanding, twisting cone or vortex. Most aircraft have ailerons located somewhat inboard of the wing tip to avoid this disturbed flow and thus any adverse influence on aileron function. When a wing is shortened and the aileron is not relocated relative to the tip (which is rarely done), the vortex may affect aileron effectiveness.

During World War II a German scientist, Sighard F. Hoerner, investigated a variety of wing tip geometries. In addition to theoretical work, he experimented with in-flight photography to record vortex patterns shed by different tip configurations. The vortex patterns were made visible by generating smoke at the wing tip. After the war, Hoerner was one of many German scientists that came to the United States. Working for the Air Force, he prepared a report on his work in Germany with tip vortices.[1] His work had no impact on race teams participating at Cleveland in the late 1940s.[2] Indeed, Hoerner's work was not published in this country until 1949.

When racing became popular again in the late 1960s, Hoerner's work stimulated thinking about modifying wing tip geometries on racing airplanes. The first person to consider wing tip geometries was Lockheed test pilot Darryl Greenamyer. He acquired a Grumman F8F-2 *Bearcat* and together with a team of fellow Lockheed engineers he began modifying the fighter for all-out speed. The already stubby *Bearcat* wing was made even shorter, leaving only marginal aileron surfaces. Lockheed aerodynamicist Mell Cassidy designed a new wing tip for the racer to move the tip vortex away from the outer edge of the short span ailerons. Cassidy's tip design incorporated a concave underside that faired to a very thin edge along the upper contour. The result was satisfactory aileron response. This concept was picked up by other technicians and pilots who added their own flair to tip designs. When these new wing tips began appearing they were erroneously dubbed "Hoerner tips." None of Hoerner's experimental wing tip configurations included concave shapes. Perhaps a proper nomenclature for the concave geometry is the "Cassidy wing tip," in recognition of this innovative Lockheed engineer.

How effective are these custom wing tips? Some twenty years since their introduction, many modified racing wing tips are still simple rounded surfaces. What about the vortex? It is obviously still present. It has to be, if the wing is producing lift. It would appear that enough aileron authority remains on the shortened *Mustang* wing to provide satisfactory control. In more recent custom tip designs, small vertical fences are added to the outer edge of the aileron to prevent spanwise flow when the controls are deflected.

The P-51 racer known as *Strega* is a good example of experimentation with wing tip design. When *Strega* first raced it had a modified raked wing tip borrowed from another *Mustang*, *Precious Metal*. After the first race sea-

E.D. Weiner was an early and active participant when unlimited class racing resumed in the 1960s. Changes were limited to a reduction in wingspan, a highly tuned dash 9 Merlin and the addition of a tank in the cockpit for antidetonant fluid. This picture was taken at the 1966 races at Lancaster, California. Photo Credit: Dusty Carter

"Stilleto," shown here on takeoff at Bakersfield, is one of the most highly modified Mustangs to ever fly. The wings were drastically reduced in span as was the horizontal stabilizer. Gone is the distinctive belly scoop and of course, the airplane sports a low profile canopy assembly. The airplane is shown here at the Bakersfield Air Race. Photo Credit: Neal Nurmi

A different view of the clipped wing modification on a Mustang is seen here on John Crocker's "Somthin' Else." John also has long graceful wing fillets and a cropped horizontal stabilizer. The airframe modifications are the product of engineer Jim Larsen. This is the 1980 version of the racer as it appeared in Reno. Photo Credit: Neal Nurmi

Race 19 was competed by Dave Allender as the "Wayfarers Club Lady" during the late 1960s with essentially a stock airframe. The red P-51D was modified drastically in 1978 with a small bubble canopy, clipped wings and horizontal tail. Unfortunately, the aircraft never raced in this configuration and was reportedly reconverted to a stock Mustang at a later date. This is how the airplane appeared in February, 1979, while at Hollister, California. Photo Credit: William Larkins

Detail of the cockpit canopy is shown in this photograph of John Crocker's racer. Also apparent is the excellent surface finish on the airplane. Photo Credit: Neal Nurmi

son, a new set of wing tips were fashioned and installed. They were basically just a rounded contour in cross-section. Small fences were added on both the upper and lower inboard side of the tip adjacent to the aileron. According to race pilot Bill Destefani, he could see no difference in airplane handling quality between the original and second set of wing tips. As a slight bonus, the new wing tips were a bit lighter.

The most radical aerodynamic modification ever attempted on a *Mustang* was the installation of a swept wing. John Dilley spent untold amounts of money and time adapting a Learjet wing and horizontal stabilizer to a P-51 airframe. The end product was a stunning racer. Unfortunately, performance of this unique configuration was never demonstrated on a pylon course. Engine problems beset the Dilley race team throughout the 1988 Reno race week. Subsequent to the races, the airplane crashed and the efficacy of this modification remains to be proved.

Another new feature appeared during the 1987 Reno races. In reality, it was not a new technical innovation. Rather, it was the use of propeller cuffs on a highly modified racing *Mustang*. During World War II, propeller manufacturers developed a rubber-like cuff that fitted around the propeller blade adjacent to the hub. The intent of the cuff was to provide an improved airfoil shape in a region where the propeller blade makes a transition from a round shaft to an airfoil. Cuffs simply extended the airfoil shape in close

to the hub and provided a marginal improvement in propeller efficiency. The blade itself could not be made into an airfoil shape near the hub because of stress concentrations that would lead to propeller failure. Cuffs were used to improve airflow near the hub for better cooling on radial engines. In the case of the P-51 *Mustang*, cuffs were thought to provide better ram air conditions at the carburetor duct inlet.

Bill Destefani's record setting *Strega* was the first to appear with propeller cuffs. According to *Strega* crew chief Bill Kerchanfaut, "...the cuffs were (race pilot) Bob Love's idea. He always thought the engine performed better with cuffs." *Strega* set a new closed-course record at Reno that year. And the engine performed flawlessly.

Someone once said, "... there really is not much to modern air racing. After all, a P-51 is a P-51. You simply paint them different colors but they are all the same." But in reality, building a truly competitive racer is a culmination of detailed attention to every aspect of aerodynamic design.

Notes

1. Hoerner is probably best known in the aeronautical community of the United States for his self-published compendiums on aerodynamic drag.
2. The single exception to this statement is the F2G racer prepared by Cook Cleland for the 1949 Thompson Trophy Race. Cleland had shortened the wing span (and correspondingly the ailerons) to a point where aileron effectiveness may have been marginal. To counteract this, he installed flat end plates along the entire chord of the clipped wing tip to eliminate span-wise flow on the aileron.

Cliff Cummins taxis "Miss Candace" out for takeoff in Reno. Note the shallow belly scoop, cockpit canopy treatment and wing tip design including small fences just outboard of the aileron. Photo Credit: Neal Nurmi

This racing Mustang was named "Habu" and raced for several years in Reno and other locations. The 1982 version shown here incorporated vertical shrouds or fairings on either side of the fuselage where the heated air exited the belly scoop. This was an attempt to control and straighten the air flow in this region of the airframe. Photo Credit: Birch Matthews

Another detail photograph of "Habu" reveals the wing tip treatment, including the fence installed to stop spanwise flow on the aileron due to the close proximity of the wing tip vortex. This all-black P-51D later crashed fatally. Photo Credit: Birch Matthews

The only racer to adopt a unique wing tip treatment during the post-war Thompson Trophy races was Cook Cleland's 1949 Goodyear F2G Corsair. The wings were severely clipped and the vertical fences were employed to enhance aileron authority. Photo Credit: Birch Matthews

Chapter Three
MERLIN MAGIC

Prologue. To even the most casual observer, Reno air racing is a cacophony of sights, sounds, and even smells, sufficient to confound the human sense. Those that chronicle air races only relate their visual recollections of the event frequently laced with statistical data to the third decimal place. But there is a story behind the sounds heard at Reno, particularly with respect to the unlimited class racers. *Mustangs* typically dominate each year's entry list. And the audio output of a racing *Merlin* engine under full steam is something unique. Multiplied by a full slate of entries, as during a Reno Gold Championship Race, the sound is truly awesome. It is a sound that almost defies adequate description, but once heard is seldom forgotten. Indeed, the *Merlin* sound is a blend of propeller tips turning at near sonic velocity, coupled with the whine of over-stressed gears and

staccato combustion noise. This chapter is devoted to providing some understanding of what is required to build a racing *Merlin* engine and thus give some added meaning to that wonderfully distinctive and "awesome" sound.

Historical Perspective. Twelve-cylinder, V-shaped, liquid-cooled engines have long been used for high-speed aircraft applications. Early V-12s built by Renault appeared during World War I. Improvement of the breed was rapid during the next two decades. A figure of merit for all aircraft engines is the ratio of engine dry weight to power developed. The trend for liquid-cooled V-12s is shown in the accompanying curve over a time span of 70 years. The 1916 Renault engine produced 220 horsepower and weighed over 800 pounds. The weight-to-power ratio was 3:66. As early

Rolls-Royce Merlin racing engine on display in Reno. The mammoth two-stage, two-speed supercharger mounted on the rear of the engine is evident in this photograph. Photo Credit: Al Hansen

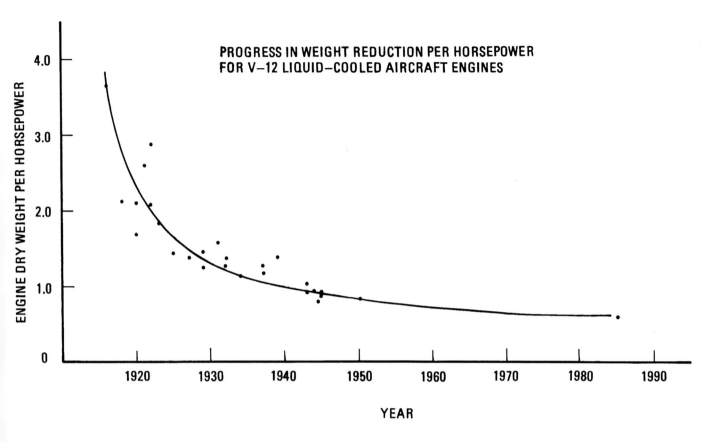

**PROGRESS IN WEIGHT REDUCTION PER HORSEPOWER
FOR V–12 LIQUID–COOLED AIRCRAFT ENGINES**

This curve illustrates the progress in weight reduction per unit of horsepower for liquid-cooled V-12 aircraft engines as a function of time beginning with World War I to the present.

as 1920, V-12 engines had an improved ratio of around 2:3 and the advent of World War II brought this figure to near unity. Preeminent in this respect was the Rolls-Royce *Merlin* engine. Contemporary Reno unlimited pylon racers using *Merlins* achieve a weight-to-power ratio of less than 0.6, a rather astonishing value for World War II vintage engines.

Although the apparent tangle of metal, plumbing, cable and wiring under the cowling of a *Mustang* may appear complex, the fundamental processes of piston engine operation are relatively straightforward. A mixture of fuel and air, called a "charge," is inducted sequentially into each engine cylinder. The charge is compressed by a piston and ignited by firing a spark plug. High-temperature combustion gases expand and force the piston downward to the end of its stroke. Linear motion of the piston is translated by a connecting rod into rotating movement of the crankshaft. When the power stroke is complete, the piston reverses direction and forces residual exhaust gases out of the cylinder exhaust valve ports. This process is repeated when the pistons once again move downward drawing fresh charge into the cylinders through intake valve ports. Crankshaft counterweights provide the necessary balance and momen-

tum to maintain rotation between piston power strokes.

The process just described is termed a four-stroke cycle and, as indicated, consists of intake, compression, combustion (power) and exhaust piston strokes. Rolls-Royce chief engineer and superb aerodynamicist, Sir Stanley Hooker, once facetiously remarked that the four-stroke engine has one stroke for producing power and three for wearing the engine out. Before the advent of aircraft gas turbines, however, the four-stroke piston engine was without peer.

Fuel-air mixture ratio varies depending upon desired engine operation. To achieve maximum power, a fuel-air ratio of about 0.09 is required. At this ratio, one pound of gasoline is mixed with 11 pounds of air. If the weight of air processed by an engine is increased per unit of time, power output will be proportionately higher because more fuel (chemical energy) is simultaneously added to maintain constant mixture ratio. Early aircraft engines were "normally aspirated" in that charge air was drawn from the local atmosphere. At sea level, weight density (pounds per cubic foot) of air is at a maximum. Air density decreases as altitude above sea level increases, depending upon local barometric pressure and temperature conditions. Thus, power output of normally aspirated engines is reduced with increasing altitude because air density is diminished. To overcome this inherent limitation, charge air must be compressed to maintain or increase the weight of air processed by the engine. Different types of compressors have been employed to increase the air pressure supplied to aircraft engines; however, the centrifugal blower is most widely used.

Blowers are commonly called superchargers, a name derived from the basic terminology for the fuel-air mixture or "charge" supplied to the piston engine. Supercharger technology developed rapidly during the late 1920s and the decade that followed. The capacity of the basic *Merlin* engine design to accept increasing degrees of supercharging was perhaps its greatest single attribute. At conception, the *Merlin* produced something in excess of 800 horsepower. By the end of World War II, Merlin variants developed more than 2,000 horsepower. Current racing *Merlins* have generated as much as 3,000 horsepower.

The Merlin Heritage. The driving force behind the Rolls-Royce firm was Sir Henry Royce. A meticulous craftsman of humble origins, Royce's interest in the fledgling automobile business eventually brought him in contact with C.S. Rolls, pioneer balloonist and auto racer. The two men formed Rolls-Royce Ltd. to produce motor cars of the finest quality.

It was C.S. Rolls, however, who first became intrigued with flying heavier-than-air machines. Coincidentally, he rapidly lost interest in automobiles. In 1910, Rolls made the first double crossing of the English Channel in an airplane. Tragically, he was killed on 12 July of that same year during a flying meeting in Bournemouth, England. Structural failure in the airplane he was piloting resulted in a fatal crash. Frederick Henry Royce, did not share his colleague's enthusiasm for aviation and Rolls' accidental death had a profound effect upon him. Royce gave no thought to aviation ventures. One wonders if Rolls-Royce Ltd. might have built airframes as well as engines had C.S. Rolls lived.

World War I brought the company into design and manufacture of aircraft engines. This led to the Rolls-Royce *Eagle* series, first in a long line of engines named for birds of prey. The *Eagle* was followed chronologically by the *Hawk, Condor, Kestrel* and *Buzzard* engines. In 1928, Rolls-Royce discussed the possibility of using their engines in airframes contemplated by both Supermarine and the Gloster Company for the 1929 Schneider Trophy Race. Britain's Air Ministry finally guaranteed government support for the race in late February of 1929. This decision having been made, Supermarine accepted Royce's proposal. It was a fortuitous acceptance for both companies. The racing engine

series developed by Rolls-Royce was truly a progenitor of the *Merlin* engine. Supermarine's aerodynamic efforts ultimately led to the Spitfire, a World War II benchmark in fighter aircraft.

The approach selected by Royce for the 1929 Schneider racer was to modify and supercharge a normally aspirated 825 horsepower *Buzzard* engine. The end product was the Rolls-Royce R engine which produced about 1,900 horsepower and powered a Supermarine S.6 racing floatplane to victory in the Schneider race. In 1931, the Schneider Trophy Race was held for what was to be the final time. Rolls-Royce engineers improved the R series engine until it was capable of 2,300 horsepower. Installed in the 1931 Supermarine S.6B airframe, this combination won permanent possession of the Schneider Cup for Great Britain.

Rolls-Royce engineering evolved a truly elegant solution to increasing power of the *Buzzard* engine. The heart of this dramatic power increase centered on adapting a two-sided centrifugal blower to increase the mass flow of air processed by the engine. This, coupled with more rugged construction and an exotic fuel blend, resulted in a winning combination.

As 1932 drew to a close, Rolls-Royce realized that advances made with their *Kestrel* engine series together with the experiences gained from the R engine development provided a basis for a new design that promised world leadership in liquid-cooled aircraft engines. This new concept centered on a 1,650 cubic-inch displacement design initiated as a private venture.[1] Design of what was eventually to become the *Merlin* began two years after the Allison V-1710 engine development commenced in the United States. Clearly similar in dimension and displacement, the Allison never matched its British counterpart in performance. The *Merlin* engine resulted from a confluence of three factors: two decades of engine development experience; a work force dedicated to quality craftsmanship; and, technical leadership molded by Sir Henry Royce.[2] Ironically, Sir Henry suffered failing health during this period and his direct involvement in what was to become the company's most famous aircraft product was limited. Frederick Henry Royce died on 22 April 1933.

The burden of developing the *Merlin* fell to the talented Rolls-Royce staff, including A.G. Elliot and E.W. Hives. What resulted was a liquid-cooled aircraft engine composed of 12 cylinders in two 6-cylinder banks, separated by 60 degrees of included angle. The bore and stroke of each cylinder was 5.4 inches and 6.0 inches, respectively, for a total displacement of 1,650 cubic inches of swept volume. By comparison, the Allison incorporated a 5.5 inch bore with a stroke of 6.0 inches, yielding a displacement of 1,710 cubic inches. Compression ratio for the *Merlin* was 6:1 while the Allison was 6.65:1. Output for the early *Merlin* series was 880 horsepower at 3,000 crankshaft revolutions per minute (rpm). By the end of World War II, production variants of the original *Merlin* achieved maximum outputs in excess of 2,000 horsepower, more than twice the original power output with the same displacement. The approach to achieve this remarkable power increase was essentially that utilized by Sir Henry in evolving the Schneider Trophy Race R engine: development through use of stronger components, in part aided by improved metal alloys, sodium-cooled exhaust valves, improved spark plug design and use of exhaust gas discharge to augment total thrust. This latter element took advantage of energy remaining in the high temperature, sonic velocity engine exhaust gases. Allowing these gases to exhaust through properly designed stacks added measurable thrust. What evolved from all this was the epitome of liquid-cooled engine development for that era and a basis of even greater *Merlin* power for future unlimited class air racing.

Postwar Unlimited Class Racing: 1946-1949. With resumption of air racing in 1946, ascendancy of Rolls-Royce designed engines commenced. Early dominance of *Merlin*-powered *Mustangs* occurred in the long-distance Bendix Trophy Race. Both Paul Mantz and Joe DeBona rode *Mustangs* to victory in the Bendix. Indeed, *Merlin*-engined Mustangs dominated this classic race. *Mustangs* also won the closed-course Tinnerman, Kendall, and Sohio Trophy

races of that period. And in 1948, Anson Johnson won the premier Thompson Trophy Race in a D model *Mustang* using a dash 225 *Merlin* engine.

In reality, a number of different engines have powered *Mustangs* around the pylons. Table I is a listing of these engines. In the early years, many pilots simply ran their engines in stock condition at or near war emergency power. A venturesome few modified *Merlins* to operate at higher manifold pressures and crankshaft speeds. In comparison with current day practice, such modifications were relatively modest. Nonetheless, *Merlin* reliability and durability in pylon races proved a problem during this period.

Bendix Trophy *Mustangs* faired much better. In this race, the objective was to fly nonstop at or near emergency power, a goal not all could achieve. War emergency power in the military meant a maximum engine manifold pressure and speed for a specified time limit; typically not to exceed five minutes. For example, the Packard-built V-1650-7 *Merlin* had a 19,300 foot critical altitude war emergency rating of 1500 horsepower at 67 inches of manifold pressure and 3000 revolutions per minute.[3] The dash 9 *Merlin* could produce significantly more horsepower at a greater critical altitude, but only through the use of water injection. The weight and volume of water required for the 2,000 mile Bendix race made this alternative impossible.

The capacity of the *Merlin* to absorb supercharging and deliver in excess of 1500 horsepower at altitudes approaching 20,000 feet made it a very competitive engine for the Bendix

Table 1: VARIOUS ENGINES USED OR MODIFIED FOR RACING MUSTANGS

Engine	Max. Power HP	Max. Power RPM	Reduction Gear Ratio	Supercharger Impeller Diameter 1st Stage	Supercharger Impeller Diameter 2nd Stage	Gear Ratio Low	Gear Ratio High	Remarks
V-1650-3	1600	3000	0.479:1	12.0"	10.1"	6.391:1	8.095:1	Used on P-51B and C-1 through -10 variants. Also used as a replacement on later P-51D aircraft.
V-1650-7	1720	3000	0.479:1	12.0"	10.1"	5.802:1	7.349:1	Production P-51D models.
V-1650-9	1930	3000	0.479:1	12.0"	10.1"	6.391:1	8.095:1	Equipped with water injection system. Similar to V-1650-3
Merlin 225	1620	3000	0.420:1	10.25"	–	8.150:1	9.490:1	Single stage, two-speed supercharger. Engine equipped Canadian-built deHavilland Mosquito.
Merlin 500	1635	3000	0.420:1	10.25"	–	8.150:1	9.490:1	Single-stage, two-speed supercharger used in York and Lancastrian transports.
Merlin 620	1800	3000	0.471:1	12.0"	10.1"	5.790:1	7.060:1	The 600 series of engines was produced in eight variants. The 620 is representative and powered the DC-4M-1 and Canadair North Star transports.
V-1710-81	1330	3000	0.500:1	9.5"	–	8.800:1	–	Single-stage, single-speed supercharger. Used on the P-51A Mustang.
V-1710-87	1500	3000	0.500:1	9.5"	–	7.480:1	–	Single-stage, single-speed supercharger. Used on the A-36A Mustang.
Griffon	2450	2750	0.442:1	11.5"	13.4"	5.840:1	7.580:1	Griffon engine used in the Red Baron RB-51 was a hybrid composed of Griffon 57 and 74 components. The latter provided a two-speed, two-stage supercharger. Griffon 57 nose case afforded the contra-rotating propeller shafts. Stock Griffon 74 blower gear ratios are quoted. Custom gearing used on the RB-51.

race. Equally impressive, however, was the ability of this engine to operate at war emergency power continuously during the approximately four and one-half hours required to fly the Bendix. Such prolonged maximum power operation was not without precedent. Wartime development resulted in numerous *Merlin* durability tests. For example, the Army Air Force ran a dash 7 *Merlin* for three and one-half hours at 67 inches and 3000 rpm during testing to evaluate engine operation with elevated oil temperatures.

The rigors of pylon racing offer a challenge different from transcontinental events. Such races are run at low altitude for relatively short durations. Competitive engine configurations will vary depending upon such factors as local race duration, altitude, and weather conditions. Pylon race distances have varied significantly during the past 40 or

so years (see Table II). Longest were the California 1000 and U.S. Cup Races held during the early 1970s. Shortest are the current Reno Championship races. Race distance determines the amount of fuel and oil which must be carried and the extent of water injection which may be utilized. In contemporary Reno races, *Merlins* operate continuously at maximum water injection rates for this relatively short race. *Merlin*-powered *Mustangs* in the Thompson Trophy Race were limited to water injection rates of 40 to 60 percent of current practice with correspondingly lower power settings. The Thompson race was four times longer than Reno's championship race. Conversely, later 1000 kilometer (625 mile) and 1000 mile pylon races during the 1970s did not preclude use of water injection because pit stops were allowed. Both Howie Keefe and Darryl Greenamyer utilized

This photograph illustrates the power package of a Mustang and reveals the fabricated aluminum engine mount structure used by North American instead of the more conventional welded steel tube mount. The photograph was taken in the engine rebuild area of Trans-Florida Aviation, Inc., in Sarasota, Florida. Photo Credit: Roger Besecker

Table 2: COURSE DISTANCE FOR VARIOUS PYLON RACES

Event	Distance (Miles)	Remarks
California 1000	1,000	1970 only
U.S. Cup Race	1,000	1971 only
California 1000	621	1,000 kilometers in 1971
Thompson Trophy	300	1946 through 1948
Sohio Trophy	240	1946 only
Thompson Trophy	225	1949 only
Sohio Trophy	105	1947 through 1949
Kendall Trophy	105	
Tinnerman Trophy	105	
Reno Championship	73.8	See Note

Note:
Length of the Reno unlimited race course has varied since the inaugural race in 1964. This original course was 80 miles. The longest Reno race was the 1968 course which was 12 laps totaling 96 miles. The shortest was the 1980 eight-lap race of 72 miles.

water-injected *Merlins* during the California 1000 and U.S. Cup Races, respectively.

The host site for a pylon race determines the altitude in which an engine must operate. Air density diminishes with altitude and thus the weight flow of air processed by an engine decreases. Supercharging is the antidote; however, it is not without cost. Engine-driven superchargers on *Merlins* consume about 600 to 1000 horsepower at race operating conditions. Each stage simultaneously imposes a weight penalty on the airframe. Thus at postwar events in Cleveland, a two-stage setup on a *Merlin* could prove a liability with a net power loss and weight handicap in a race run at near sea level. For this reason, at least three *Mustangs* at Cleveland in 1949 ran a low-altitude *Merlin* 225 engine employing a single-stage, two speed supercharger. These aircraft were Anson Johnson's highly modified N13Y, race 45, M. W. Fairbrother's N65453 carrying race 21, and *Mustang* N37492 owned by J.D. Reed and flown by James Hagerstrom running race 37.

By contrast, Reno-Stead Airfield – host of the current unlimited classic – is situated at an altitude of 5000 feet. Competitive *Mustangs* typically run two-stage, two-speed *Merlin* superchargers. Assessing the degree of supercharging necessary for a given race location can be visualized by data shown in Table 3. Derived from International Civil Aviation Organization (ICAO) data for a standard atmosphere, this shows that in theory an engine racing at Reno requires an additional 20 cubic feet of air for each pound of fuel burned compared to the same engine running at Cleveland in the Thompson. This illustration is for standard conditions.

The actual situation can vary significantly. Temperatures at Reno are often high during the September races and the effective or density altitude can vary significantly. For example, if a race is run while the air temperature is 90 degrees, the density altitude is then 8000 feet. In this situation, the air density is about .06 pounds per cubic foot and 185 cubic feet of air is required for each pound of fuel burned. So both the local atmospheric conditions and the race site location play a role in determining the engine setup.

Contemporary Unlimited Class Racing: 1964-Present. Early years at Reno frequently saw basically stock *Mustangs* with unaltered dash 7 or dash 9 *Merlins* in competition. There were exceptions, of course, including the *Mustangs* of Chuck Lyford, Chuck Hall and later, Gunther Balz. This first decade of contemporary racing produced some *Merlins* modified with lightweight pistons, increased compression ratios, and emphasis on improved fuel distribution. Manifold pressures up to 100 inches of mercury were possible with a dash 9 engine speed of 3100 - 3200 revolutions per minute. A dash 9 *Merlin* was probably the most popular variant. Water-alcohol injection became routine. Nitrous oxide was employed by several pilots.

During these years, *Merlin* engines strained to the limit, attempting to match the Grumman *Bearcats* of Darryl Greenamyer and later Lyle Shelton. There were some closed-course *Mustang* victories during this period of air racing revival. Indeed, Clay Lacy was the first *Mustang* pilot to capture the unlimited gold race at Reno. It was not

Table 3: AIR VOLUME REQUIRED PER POUND OF GASOLINE AT STANDARD ICAO ALTITUDES
Mixture Ratio = 0.09

Location	Altitude (Ft.)	Air Density (Lb./Cu Ft.)	Air Required (Cu Ft.)	Percent Increase (%)
Schneider Trophy Race	Sea Level	0.0765	145	–
Thompson Trophy Race	800	0.0747	149	3
California 1000 Race	3,000	0.0700	159	9
Reno Air Race	5,000	0.0659	169	16
Bendix Trophy Race	25,000	0.0343	324	123

until 1972 that a highly modified *Mustang* and custom-built *Merlin* succeeded to the winner's circle at Reno. This honor went to Gunther Balz. He demonstrated that a *Merlin* could indeed provide the power and durability necessary to surpass more powerful radial-engined *Bearcats*.

The engine in Gunther's racer used cylinder heads and banks from the more rugged *Merlin* 620 transport engine combined with a dash 9 engine crankcase and supercharger. The reduction gear ratio was lowered to inhibit propeller tip speeds reaching sonic velocity while running the *Merlin* at high revolutions. This philosophy of mixing and matching assemblies from various *Merlin* marks and Packard dash numbers is now a competition standard.

Engine Modifications. What follows is a generic description of modifications to *Merlin* racing engines. Engine rebuilders differ somewhat in detail over what constitutes an optimum racing setup, but for the most part such variations are subtle in extent. Starting at the ground floor, both Packard and Rolls-Royce transport engine cases (crankcases) are used. Attached to the rear of the engine case is a wheelcase which houses gear drive trains necessary to engine operation. Table 4 lists drives located in the wheelcase of a stock V1650-7 engine together with corresponding gear ratios. Maximum engine speed for military-rated *Merlins* is 3000 revolutions per minute (67 inches manifold pressure). At this crankshaft speed, camshafts are geared to rotate at 0.5 X 3000 or 1500 revolutions per minute. At engine overspeeds of 3200 to 3800 revolutions, a camshaft still only rotates at 1600 to 1900 revolutions, an acceptable limit. Similarly, most engine pumps are turning at approximately 2500 to 3000 revolutions compared to their original design maximum of about 2400 revolutions per minute. Racing experience has demonstrated that these accessory components are capable of withstanding overspeed operation for at least limited Reno race durations. An exception is the electrical generator with a gear ratio of 2.468:1. For an

engine speed of 3000 revolutions, the generator turns 7400 revolutions per minute. During a race with an engine speed of say 3400, a generator speed of 8390 revolutions results. In earlier years at Reno, such generator speeds led to armature wire failure and floating armature brushes. Conversion to alternators with rotating armatures alleviated this problem, though high alternator drive speeds, together with engine-induced vibrations, still cause difficulties.

Behind the wheelcase is the supercharger which compresses charge air delivered to the cylinders. Competitive *Merlins* at Reno supercharge to manifold pressures well over 100 inches of mercury. Veteran unlimited pilot Jimmie Leeward has run his engine at 135 inches and 3800 revolutions, although he freely admits that *Merlin* durability becomes problematic. At 100 inches, Jimmie notes that "Merlins are very durable." Lockheed engineer Bruce Boland states that Reno championship class unlimiteds with a dash 7 supercharger can run at power settings of 110 inches and 3600 revolutions to 120 inches at 3800 revolutions.[4] Most *Merlin*-powered *Mustangs* raced at Cleveland and at Reno have used two-speed, two-stage blowers, typically from the Packard dash 7 or dash 9 engine. All run in low blower. This allows overspeed engine operation (increased power) without the additional power loss incurred by running the blower at high speed. The two speed, single-stage blower from a *Merlin* 225 was successfully run at Cleveland during the late 1940s. At Reno, however, the mile-high air density makes the single-stage blower running in high speed inadequate to the task. Manifold pressures above 85 inches of mercury are virtually impossible with this setup and certainly not competitive.

During the early years at Reno, the dash 9 supercharger seemed to be popular. Engine speeds were more modest, typically running in the 3100 to 3400 revolutions range. As engine speeds increased in the never-ending quest for more power, dash 7 blower gears became favored. The dash 7 gear ratio is lower than the dash 9. Consequently, this configuration runs at slower speeds and less horsepower is consumed driving the supercharger.

All competitive engine builders weld additional mass to *Merlin* crankshaft counterweights for dynamic balance at high speed. Rolls-Royce crankshaft counterweights thus modified have been known to fracture at race speeds. Conversely, Packard-built crankshafts seem less prone to this failure. Post-war transport engine series crankshafts are somewhat more rugged also, and are used extensively for racing. It is believed that these later series components benefitted from improved metallurgy through Rolls-Royce development work that extended into the 1950s.

Huskier connecting rods from transport engines are also favored for racing. Rods are shot peened to increase fatigue life for improved durability.[5] Connecting rod bolts are heat treated to obtain a four to five percent increase in hardness. All critical steel parts are carefully inspected, using the Magnaflux process. This process relies upon magnetic properties found in most steels. Imperfections in the surface of a forged steel connecting rod or crankshaft result in discontinuities in the applied magnetic field used in this inspection method.

Another *Merlin* modification involves use of Allison V-1710 connecting rods in place of Rolls or Packard rods. This substitution is possible because both engines have identical 6.0 inch piston strokes. First employed in boat racing engines, the conversion to Allison rods is expensive, since custom connecting rod bearings must be built to make the adaptation. The advantage obtained is greater structural strength to withstand high-speed loads imparted to the connecting rods during race operation. The Allison connecting rods are larger and stronger than their *Merlin* counterparts.

At the top end, engine builders frequently use transport series heads and banks. Stronger construction and apparently improved metallurgy of these late-model engines provide

Table 4: WHEELCASE GEAR DRIVES: V-1650-7*

Component	Gear Ratio	Remarks
Camshaft	0.5:1	
Front Scavenger Pump	0.814:1	
Rear Scavenger Pump	0.814:1	
Oil Pressure Pump	0.814:1	
Hydraulic Oil Pump	0.819:1	
Engine Coolant Pump	1.5:1	
Engine Fuel Pump	0.6:1	
Generator	2.468:1	Alternators now used
Electric Starter	104.252:1	Not used on Stilleto**
Aftercooling System Pump	1.892:1	Sometimes not used
High Blower	7.349:1	Dash 9 Ratio = 8.095:1
Low Blower	5.802:1	Dash 9 Ratio = 6.391:1
Magneto Drive	1.5:1	
Auxiliary Drive (Exhaust Side)	0.777:1	
Auxiliary Drive (Intake Side)	0.828:1	
Auxiliary Drive (Intake Side)	1.0:1	
Tachometer	0.5:1	

* Data obtained from "P-51D Fighter Airplanes," Report No. NA-8248, North American Aviation, Inc., December 1944.
** Starter removed as a means of saving weight. A portable ground starter was used to drive the engine hard crank adaptor.

This is a common scene in Reno every year. Bill Destefani's highly modified P-51D, "Strega," is undergoing an engine change during the 1983 Reno National Championship Air Races. Four years later, "Strega" would win the Reno championship at a record-setting speed. Photo Credit: Birch Matthews

sought-after qualities for racing. An advantage with transport heads is the elimination of the soft aluminum head gaskets which provide a gas seal between the heads and cylinder liners of earlier Packard and Rolls engines. Transport series heads are sealed against the cylinder liners using ground and lapped surfaces.

Transport engine heads possess the additional advantage of having intake and exhaust valve openings about five percent larger than military engine heads. This provides better engine breathing when introducing fresh charge and exhausting combusted gases. Of available transport heads, 600 series components are the most desirable. The 500 series *Merlins* utilized a single-stage supercharger and developed lower rated horsepower relative to the two-stage 600 series engines. Race experience demonstrated that 500 series heads are prone to cracking between the intake valve

Engine rebuilder Mike Nixon specializes in Merlins at his "Vintage V-12s" shop. In the foreground is a Merlin with the heads and banks removed in the process of rebuild. Photo Credit: Birch Matthews

With the propeller removed (left foreground), Don Whittington's crew works on the Merlin engine of his Mustang racer in the pit area at Reno. Photo Credit: Birch Matthews

seats when subjected to race power outputs. Both Rolls and Packard heads are used for racing. Packard heads are superior in one respect. Rolls transport head perimeter tiedown studs are relatively easy to pull out. As a consequence, virtually all transport heads use helicoil inserts. These are seldom required for Packard components. This difference between Packard and Rolls heads is again attributed to subtle variations in metallurgy, or the casting process.

An alternative engine head configuration developed by the late Dave Zeuschel involves welding filler into the seal counterbore on Packard dash 9 heads. The surfaces are then machined and lap finished. A dash 9 cylinder skirt is used in conjunction with 500 series liners. Thus the propensity of 500 series transport heads to crack under stress loads due to high-speed operation is eliminated; however, the improved head seal configuration is retained. Innovations such as this help keep 45-year-old engines operational.

In a similar fashion, cylinder liners can be reworked for continued use. Liner hardness is an important factor with respect to wear from continued translation of the piston and rings. Rolls-Royce greatly improved the hardness of transport liners over that achieved for their military engines. The 600 series liners had the highest hardness values approaching that of chromium. Indeed, chrome alloy piston rings must be carefully run in to obtain proper seating of the ring.

Very early engines coupled the propeller directly to the

crankshaft. Engine speeds rapidly increased as development proceeded and propeller structural loads due to centrifugal force quickly became excessive. For this reason reduction gear drives are used to slow the propeller speed relative to the crankshaft. Propellers convert engine shaft horsepower into propulsive thrust. In general, large diameter propellers are more efficient in that they process large masses of air flow. As engine speeds increase, propeller tip velocities approach the speed of sound. At sonic velocity, propeller efficiency drops rapidly. Indeed, the propeller begins to act as a brake on aircraft forward velocity, even with increased engine power output. For this reason, racing aircraft often use propellers of somewhat shortened diameter to forestall onset of sonic tip velocities. This approach has decided limits with respect to propeller design and efficiency.

Reasonable propeller tip velocities are obtained by lowering the reduction gear drive ratio. Stock Packard dash 7 *Merlins* use a reduction gear ratio of 0.479:1. Thus at a war emergency power using 3000 crankshaft revolutions, the propeller is running at a speed of only 1437 revolutions, or less than half the engine speed. This stock reduction gear ratio is adequate for moderate overspeed engine operation (3100-3300 rpm) and was the norm at Cleveland during the late 1940s as well as the early years at Reno. In later years, *Merlins* were run at higher speeds (3400-3600 rpm) and a lower gear ratio had to be employed. Engine builders resorted to installing transport reduction gears in the nose case (providing a ratio of 0.420:1) to maintain reasonable propeller tip velocities. More recent *Merlins* have been run at speeds as high as 3800 to 4000 revolutions per minute. To facilitate these speeds, custom reduction gears are used with ratios under 0.400:1. Selecting the correct gear ratio for a specific race is a complex calculation, contingent upon such considerations as desired engine speed, anticipated air temperature, and barometric pressure as well as the propeller diameter. This degree of sophistication was employed in the setup of the racing *Merlin* for "*Dago Red.*" Such attention to detail led *Dago Red* to victory in the 1982 Reno Championship Gold Race.

If previous *Mustang* victories at Reno were the result of superb technical effort, performance of the *Merlin*-powered "*Strega*" during the record-setting 1987 Gold Championship Race can only be described as flawless. Indeed, Dwight Thorn's engine setup using dash 9 gears with the supercharger operating in low blower coupled with Allison connecting rods may represent the ultimate in racing *Merlins*. Employing the stronger rods no doubt contributed to the as-tounding durability of this *Merlin* throughout the Reno '87 race week. Under the meticulous supervision of crew chief Bill Kerchenfaut, *Strega's Merlin* performed infallibly at a reported 135 inches manifold pressure and engine speeds well in excess of 3000 revolutions.

Engine Cooling. Racing *Merlins* release tremendous quantities of heat due to combustion. If stock radiators are retained on racing *Mustangs*, cooling augmentation is imperative. Engines operating at high manifold pressures and speeds release correspondingly more heat than their stock cousins. Waste heat introduced into the engine coolant and oil must be dissipated or redline temperatures will be exceeded with accompanying catastrophic results. Methods of heat dissipation are outlined in Table 5. Each approach is valid; however, the method selected must accommodate specific high-speed flight requirements. Pylon racing at Reno demands maximum cooling for perhaps 12 minutes at most. Under these conditions, spray bar cooling augmentation has proved the optimum choice.

Cooling radiators in stock *Merlin*-powered *Mustangs*

Table 5: ENGINE COOLING OPTIONS FOR HIGH SPEED AIRCRAFT USING LIQUID-COOLED AIRCRAFT ENGINES

Method	Configuration	Remarks
Surface Radiators	Airframe surface or skin incorporates coolant passages. High-velocity low-temperature air passing over the skin removes heat by convection from the oil and engine coolant pumped through their respective passageways.	This technique used on various high-speed and racing aircraft during the 1920s and 1930s. Method required large surface areas and reduced airfoil efficiency when wing surfaces were used. Coolant passages were copper because of its high thermal conductivity; however, this imposed a weight penalty.
Fin & Tube Radiators	Compact fin and tube radiators transfer heat from the hot liquid in the tubes by conduction through integral fins exposed to the airstream. Heat is removed from the fins by convection to the air moving through the radiator core. Pressurized cooling systems are used to raise the boiling point of the coolant allowing smaller radiators with reduced aerodynamic drag.	Compact efficient aircraft radiators are suitable for ducted air scoops such as used on the P-51 Mustang. Air entering the scoop is slowed in a diverging section ahead of the radiator core with a corresponding increase in static pressure. Heat from the engine coolant (oil, etc.) is tranferred to the airstream simultaneously elevating the air temperature. High temperature air is then accelerated in a converging section of the duct to a small exit area. Passing the heated air through this nozzle imparts a measurable thrust. This partially offsets drag induced by the presence of the duct and radiator core.
Coolant Boiling	Engine coolant is allowed to elevate in temperature to just below boiling and then "flashed" to steam upon leaving the engine. The vapor is routed through an air-cooled condenser to return it to the liquid state. Oil cooling has been accomplished by immersion of the radiator in a water-cooled bath. Heat is removed from the high temperature oil into the bath which boils at 159 degrees F. Vapor is simply vented overboard. Oil temperature is thus maintained at about 212 degrees F.	The Rolls-Royce Goshawk utilized this cooling principle in a limited number of service aircraft, but not without reliability problems. The Messerschmitt Me 209V1 powered by a highly modified Daimler-Benz DR-601A engine used a boiling system to establish the world speed record in 1939. This technique was used by Darryl Greenamyer in his world record setting F8F-2 Bearcat and also by Mike Carrol in his ill-fated Cobra III project. High performance flight time is obviously limited by the amount of water mixture carried in the boiler.
Spray Bar Systems	Conventional or stock radiators are equipped with water spray nozzles located in front of the heat exchangers. Atomized water droplets are sprayed on the radiator fins to remove additional heat when the engine is operated such as to produce thermal loads above the radiator design capacity.	Spray bar systems are commonly used on all competitive unlimited racers of the current era. For radial engines, spray systems are used on the oil coolers. Liquid-cooled Merlins employ water spray bars for the engine coolant, oil and supercharger aftercooler radiators. About 100-110 gallons of spray bar water is carried during a Reno championship race. At maximum power, spray bar water will last about twelve minutes.

are sized to dissipate waste heat generated at war emergency power. At higher power settings for racing, additional waste heat must be removed. For example, the theoretical chemical energy released at say 1500 horsepower is approximately 18 million Btu's per hour (300,000 Btu's per minute). A racing *Merlin*, generating twice as much power, results in a theoretical total heat release, approaching 3 million Btu's during the approximately 10 to 12 minute race.[6] This additional 3 million Btu's (actually significantly less when various thermal efficiencies are considered) could be removed by adding more or larger cooling radiators. In at least one instance, this approach was utilized. The 1946 Thompson Trophy-winning Bell P-39Q *Cobra* II added a second oil radiator, located in a duct beneath the wing. This solved a high temperature oil frothing problem but added airframe weight and drag.

The optimum solution for Reno pylon racing is spray bar cooling. The amount of heat required to vaporize water is approximately 1000 Btu's per pound of water. Thus by spraying water droplets on heated radiator surfaces additional heat is removed through water evaporation. Using the theoretical numbers, this would imply that some 3000 pounds of water would have to be carried onboard the airplane during a race. Fortunately, this is not the case and less than 1000 pounds is actually required. In addition to the thermal factors that lower the theoretical heat release, the engine is also cooled because the mixture ratio used in a race is fuel rich. Fuel evaporation plays a significant role in engine cooling.

The first spray bar cooling system employed on a *Mustang* occurred in 1964 at Reno. The aircraft was Chuck Lyford's beautiful white P-51D, sponsored by the Bardahl Company. This aircraft was powered by a Dwight Thorn-built V-1650-9 *Merlin*. In a typical Reno race, championship class *Mustangs* consume seven or more gallons of water per minute through the spray bar nozzles.[7] This rate of spray bar flow allows the pilot to race with the coolant door closed to minimize aerodynamic drag. To achieve this drag reduction, even relatively stock racing *Mustangs* usually employ spray bar systems though water throughput is reduced to about two and one-half gallons per minute.

Because the laws of physics are always with us, utilization of a spray bar system to remove excess heat is not without penalty. The timed portion of the championship race lasts about 10 minutes. Additional race power is required to accelerate down the "chute" and run the initial lap around the course to the home pylon when timing begins. This means that about 12 minutes worth of spray bar water is required. For this overall duration, typically 80 to 90 gallons of water may be consumed. By using a thin bladder in place of one wing 92 gallon fuel cell, about 110 gallons of water can be carried for the spray bar system. This imposes a weight penalty of over 900 pounds at takeoff. As with fuel, the water is consumed during the race so airframe gross weight is continually reduced. Conversely, the power-to-weight ratio continually improves as the race progresses – a decided advantage over other potential heat removal schemes. Any discussion of spray bar cooling is incomplete without acknowledging Lockheed engineer Pete Law, who has perfected this cooling technique. Most Reno racers utilize one of his systems.

In a similar vein, recognition is due to the builders of racing *Merlin* engines. Names such as Jack Hovey, Mike Nixon, John Sandberg, Dwight Thorn, and the late Dave Zeuschel are relatively unknown to most air racing stalwarts. Intimately known within the racing fraternity, each has toiled to perfect the ultimate *Merlin*. It is also worth noting that all have built upon the original *Merlin* engine design, a truly elegant solution to the requirement for a liquid-cooled V-12 powerplant.

Mustang Powerplant Addendum. Emphasis in this chapter has justly concentrated on Rolls-Royce *Merlins* and license-built Packard engines. As a historical footnote, *Mustangs* have raced with other engines. During the late 1940s, at least two *Mustangs* flew with Allison engines. In 1981, history was repeated when Ed Maloney (Planes of Fame Air Museum) entered a P-51A powered by an Allison V-1750-81 engine.

Conceived by N.H. Gilman, manager of the Allison Engineering Company in Indianapolis, Indiana, the original V-1710 was designed to produce 750 horsepower some two years before work began on the *Merlin*.[8] Through the trials of America's Depression years, Allison's early support was furnished by the U.S. Navy for their airship program. Belatedly, the Air Corps accepted the liquid-cooled Allison engine for evolving pursuit aircraft, notably Lockheed's P-38 *Lightning*, Bell's P-39 *Airacobra* (and later P-63 *Kingcobra*) and the P-40 *Warhawk* produced by Curtiss. North American Aviation also designed their prototype and early production *Mustangs* around the Allison. But the *Mustang's* dash 81 Allison, which developed 1330 horsepower, lacked adequate supercharging to bring North American's fighter to its ultimate military potential. Although generally considered structurally stronger than a *Merlin*, the Allison never matched its counterpart in racing. It forever lacked a comparable supercharger.

Perhaps the ultimate *Mustang* powerplant combination involved a modified Rolls-Royce *Griffon*. Design of the *Griffon* began in 1939. Equal in volume to the Rolls-Royce R engine, the *Griffon* has a displacement of 2239 cubic inches, a 36 percent increase over the Merlin. Rolls very cleverly designed the *Griffon* to fit into *Merlin*-powered airframes with minimal modification. Thus the RB-51 *Red Baron* crew was able to adapt the *Griffon* into a *Mustang* airframe. This *Griffon* was a composite engine consisting of a dash 57 engine turning counter-rotating propellers, coupled with a dash 74 blower. The resulting combination was fed by a Pratt & Whitney R-2800 carburetor and water-injection regulator. This potent 3400 horsepower engine was the creation of Randy Scoville and Dave Zeuschel. The result

was a powerplant which produced a world piston engine speed record of 499.018 miles per hour plus four championship race victories including the 1977 and 1978 Reno National Championship Gold Races, a truly remarkable achievement.

The only other *Griffon*-powered *Mustang* to appear at the Reno races was one built by Don Whittington of Fort Lauderdale, Florida. Unfortunately, the aircraft was plagued with problems and Don aborted before the start of the 1988

Power generated by the Merlin engine is converted to thrust with the four-bladed Mustang propeller. This picturesque view was taken of Don Whittington's "Precious Metal" as it sat in the Reno pit area before a race. Photo Credit: Birch Matthews

The "Red Baron" racing team installed a Rolls-Royce Griffon engine in a Mustang airframe. The mammoth size of the engine is illustrated in this photograph as a crew member works on the aircraft during the 1978 Reno Air Races. Photo Credit: Chuck Aro

This profile of Cliff Cummins' "Miss Candace" shows the power package uncowled during an engine run up at Reno. Photo Credit: Chuck Aro

Reno Gold Race. The propeller governor for the counter rotating propellers failed, sending all six blades into flat pitch. He made a wheels-up, forced landing in Lemon Valley, east of the airport. The beautiful racer was extensively damaged.

Notes

1. Virtually all historians recount the fact that the Merlin engine began as a private venture with corresponding Rolls-Royce nomenclature of P.V.12. In most instances, the reader is allowed to infer that the British Air Ministry had little if any interest in the project. Major G.P. Bulman, Ministry of Supply and a Fellow of the Royal Aeronautical Society, commented, ". . . [the Merlin] began without Air Ministry support. Well, the support was offered but it was not accepted. The firm prepared to go ahead with it as a private venture, no doubt because they thought they would be free to deal with ultimate royalties and so on, but it was not long before they came along and said we will accept your offer of a contract." Whatever the circumstances, development of the Merlin, named after a member of the falcon family of birds, proceeded boldly.

2. There is also strong evidence to suggest that the Allison suffered from inconsistent support and changing requirements that bordered on interference. See, for example, "The Curtiss D-12 Aero Engine," *Smithsonian Annals of Flight*, Number 7, Smithsonian Institution Press, Washington, D.C., 1972. Pages 106-107.

3. Critical altitude is the maximum altitude at which a supercharged engine can deliver full sea level power. Data obtained from "Performance Calculations for Model P-51D Airplane," North American Aviation, Inc., Report No. NA-46-130, 6 February 1946.

4. Appendix A contains a further discussion on supercharging.

5. Shot peening is a surface treatment which increases the compressive strength of the metal.

6. A moderate size home is warmed by a gas-fired furnace with an input rating of around 150,000 BTu's per hour. Thermal energy released during a Reno championship race in one Merlin is probably sufficient to heat this home for almost 40 hours during the coldest days of winter.

7. *Stilleto* requires up to nine gallons of spray bar water per minute. Race consumption may therefore be as much as 108 gallons for this aircraft, often making the final lap interesting, if not a bit tenuous.

8. When founder James A. Allison died in 1928, his company was ultimately purchased by the General Motors Corporation. The organization remains a division of GM to this date.

Chapter Four
MAGIC POTIONS

Depending upon one's perspective, aircraft piston engine development may be viewed from strides made in metallurgy, supercharging, cooling technology, lubrication, and engine design configuration. Absolutely critical and perhaps most important to aircraft engine progression was the evolution of high-performance aviation fuels. Without such fuels, even the finest metallurgical advances would not have sufficed. Supercharging would have been of marginal use. Fuel research and development, however, allowed engine designers to conquer the beast of detonation, or "knock," and achieve rather astounding power outputs from *Merlins*

and other well known engines.

The late C.F. Kettering of General Motors stated the relationship between fuels and internal combustion engines when he said, "We fully realized that it was the combination of engines and fuels and not either one of them alone that develops useful power." This is certainly true with respect to racing engines. Maximum useful power from a *Merlin* engine is very dependent upon the quality of fuel employed. Historically, high performance racing fuels include both gasoline blends and various alcohol-based combinations. Gasolines are produced by distilling, or "cracking," crude

Chuck Lyford's beautiful Bardahl-sponsored Mustang runs up in the pit area at Reno during the 1967 racing season. Chuck ran a Merlin with the first spray bar system designed to augment the engine cooling system by injecting an atomized water-methanol spray over the radiators to dissipate excess heat generated by high power settings used during a race. This photograph was taken during the 1967 Reno Air Races. Photo Credit: Birch Matthews

oils while alcohols are synthesized from various hydrocarbons such as coal, natural gas and petroleum products.

Alcohol Fuels. Prior to development of truly high octane aviation gasolines during the 1930s, alcohol blends were frequently used in high performance racing engines. There were at least two factors influencing this trend. During World War I and into the 1920s, available gasolines were not only noisome but of perhaps no more than 50 octane rating.[1] As such, they were highly susceptible to detonation, or as it was commonly called, knock. And secondly, especially in Europe, alcohol production was typically a government-controlled monopoly. Excess alcohol was directed into various fuel markets. Thus in early years, the quality of alcohol-gasoline blends varied with supply and various demands such as heating, lighting, and motoring fuels. Racing participants increasingly resorted to precisely mixed alcohol-based fuels to facilitate high compression ratio or supercharged engine operation without detonation.

Although of lesser chemical energy than gasolines, alcohol fuels provide detonation resistance when used in supercharged engines. The British, for instance, used an alcohol-based fuel in their 1931 Schneider Trophy winning Supermarine S.6B racer. The S.6B powerplant was a Roll-Royce 2239 cubic inch R engine, supercharged to deliver over 2300 horsepower when operated on a blend of 60 percent methyl alcohol (methanol), 10 percent acetone and 30 percent benzol. Benzol is a colloquial term applied to mixtures of benzene and toluol.[2] A mixture commonly used in the United States for motor racing during the 1930s was benzol 90s. This nomenclature indicated that its volatility was high: 90 percent of the mixture boiled upon reaching 212 degrees Fahrenheit.

Although alcohol blends and alcohol-gasoline combinations provided detonation resistance for supercharged engines, their limitation is lower energy content per pound relative to high-grade gasolines. The chemical energy content of a fuel is defined as its heating value and measured in terms of British thermal units (Btus) per pound. This is the amount of heat required to raise one pound of water one degree Fahrenheit in temperature. The inherent disadvantage of using alcohol-based fuels in high performance racing engines is seen in Table 1 which is a list of some common fuels, including aviation gasoline.

Heating values given in this table show, for instance, that a racing airplane using a supercharged engine would have to carry more than twice as much methyl alcohol as aviation gasoline to achieve the same power setting during a race of fixed distance. This disadvantage is compounded due to the fact that methyl alcohol is 10 percent heavier than gasoline. Even though fuel is burned off during the course

Supermarine S.6 N247 powered by the Rolls-Royce R engine fueled with a 78 percent benzol, 22 percent Romanian straight run gasoline. This combination won the 1929 Schneider Trophy Race at 329 mph. Photo Credit: Vickers Armstrong

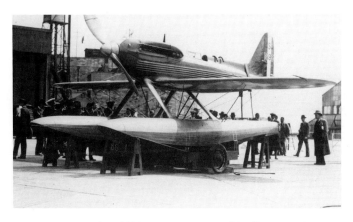

Supermarine S.6B S1595 using an uprated Rolls-Royce R engine won the 1931 Schneider race. Rod Banks blended 70 percent benzol, 10 percent methanol and 20 percent California straight run gasoline. Photo Credit: Vickers Armstrong

Supermarine S.6B S1596 set the world's absolute speed record of 407 mph. To develop more power, fuel was changed to 30 percent benzol, 60 percent methanol and 10 percent acetone which allowed greater supercharging. Photo Credit: Vickers Armstrong

of a race, the initial fuel weight penalty and volume requirement at takeoff is quite significant.

A comparison of methyl alcohol with aviation gasoline is perhaps an extreme case. In reality, supercharged engine performance may be obtained by blending various alcohols both with and without gasolines. The objective is to achieve detonation resistance while still maintaining some reasonable energy content and other important fuel characteristics. This is why benzol, with its relatively high heating value, was usually a fuel constituent in many racing engines before World War II.

For their successful record run of 1931, Rolls-Royce engineers utilized a blend of methyl alcohol, benzol and acetone, upon the advice of F.R. (Rod) Banks. This fuel cocktail, combined with the R engine and Supermarine S.6B airframe, produced an absolute speed record of 407 miles per hour; a phenomenal velocity achieved less than three decades following man's first tenuous powered flight. It is interesting to note that the 1931 fuel blend resulted in

a heating value of about 11,600 Btus per pound of fuel. Had high octane aviation gasoline of World War II been available in 1931, the Supermarine S.6B fuel load would have been reduced some 40 percent.[3]

Alcohol-based fuels have enjoyed sporadic usage among post-World War II and contemporary unlimited class air racers. In addition to weight and tank volume penalties, alcohols chemically attack materials commonly used for fuel system seals and tank bladders. Lower alcohol blend heating values also require larger capacity fuel pumps to deliver an equivalent amount of energy to the engine, and to accept these higher flow rates, carburetor jets must be enlarged.

Four unlimited class air racers have attempted to use alcohol-based fuels since World War II. The first was Chuck Brown's P-39Q-10 *Airacobra*, entered in the 1948 National Air Races. This racer was powered by an Allison V-1710-G6 engine with the auxiliary stage supercharger removed and the engine stage supercharger regeared to an

Table Six: PROPERTIES OF COMMON FUELS

Fuel	Heating Value Btu/Lb.	Weight Lb/Gal.	Heat of Btu/Lb.	Octane Rating
Aviation Gas	18,800	6.0	130	115/145
Xylene (91% Pure)	17,800	7.2	145	Unknown
Toluene	17,500	7.2	150	98
Benzene	17,300	7.3	170	88-110
Acetone	12,300	6.6	170	100
Ethyl Alcohol	11,600	6.6	390	99
Methyl Alcohol	8,600	6.6	470	90-100
Rolls-Royce #1	17,600	7.0	160	96
Rolls-Royce #2	16,700	7.0	192	95
Rolls-Royce #3	11,600	6.8	350	92
Benzol 90s	17,500	7.3	162	95-100
Methyl Alcohol & Nitromethane	7,800	7.2	425	Unknown

Notes:
1. Acetone was used as a mixing agent.
2. Rolls-Royce Mixture #1 consisted of 78% benzol and 22% gasoline from Romanian fields with 3.3 cc of tetraethyl lead added. It was used in the 1929 Schneider Cup Race.
3. Rolls-Royce Mixture #2, used in the 1931 Schneider race, was 70% benzol, 10% methyl alcohol and 20% gasoline from California fields with 3.3 cc of tetraethyl lead added.
4. Rolls-Royce Mixture # 3 consisted of 30% benzol, 60% methyl alcohol and 10% acetone with 4.1 cc of tetraethyl lead added. This blend was used in the successful world speed record of 1931.

This Sea Fury Mk F.B. 11 was modified to allow its Wright R-3350 to burn a methanol-nitromethane mixture. Teething problems at the 1987 Reno races resulted in replacement of the engine with a gasoline-burning R-3350 just prior to the races. Photo Credit: Birch Matthews

8.8:1 ratio to increase fuel-air charge weight flow. The engine was prepared by Allison engineer Don Nolan to produce maximum race power. His preparation included consideration and testing of alcohol-based fuel blends. According to Nolan, ". . . Flight tests were conducted with several fuels, principally methanol, benzene, and acetone mixtures. Complete recarburization was accomplished to match these requirements. Speed-power data were obtained which showed the aircraft to fly at speeds in excess of 438 miles per hour, true air speed (power set at 115 inches manifold pressure and 3350 revolutions per minute) on a measured mile course. Comparative runs were also made using 2-4-4 tri-methyl butane (from Shell Oil Company)

and water injection which showed reasonably good data as compared to the alcohol fuels with correspondingly less consumption. The decision was made to sacrifice the slight performance margin with the alcohol blends for a guarantee of a sufficient quantity (of fuel) for the race."

With the return of unlimited air racing at Reno in the 1960s, David Maytag entered a P-51D *Mustang*. During 1967, the *Merlin* engine setup was modified in a unique dual fuel configuration. Conventional aviation gasoline was used for start up, taxiing, takeoff, and landing. High power race operation was to be conducted using methanol. This complex approach to an alcohol-fuel racer was the design product of Douglas Aircraft powerplant engineer, Al Heinike.

John Sandberg ran this rare Bell P-63 C-5 Kingcobra for a number of racing seasons. The aircraft was at one time equipped with a dual Garrett turbocharger setup. The fuel system was revised to burn methanol. Engine reliability problems plagued John and he reverted to aviation gasoline. Photo Credit Vlado Lenoch via Dick Phillips

In his own precise description, "the methanol system was installed parallel with the existing gasoline system except that methanol was injected at the intake valves while the aviation gasoline was injected at the blower inlet in the normal manner." Maytag's crew custom built the methanol injectors and calibrated them by flowing methanol through the injectors and catching the fluid in milk bottles! Maytag *Mustang* pilot Russ Schleeh stated that during flight he could "pull 110 inches manifold pressure using antidetonant fluid with aviation gasoline, but needed only 85 inches manifold pressure with methanol for about the same engine power levels."

The Maytag *Mustang* methanol-fueled engine project came to an unhappy ending. On the day before the Maytag crew was to leave for Reno and the races, Russ was flying a last test flight over California's Mojave desert. Applying power while running methanol, Russ's engine blew, forcing him to make an emergency landing at Palmdale Airport. David Maytag lost interest in the project and it died aborning.

It was not until 1974 that race enthusiast, John Sandberg, gave alcohol fuels another shot. Armed with Don Noland's experimental data from 1948, John modified the Allison V-1710 engine in his Bell P-63C racer, Miss Tipsie, to run on methanol fuel. Methanol was port-injected using a Hillborne fuel injection system. Wet wings were used with a methanol-resistant sealant which provided sufficient fuel capacity for the Reno race course. Stainless steel was used throughout the fuel feed system. Even more adventuresome was incorporation of two Garrett turbochargers, one for each six-cylinder bank of the Allison. The engine was capable of up to 110 inches of manifold pressure, an impressive achievement. In spite of all his effort, John found the reconfigured Allison unreliable for racing and reverted to gasoline the next year.

Tex Johnston flew this Bell P-39Q-10 to victory in the 1946 Thompson Trophy Race. To overcome an oil frothing problem, his crew added a second oil cooler radiator in a belly scoop beneath the airframe to dissipate extra heat generated by race power operation of the Allison engine. Spray bar cooling augmentation eliminated the need for additional radiators in current Reno racers. Photo Credit: Bell Aerospace Corporation

The most recent attempt to employ alcohol-based fuels in an unlimited racer occurred during 1987. In Reno that year, Eric Lorentzen of Levolor-Lorentzen, Inc. entered a striking Hawker Sea Fury F.B. 11, incorporating a methanol-fueled Wright R3350-26WD radial engine. An electronic computer-controlled fuel injection system was utilized and the fuel feed system made compatible with methanol. In reality, the fuel was a methanol-nitromethane blend and, based upon dynamometer tests, the Levolor people claimed power output in excess of 4000 horsepower. This is an impressive 40 percent increase over a stock R3350. To feed this monster, fuel tank capacity was increased from 240 gallons to 301 gallons. Engine problems plagued this new racer, and by race weekend the methanol engine had been replaced by another R3350 burning conventional aviation gasoline.

Aviation Gasolines. Petroleum engineers brought high-performance gasolines to reality during the 1930s and development continued during World War II. These advancements allowed engine designers to routinely increase power by boosting manifold pressures to higher and higher magnitudes. The consequences of improved fuels were evident during the war as numerous fighter aircraft, including the *Mustang*, were able to operate effectively at altitudes above 20,000 feet by using more supercharging.

The topic of gasolines is simultaneously broad and technically complex. Fuel research and development is the province of chemists, although one suspects such research also contains a motivating dash of ancient alchemy, a Middle Ages philosophy principally concerned with turning baser metals into gold. How better to describe the transformation and monetary return from crude oil into high-performance aviation gasoline?

Aviation fuels consist primarily of four different series of hydrocarbons: aromatics, naphthenes, olefins, and paraffins. During the early years of aviation, gasolines were obtained by simple distillation of crude oils to obtain the lighter fractions -those hydrocarbons with boiling points of say 100 to 300 degrees Fahrenheit. These were so-called "straight run" gasolines and varied in quality from wretched (perhaps 50 octane) to moderately acceptable (approaching 70 octane). Their consistency and quality, if you will, was dependent upon the oil fields from which they were derived. Thus, the racing technician of the late 1920s and early 1930s sought gasolines from fields rich in aromatics or naphthenes, which possessed the highest and second highest anti-knock qualities, respectively. Aromatics, incidentally, had concentrations of benzene and toluene which by themselves were useful anti-knock ingredients in fuel blends during this era. With this logic, it is understandable that Rod Banks

selected California straight run gasolines as one fuel constituent for the 1931 Schneider Trophy Supermarine S.6B racer. California crudes were known to have high aromatic content. To deal with the high degree of supercharging employed in the R engine of the S.6B, Banks further improved his potion by adding large doses of methanol and benzol together with a lacing of tetraethyl lead. This chemistry yielded an octane rating of about 95 and a corresponding heating value of 17,500 Btu per pound. Earlier, for the 1929 Schneider Race, Banks mixed benzol with Romanian gasoline, high in naphthenes, and fed it to the Rolls-Royce R engine powering the Supermarine S.6. Logistically, Romanian gasoline was in relatively near proximity to Great Britain. Simultaneously, Rolls enjoyed a reasonable amount of time in which to prepare their racing engine. By contrast, precious little time existed for development and preparation of Britain's 1931 Schneider entrant, the S.6B. With attention to detail and seeking every advantage, Banks no doubt selected the marginally improved anti-knock quality of the distant California straight run gasoline. Britain's victory was the sum of all parts played in this international race project, not the least of which was the fuel blend.

With the passage of time, petroleum engineers and chemists became more sophisticated in cracking crude oils and in blending constituents to achieve consistent quality standards and octane ratings independent of the crude source. Thus it was that American racers of the Depression years had access to 87 octane fuel which would allow moderate supercharging. One hundred octane aviation gasoline was in laboratory quantities by 1934. In a few short years, it was the Army Air Corps standard, and higher performance fuels were in the offing. These latter gasolines would be race tested at Cleveland following World War II.

Unlimited racers entered in the 1946 and 1947 National Air Races in Cleveland basically relied upon commercially available aviation gasoline having a performance number of 100/130.[4] Contemporary reports suggest that some of the entries further modified their gasolines to a limited extent with additives, hopefully to further suppress detonation at race manifold pressures.

In 1948, Shell Oil introduced a limited quantity of what was billed as an outstanding new fuel called Methyl Triptane-1. The basis for triptane was actually not very new at all. This fuel was first formulated and reported in scientific literature during 1922 by Chavanne, a Belgian chemist.[5] It was subsequently made in laboratory quantities and first tested in an engine during 1926. By 1938, triptane had been tested in a supercharged engine, and at this point, Wright Field engineers became interested in its possibilities. Research, development, and limited production of triptane continued during World War II by General Motors Research Laboratories under sponsorship of the Army Air Forces. Results were impressive. Tests revealed that an Allison V-1710 engine with a rated takeoff power of 1500 horsepower could deliver up to 2500 horsepower using a mixture of 60 percent triptane and 40 percent 100 octane aviation gasoline. Introduction of triptane fuel by Shell for the 1948 races was perhaps an advertising coup d'etat over rival Standard Oil of Ohio, one of the race sponsors. Shell's triptane had a performance number of about 200/300 and was practically free from any destructive detonation tendency. Without doubt it was the pinnacle in aviation gasoline development for reciprocating engines.

Triptane was available again for the 1949 races. Both Bill Odom and Anson Johnson loaded this fuel into their highly modified *Merlin*-powered *Mustangs*. Aviation Week magazine indicated that both added four cubic centimeters of tetraethyl lead per gallon of triptane racing fuel. Not to be outdone during the 1949 races, Standard Oil offered an improved aviation gasoline with a performance number of 130/170. In essence, use of these racing fuel blends meant that engines were structurally limited and not fuel performance or detonation limited. Prolonged operation at extreme pressures and temperatures could still result in engine failure but not necessarily because the gasoline used caused detonation.

Fuel Additives. In a broad sense, there are two convenient categories of fuel additives. The first category involves additives blended directly into aviation gasoline while the second consists of fluids introduced at some point into the engine induction system. Both categories are designed to allow the race pilot to extract more power from a highly boosted engine.

Power developed by reciprocating engines is fundamentally related to the quantity of air put through each cylinder per minute. Although both fuel and oxygen in air are required for combustion, fuel represents only about two percent of the mixture volume. Thus the engine is essentially an air pump. Improved power output from a *Merlin* or any racing engine is accomplished by operating at increasingly higher manifold pressures through supercharging. Some attempts have been made to run *Merlins* at compression ratios greater than the stock 6:1 ratio. Increasing compression ratio yields higher efficiency, which means more energy is extracted from the charge of fuel and air introduced into the cylinders. Results from this approach have been limited. Higher manifold pressure operation is the most productive means of achieving race power output and is the technique most commonly used today.

Application of these extraordinary manifold pressures can result in the phenomenon of detonation. At moderate manifold pressures, ignition of the compressed fuel mixture produces smooth, stable combustion within the engine cylinders. At higher manifold conditions, gas temperatures and pressures within the cylinders increase dramatically. Ignition and combustion of the gasoline vapor starts in a normal progression but then a threshold pressure and temperature is reached beyond which remaining unburned fuel spontaneously explodes or detonates. Consequent pressure peaks in the cylinder are extreme, amounting to some three or four times a normal combustion pressure rise on the piston surface. Engine components are subjected to abnormal forces and temperatures. In the limit, structural failures occur. Detonation problems in high performance engines can be acute, as witnessed by the innumerable engine failures over the years of unlimited class racing. It was the propensity of early gasolines to detonate that forced engineers to use anti-knock alcohol-based fuels in supercharged engines during the early years of aviation.

The petroleum industry attacked detonation problems by increasing the octane rating of aviation gasolines using refining and blending techniques. As noted earlier, 100 octane fuel became the standard for military aviation in the United States and Britain during World War II. In addition to raising octane rating, various additives were used to retard the onset of detonation. The most commonly recognized additive is tetraethyl lead, used in quantities typically one to six cubic centimeters per gallon of gasoline. Developed by Thomas Midgley, Jr., and associates, it is a remarkably effective compound.

There are many other chemical compounds capable of reducing detonation in aviation gasolines. In his classic book, *The Internal Combustion Engine*, C.F. Taylor lists 45 compounds known to have a positive effect on detonation. Standard Oil of Ohio modified its 100/130 grade gasoline to National Air Race competitors with aromatic compounds including benzene, toluene and xylene. These additives provided good antidetonation qualities for supercharged racing engines.

With today's military and commercial aviation emphasis on turbine engines, refinery development and production centers on jet fuels. As a consequence, specialized racing fuel blends are not available from major refiners. Aviation gasoline available at Reno is 115/145 performance number. To this some of the competitors add tetraethyl lead.

High performance fuel technology for present day unlimited class racers is not significantly different from that of earlier years. Aromatic compounds, such as toluene, are still used to inhibit detonation. Another additive sometimes used in contemporary racing fuels is methylcyclopentadienyltricarbonyl. Because of its awesome chemical nomenclature, this compound was marketed by the Ethyl

David Maytag owned this chocolate-colored P-51 and it was flown by Russ Schleeh. It was converted to an unusual dual fuel system in 1967. Standard aviation gas was used for takeoffs and landings while methanol was injected for pylon racing. Russ lost an engine during a test flight right before the 1967 Reno races and the system was never used in competition. Photo Credit: Dusty Carter

Corporation under the trade name Combustion Improver No. 2 or simply CI-2. It was originally used as a fuel oil additive in the electric utility industry; Ethyl Corporation hoped to expand its use as an antidetonant additive in gasolines to replace tetraethyl lead. This did not occur. Today, Ethyl markets this product under the name MMT. With MMT added to 115/145 aviation gasoline, a performance number of about 170 is obtained.

The second class of additives used in racing is not blended into the fuel. Rather, these fluids are injected directly into the engine induction system. This category includes water, nitrous oxide and nitromethane. Water injection is virtually mandatory at high engine power levels. In reality, the fluid used is usually a 50 percent mixture of water and methyl alcohol, and formally called antidetonant injection liquid. A water-alcohol mixture was originally used during World War II to prevent the liquid from freezing in cold weather climates or during high altitude operations. This mixture has been retained for unlimited pylon racing aircraft because it yields better engine performance than straight water injection.[6] As the antidetonant liquid vaporizes, incoming supercharged fuel-air mixture temperature is

reduced through evaporative cooling. The fluid reduces engine combustion about 300 to 400 degrees Fahrenheit, which acts to suppress detonation.

Significant quantities of antidetonant fluid are required for a *Merlin* racing engine. The amount consumed during a race depends upon the engine mixture ratio setting and whether or not an aftercooler is used at the supercharger outlet. In the absence of an aftercooler and at relatively lean mixture ratios, combustion temperatures are high. At these conditions, antidetonant injection is consumed at a rate of about 0.8 to 1.0 pound per pound of fuel burned. A somewhat fuel-rich mixture, together with supercharger aftercooling, requires less antidetonant injection with flow rates around 0.4 to 0.5 pound per pound of fuel. The precise amount of injection is determined by measuring the engine air induction temperature. This in turn is influenced by the outside air temperature. On such subtleties are races won.

Merlin-powered unlimiteds at Reno carry around 40 gallons of antidetonant liquid for the 10 minute duration championship race. By comparison, Thompson competitors used antidetonant injection at something like 0.3 to 0.5 pound per pound of fuel consumed while running with

Chuck Brown flew the diminutive Bell racer in 1948. Chuck held the lead for nineteen laps before a fuel vapor lock problem forced him out of the race. Photo Credit: Emil Strasser

manifold pressures ranging from 70 to 110 inches of mercury. Even at lower consumption rates, Thompson pilots found it necessary to carry in excess of 100 gallons to sustain high power during much of the approximately one-half hour race. The weight penalty imposed on a *Mustang* carrying this much antidetonant liquid amounted to about 800 to 1,000 pounds at race takeoff.

Another injectant periodically employed with *Merlin* engines is nitrous oxide, a compound containing about 36 percent by weight of oxygen. This was a technique originally developed in Germany during World War II. Injection of nitrous oxide requires additional fuel to maintain the desired engine fuel-air mixture ratio. As a consequence, more chemical energy per charge is introduced into the engine cylinders on each power stroke, providing more horsepower. In addition to increased fuel input, nitrous oxide provides evaporative cooling and increased charge density. In a typical racing engine setup, liquid nitrous oxide is stored under pressure in bottles (tanks) of 24 pound capacity. In practice, the bottles are not filled to capacity and usually carry around 20 pounds of the substance. This leaves sufficient tank volume available in the bottle to accept nitrous oxide vapor without venting overboard as the liquid temperature rises. The injection system incorporates on-off solenoid-operated valves, controlling the nitrous oxide injection as well as added fuel flow (1.5 pounds of fuel per minute) to produce an incremental power increase of approximately 200 horsepower. Used with some restraint, nitrous oxide injection can marginally add power output to the racing engine when needed. It is advantageous for power surges in sprint situations. Used to excess or for prolonged periods, nitrous oxide injection quickly results in engine structural failure.

Nitromethane is a liquid compound consisting of carbon, hydrogen, nitrogen, and oxygen. Because oxygen is present in this compound, combustion is possible without the addition of air. The potential of "nitro" as a fuel or fuel additive has been well understood since the 1940s, and indeed has been used in other forms of motor racing. Standard Oil of Ohio reportedly offered a special antidetonant fluid to unlimited pilots entered in the Thompson Trophy Race. It was suggested that this particular antidetonant injection blend would result in up to 15 percent more power output from the engine. From speculation, it has been concluded that the Sohio fluid probably contained a stabilized form of nitromethane. Nitro has been used in contemporary unlimiteds, including Darryl Greenamyer's F8F Bearcat and the Red Baron *Mustang*, prior to the installation of a Griffon engine in the latter. Reportedly, nitro was added to the aviation gasoline used in the Red Baron *Merlin*, with catastrophic results in 1974. The engine exploded during the championship race at Reno. One piston was actually blown out of the aircraft onto the desert floor and never found. It was postulated that some of the nitromethane stratified in the fuel tank or fuel feed system, resulting in an excessive amount reaching one or more cylinders. More recent applications of nitromethane have been successfully accomplished by mixing the compound with antidetonant solution.

Detonation Suppressing Chemical Compounds. The relentless search for fuel chemistry to suppress detonation in piston engines was eventually resolved by Thomas Midgley, Jr., and T.A. (Tab) Boyd, who empirically discovered the pacifying effects of minute quantities of tetraethyl lead in gasoline. There was more than a touch of irony in their chemical endeavors. Both were mechanical engineers! In his highly readable book, *I Kept No Diary*, Air Commodore R.F. Banks relates the genesis of the Midgley-Boyd research. In 1917, America was fully engaged in "the war to end all wars." As a consequence, there was a shortage of gasoline for domestic consumption to power home generators for lighting, especially in rural areas. To offset this shortage, kerosene was distributed as a substitute. As it so happened, Charles (Boss) Kettering's Dayton, Ohio-based Delco Corporation was a major supplier of home lighting sets. Reacting to widespread complaints of engine knock or detonation in these devices when fueled with kerosine, Kettering turned to co-workers Midgley and Boyd with simple direction: "Find the cause; cure it." Thus began a four year search for a solution.

According to Rod Banks, the most valuable guidance received by Midgley was provided by Dr. Wilson of Standard Oil (Indiana) who suggested study of the Periodic Table of elemental atomic weights.[7] Midgley found from experimentation that compounds containing elements with higher atomic weights indeed had better antidetonation properties. This led to consideration of metallic lead, which was relatively abundant and inexpensive. The problem was then narrowed to determining a suitable organic lead compound miscible in gasoline. By 1922, Midgley and Boyd experimented with tetraethyl lead, an elemental compound consisting of carbon, hydrogen, and lead. Miscible in gasoline and at very low concentrations, this lead compound suppressed detonation to a remarkable degree. It

was to become the basic additive to gasolines for decades to come. Using tetraethyl lead in gasoline was not without penalty. In commercial use, other additives were also necessary lest oxidized lead deposits from the combustion process result in fouled spark plugs and ruined exhaust valves. The lead deposit problem was resolved by adding two more ingredients to the recipe: ethylene dibromide and ethylene dichloride. With these problems resolved or at least under control, high performance engines became practical. Lead additives are still used today in racing engines at Reno.

Notes

1. This is an estimate of the octane number. The octane and later performance number of classifying gasolines did not then exist.
2. Benzene and toluol (a commercial form of toluene) are both hydrocarbons possessing good anti-knock qualities for supercharged engines .
3. Octane rating of fuels is based upon comparative testing with mixtures of normal heptane which detonates easily and iso-octane which is quite resistant to detonation. These two fuels have arbitrary octane ratings of O and 100, respectively. To determine an octane number, tests are conducted in a special unsupercharged engine at standard conditions using a relatively lean fuel-air mixture ratio. Test engine compression is increased until the onset of detonation is reached. Thus through comparative testing, a gasoline exhibiting a tendency to detonate at the same point as a mixture of 80 percent iso-octane and 20 percent heptane would be rated at 80 octane.
4. Aircraft engines frequently operate for periods of time at richer mixture ratios

Don Noland's 1948 Bell P-39Q-10 creation is seen here on the Thompson Trophy race course. Noland considered and tested methanol fuel combinations with this racer but eventually resorted to high octane triptane aviation fuel for the Thompson race. Photo Credit: Emil Strasser

as during takeoff and climb. As more fuel is added, the charge cools and resistance to detonation increases. To account for this phenomenon, the performance number rating system for gasolines was developed. Test engines used in grading fuels could vary mixture ratio as well as manifold pressure (supercharging). An aviation fuel performance number of 100/130 thus indicated that at lean mixture ratio the gasoline had an octane number of 100; however, at richer mixture ratios, the manifold pressure could be increased 30 percent with a corresponding power increase before detonation occurred.

5. The precise chemical nomenclature for triptane is 2, 2, 3 trimethyl butane. The name "triptane" was not coined until 1943.

6. Addition of methyl alcohol is believed to result in finer atomization of the injected liquid due to a lowering of surface tension forces of the mixture in contrast with straight water. A more uniform distribution of vapor within the engine manifold is also thought to occur.

7. The Periodic Table was conceived and produced by Dimitry I. Mendeleyev in 1896. It lists the atomic weights of all the elements. The lightest element, for instance, is hydrogen at 1.00. In comparison, lead has an atomic weight of 207.

This unique photograph was taken at the start of the 1947 Kendall Trophy Race and illustrates three different models of the Mustang. In the lead is race 15, a P-51A. Trailing in third position is a P-51B, race 34. Below is race 77, a P-51D Mustang. Photo Credit: Warren Bodie

Part II
Win, Place and Show

Air Racing *had its beginning with the invention of the free balloon. Aero Clubs were formed in Europe and the United States in the late 1800s to promote the sport of ballooning and balloon racing. In 1899 the first cross-country race for balloons was sponsored by James Gordon Bennett, owner of the New York Herald newspaper. J.G. Bennett was a very wealthy newspaper tycoon who gained worldwide notoriety when he sent newsman H.M. Stanley to Africa in search of Dr. Livingston.*

Apparently the sport of racing had sparked his interest in a similar manner because Bennett provided trophies and prize money for both auto and balloon racing. With the advent of the "aeroplane," Aero clubs were expanded to embrace this new flying machine. Aero Clubs of Europe and the United States sponsored the first International Air Meet in Rheims, France on the plains of Bethaney where Joan of Arc once stood. James Gordon Bennett provided a trophy and prize money for the pilot and aeroplane flying two laps of a closed course at the highest speed. The only American entrant, Glenn Curtiss, won the trophy at a speed of 47.65 mph. The James Gordon Bennett Trophy race continued until 1914 when all racing ceased due to World War.

Other wealthy men were also drawn to air racing, and in 1913 Jacques Schnieder, a member of the Schnieder Arms family, provided prize money and a trophy for a racing event for seaworthy aeroplanes. This race was also interrupted by the World War, but resumed after the war and continued until 1931. The Schnieder race became a truly international affair after its resumption with participation from the United States as well as many European countries. When the United States Navy entered their Curtiss racer it set a precedent in this country of a government-funded racer. Prior to this, racing airplanes were often funded and built by wealthy individuals or business entrepreneurs. The U.S. Navy went on to win two Schnieder races but subsequently fell victim to a very well-prepared British race team. The British went on to permanently secure the Schnieder Trophy in 1931 with their Supermarine S6B.

The Pulitzer Trophy Race, like the James Gordon Bennett Trophy Race, was sponsored by newspaperman Ralph Pulitzer, owner of the New York "World." Ralph was the middle son of Joseph Pulitzer, noted for the Pulitzer Literary awards. His brothers Herbert and Joseph, Jr. were also involved in the newspaper business but Ralph was responsible for establishing various point to point, town-to-town and cross-country races prior to the closed-course event initiated in 1920. The Pulitzer Trophy Race became the main event for post-World War air meets held in the United States, with the Army and Navy entering their specially built racers. In some cases these racers were identical to the Schnieder racers but equipped with wheels in place of floats. The dominant air meets throughout the U.S. were military shows until 1929.

The National Air Races of 1929 changed air racing to a civilian event with only limited participation by military aircraft. The Nationals were managed by the entrepreneurial team of Cliff and Phil Henderson. The main event was scheduled for Labor Day. It was a free-for-all race for any size airplane with any size engine. A week before this race, a

Using a Kodak 616 camera, photographer Emil Strasser captured this P-38 and trailing P-51D turning home pylon. Quite a feat, in retrospect. Photo Credit: Emil Strasser

small black and red low wing racer flew into Cleveland and was immediately hangered. Because it was kept out of sight, the press promptly dubbed it "The Mystery Ship." To this day, the Travel Air Company's Model R is most often referred to as the Travel Air Mystery Ship. The Travel Air handily beat all competitors, including the military, to win the feature race. This set the stage for civilian domination for the next nine years of air racing.

The principle pylon event at the National Air Races became known as the Thompson Trophy Race. When air racing resumed in 1946, the Thompson was again the premier challenge. The origin of this race is of historical significance because of its ultimate impact on the sport of unlimited class racing today. The 1929 National Air Races were the beginning of what is generally called "The Golden Age of Air Racing." It was a true extravaganza, with seven cross-country races, or "derbies," plus thirty-five pylon races, embracing everything from multi-engined transports, Navy fighters, small-engined racers, and an event called a "Free-for-all-Speed Contest" – this was Event Number 26 in the busy race schedule.

In August of 1929, a representative of the National Air Races arrived at the Clarkwood Road offices of Thompson Products, Inc., to see Lee Clegg of the company's sales staff. The air race representative was looking for sponsorship and a trophy for one or more of the scheduled events. This was the first year the races were to be held in Cleveland and Thompson Products produced a line of aviation products. The association with aviation as well as the timing offered promise to Clegg. He called upon company Publicity Manager, Ray Livingston, to join the meeting. What the two men found was that what promised to be the most exciting race on the extensive program as yet had no sponsor. This was Event 26. It was a race for any type of plane, engine, supercharger, or fuel. There were really no restrictions. In short time, the company agreed to sponsor this event.

With the concurrence of Charles E. Thompson, company founder and president, Ray Livingston drove to the Webb C. Ball Company on Euclid Avenue in downtown Cleveland in search of a suitable trophy. Webb C. Ball was a noted purveyor of jewelry and fine art objects. Livingston settled on a large, shiny loving cup for twenty-five dollars. For an additional ten dollars, Ball agreed to engrave the cup. Doug Davis, in the Travel Air Model R, won Event number 26 at a speed of 191.1 miles per hour. This was the almost casual beginning of the Thompson Trophy Race. Thompson employee Fred Witt remembered standing by a fence in front of the grandstands waiting for the victor to land. When Davis pulled up and shut down his engine, Fred hopped the fence with the lovinig cup under his arm and rushed out to the racer to present the trophy.

In winning Event 26, Davis finished in front of all the free-for-all racers, including enteries by the Army and Navy. His victory over the service pursuit planes gained widespread media attention and editorial comment about the state of our military preparedness. Ray Livingston concluded this was an opportune time to present management with a proposal establishing a permanent Thompson Trophy and race. He put his ideas forth to both Fred Crawford and Lee Clegg. The idea was carried to Charles Thompson and approved. The proposed race concept was next submitted to the National Aeronautic Association, where approval was also granted. On December 21, 1929, Charles E. Thompson announced to the press his plans for creating the "Thompson Trophy" and sponsoring an international free-for-all race for the fastest land plane participating in future races.[1]

Fred Crawford of Thompson Products had little good to say about any existing trophies. He considered most to be abominations. Crawford wanted something unique, a symbol. Fred Witt prepared a description of the symbolism Crawford believed the trophy should express. His description became a specification. A competition was proposed to select a creative concept for the new trophy. The company turned to Dr. Henry Turner Bailey, president of the prestigious Cleveland Art School for assistance. With Bailey's help, a competition was established, with five prominent sculptors participating. With that settled, a panel of judges was formed to select the winning concept. Livingston contacted prospective judges. Five men agreed to participate. The judges were Orville Wright and the United States Secretaries for the Army, Navy, and Department of Commerce, F. Trubee Davidson, David S. Ingalls, and Clarence Young, respectively. These four, along with Dr. Bailey of the Cleveland Art School, reviewed sketches and then plaster models from each sculptor. Near the end of May, 1930, the winner was selected and announced to the press. Walter A. Sinz of Cleveland was the winner of the competition.[2] Several months later the sculpture was completed and cast in bronze. It would be awarded for the first time during the 1930 National Air Races in Chicago. The first "Thompson" was won by C.W. "Speed" Holman in a newly built Laird racer at a speed of 201.91 miles per hour. Except for the war years, the Thompson was run every labor day weekend through 1949.

The demise of unlimited class or free-for-all air racing after the 1949 National Air Races ended an era. There would be no more Thompson Trophies for piston engine racers. The National Air Races ended on a tragic note. Bill Odom, piloting a very modified P-51 Mustang in the Thompson, crashed into a house in Berea, Ohio, killing a woman and her child. The accident drew headlines from coast to coast. Locally, community hostility toward the races was manifest. Uncertainty about the future of air racing in Cleveland, or any other place for that matter, was the subject of speculation. Plans were laid for future racing. Attention was focused on making the races safer and on the possibility of creating a new class of racers with less power than the ex-military fighters. In the end, the Korean War broke out in the spring of 1950 and military participation in air shows and races was banned. Men and material were once again going to war and the thought of air racing melted away.

It was not until 1964 that unlimited class air racing was reborn. Bill Stead, a sportsman and rancher from Reno, Nevada, had long been interested in racing. Bill had been active in hydroplane racing and speed seemed to be in his blood. On at least one occasion, he visited people in Cleveland to discuss the possibility of a Cleveland-style air race near Reno. When the State of Nevada began discussions on how to celebrate the Centennial of their statehood, Stead saw an opportunity to have air racing considered a part of the celebration. He was successful in gaining the support of officials, both locally and from the state.

Bill Stead started with virtually nothing. He scratched a couple of runways out of the Nevada desert, brought in viewing stands, and gathered together a lot of the folks involved with hydroplane racing. The free-for-all race class of earlier days became the unlimited class, a term derived from hydroplane boat racing. Today, unlimited is the proper identification for a class that encompasses any propeller driven, reciprocating engine-powered aircraft. There are very few restrictions. As in the 1946 to 1949 era, ex-military aircraft have dominated the modern racing scene.

The races were held in this rather primitive setting for two years. In 1966 the event was moved to Washoe County's Stead Facility. This had been a United States Air Force Base and was used for survival training. The Stead facility was ideally suited for racing, with plenty of surfaced area for aircraft parking and pit locations. It has three runways, so emergencies could be well handled. There is plenty of area for spectators and grandstands. Above all, it is only eight miles from downtown Reno. The success of Bill Stead's idea has progressed past even his fondest hopes. The Reno Championship National Air Race is the longest annual event in air racing history. Cleveland had ten years of "Golden Years of Air Racing" plus another four in the post-war period. Reno has passed the silver anniversary milestone.

Notes
1. *New York Times*, December 22, 1929, page 23.
2. *New York Times*, May 22, 1930, page 9.

Chapter Five
NATIONAL AIR RACES: 1946-1949

Earl Ortman's third place winner in the first post-war Thompson race sits alone in the snow at Cleveland Airport during the winter of 1946. With little time to prepare, Earl clipped the wings on this Mustang and then refashioned the stock wing tips to accommodate the slight increase in chord. Note the flat spot where the wing tip light was originally installed. Photo Credit: Logan Coombs via Bill Larkins

Earl Ortman hopes for the best before the 1946 Thompson race in this publicity photograph. Photo Credit: Bob Burke Photographers

To spectators and racing devotees of pre-World War II National Air Races, the sights, sounds, and speeds of this autumn classic were unalterably changed in 1946. Surplus military fighter aircraft sold to civilians by the War Assets Administration totally dominated entry rosters in the unlimited pylon events. Gone were the little Menasco-powered racers of Steve Wittman, Art Chester, Keith Rider and Benny Howard. Gone were the free-for-all class of Gee Bees, Wedell-Williams and Lairds and their designers: The Granville Brothers, Jimmie Wedell and Matty Laird. In their place were the ubiquitous wartime products of Lockheed, Curtiss, Bell, and North American. Such fighter aircraft were readily available, relatively inexpensive, and technologically superior to their pre-war counterparts. In this context, North American's P-51 *Mustang* was to become one of the most popular and numerous to wear civilian dress and participate in air racing.

The Chamber of Commerce had been a key part of air racing in Cleveland before the war. Chamber members retained the idea of resuming a Labor Day event as soon as possible after the war ended. On September 16, 1945, Cleveland newspapers carried a story released by Albert J. Weatherhead, vice president of the Chamber of Commerce, which was headlined: "National Air Races to be held next

Mustang owner Sep Mighton (left) and Earl Ortman (right) take time out for a photograph early in race week at Cleveland. Hats and double-breasted suits were in fashion at the time. Photo Credit: Maryette Ortman

summer." The release went on to state that jet races were being considered and the old race course would require some alteration due to the NACA engine research laboratory located on the northwest side and hugh bomber plant along the south end of the airfield. Two months later, a new organization was formed. It was called the "Air Foundation" and had a goal of raising $250,000 for research and education. The first function of this new group was to provide financial assistance to a National Aircraft Show, scheduled for January 1946, and for the National Air Races at Cleveland airport in the summer of that same year. Four businessmen from Cleveland formed the nucleus of this group. They were Frederick C. Crawford, president of Thompson Products, Inc. (now TRW, Inc.); Albert J. Weatherhead, Jr., president of Weatherhead Co.; A.C. Ernst, managing partner of Ernst & Ernst; and W.T. Holliday, president of Standard Oil of Ohio. Fred Crawford was the man instrumental in establishing the Thompson Trophy Race in 1930. He continued to play a very significant role in the pre-World War II racing group.

The 1946 resumption of air racing really got underway when Crawford was elected president of the Air Foundation and Benjamin T. Franklin was made general manager, a position held by Cliff Henderson before the war. Franklin became affiliated with the National Air Race group in 1932 when he was appointed Director of Regional Activities, a position he held through the 1939 races. Ben Franklin also served as executive vice president for the Cleveland National Aircraft Show held in January, 1946.

At this point in time, race management signed a five year lease for the Cleveland airport race site and obtained a five year race franchise from the National Aeronautics Association. The latter association would provide an avenue for validation of racing records with the Federation Aeronautique Internationale. The Federation was an internationally recognized group verifying all aviation records.

In early spring details of the 1946 National Air Races were released to the press. The race would take place over four days; the course was revised to accommodate anticipated higher speeds. A special race committee was formed to establish rules and regulations. It was a prestigious group, with Lt. Gen. Jimmy Doolittle heading the committee and assisted by members Benny Howard, Roscoe Turner, Tony LeVier, Earl Ortman, and Jackie Cochran. Cooperation from the military had been secured. By May, a schedule of events was formalized and prize money to the tune of

From left to right, Tony LeVier, Mrs. Alvin Johnston, Tex Johnston, Fred Crawford, Maryette Ortman and Earl Ortman pose along side the 1946 Thompson Trophy-winning Bell P-39 "Cobra II," shortly after the race. Photo Credit: Bob Burke Photographers

$105,000 was in the bank! Once again, the Thompson Trophy Race would be the premier pylon racing attraction. The Thompson would be conducted in two classes; one for jet-powered aircraft over a thirty mile quadrangular course,[1] and the second for piston engine aircraft over the same course for ten laps, resulting in a 300 mile race. Other events were scheduled for women pilots, jet aircraft speed runs plus various air show events.

Despite the fact that post-war competitors began with mass produced aircraft designs, American ingenuity soon prevailed. Racing modifications evolved right from the start in 1946. The relatively short, elapsed time between the end of World War II and the decision to stage a revival of the National Air Races precluded drastic alterations to most racers that first year. Typically, preparation consisted of simple airframe weight reduction and modest aerodynamic cleanup, with emphasis on paint and polish.

Representative of racing *Mustang* state-of-the-art in 1946, was Earl Ortman's entry in the Thompson Trophy event. A noted pre-war racing pilot, Earl participated in the 1946 races quite by chance. During the spring of that year, he was employed by the Spartan Aircraft Company in Tulsa, Oklahoma, to test their prototype Model 12 Executive

which was designed for the post-war civil market. At the same time, P.J. "Sep" Mighton, Tulsa owner of a precision manufacturing company, purchased a surplus Bell P-39Q-15-BE *Airacobra*. A plain talking Westerner with flying time in T-6 *Texans*, Sep bought the P-39 in Ponca City, Oklahoma, because he was enamored with the *Airacobra*. In Sep's own words, ". . . It was available and it was cheap."

Sep's wartime fighter attracted a lot of curious attention, including that of Tulsa airport manager Marvin Sellinger. In an ensuing conversation with Mighton, Sellinger asked, "What are you gonna' do Sep, race it? There's a guy named Ortman out here that used to race. You ought to team up with him." From this chance conversation was born the Ortman-Mighton Aviation Company, formed expressly for the purpose of entering the 1946 National Air Races.

Ortman's varied wartime experience as a ferry pilot convinced Sep Mighton that there were better alternatives for pylon racing than the P-39 *Airacobra*.[2] Consequently, both men visited Altus Air Force Base to look at surplus Bell P-63 *Kingcobras*. No purchase was made. Earl definitely wanted a *Mustang* for the Thompson Race; however, none were available at the time. Earl and Sep next turned their attention to the Bendix Trophy Race. For this transcontinental

The clipped wings on Ortman's racer are evident in this photograph. The aircraft sits just across from the Sky-Tech hangar on the northeast side of the Cleveland airport. Photo Credit: Pete Bowers

This is a rare photograph of George Welch's P-51D, taken during the 1946 races. With engine problems, Welch was forced out of the Thompson in the second lap. Photo Credit: Pete Bowers

This stock Mustang, named "City of Lynchburg, VA," was flown in the 1946 races by Woody Edmonson. Photo Credit: Warren Bodie

competition, they purchased a Lockheed F-5G-6-LO from a Tulsa man who had four *Lightnings* and was planning to start an aerial photo service.

Still intent on acquiring a *Mustang*, the two men learned of a P-51 surplus sale at Walnut Ridge, Arkansas. During the third week in July, they finally achieved their goal and bought a *Mustang* for $3500. Licensed N65453, North American P-51D-20-NA was ferried back to Tulsa with Earl at the controls. By this time, a scant six weeks remained before the races were to commence.

In addition to the airplane purchase price, Sep paid another $200 for a water injection system to be adapted to the *Mustang's* V-1650-7 *Merlin* engine. Back in Tulsa, they realized the water injection apparatus was missing. Undaunted, and with the aid of crew chief Jack Kuepfin and a few Spartan Aircraft mechanics, Sep and Earl proceeded to ready N 65453 for the September classic.

By today's standards, their preparations were modest. Prophetically, the Ortman-Mighton team contemplated the possibility of: lowering the cockpit canopy profile; removing the belly air scoop and relocating the cooling systems; shortening the stock 11-foot, 2-inch diameter, cuffed Hamilton Standard propeller; and, reducing the 37-foot wingspan on the *Mustang*. These ambitious plans were tempered by limited time and a need to prepare three aircraft for the races.[3] Superimposed on this entire effort was the fact that Sep Mighton still had to manage his manufacturing business and Earl was obligated to Spartan for the Model 12 test program.

Weight reduction was a logical means of increasing speed. The Ortman-Mighton team accomplished this by the simple expedient of removing anything unnecessary for racing. This included everything from small clips and tie downs to cockpit armor plate, radios and low pressure oxygen bottles. The dry weight of a military D model is 7125 pounds. Although no data apparently survived, it can be reasonably estimated that race preparations for Earl's airplane resulted in an empty weight of around 6800 pounds, or about 5 percent lighter than its military counterpart.

In the brief period available to prepare their airplane, the Tulsa crew proceeded to work on the airframe. Outer wing tip panels were removed at the production break and the ailerons trimmed accordingly. Production wing tips were reworked to fit the slightly longer chord of the shortened span and then reinstalled. The resulting wingspan was 32 feet, with a corresponding area of just over 223 square feet, or about seven percent less than the military wing. Despite dire warnings from some onlookers, wing loadings remained in an acceptable range because the airframe had been lightened. Thus, clipped wings became a reasonable speed modification. In this regard, Ortman's *Mustang* was the first

to race with shortened wings, establishing a trend continued to this day.

Remaining airframe modifications were minimal. Wing tip running lights were removed and desert carburetor air intakes on the cowl cheeks were covered. Aluminum sheet metal caps plugged the six wing gun ports. For the 1946 Thompson race, the airframe was unpainted but highly polished. Earl insisted that the crew wax and buff the airframe literally up to the starting time of the race. Years later, Sep Mighton would recall that Earl became satisfied with the polishing job only after it was demonstrated, ". . . that a handkerchief would slide off the wing surface."

The Packard-built Rolls Royce *Merlin* engine in Ortman's racer received only routine maintenance and no modification, except one. The manifold boost control was deactivated, allowing Earl to operate at maximum pressure during the race. Although water injection was incorporated on later dash number *Merlins*, the V-1650-7 was not equipped with this system. Without water injection (more accurately, antidetonant injection or simply ADI), Earl was limited to engine manifold pressure of less than 70 inches of mercury. Sustained higher pressures led to destructive detonation.

Earl flew the *Mustang* to Cleveland and qualified for the Thompson Trophy Race at 344.388 miles per hour, earning

Woody Edmonson poses for a publicity shot in front of his racer that sits on the ramp at Cleveland. He placed seventh in the 1946 Thompson race. Photo Credit: Bob Burke Photographers

This Mustang was prepared for the 1946 National Air Races by technicians from North American. Undergoing an engine run up, race 61 is seen here outside the North American Aviation facility at the Los Angeles airport on 25 August 1946. Photo Credit: NAA via Birch Matthews

ninth position in the racehorse starting lineup. The team's Airacobra and Lightning entries were flown to Cleveland by two pilots enrolled at the Spartan School of Aeronautics. Earl had withdrawn the F-5G from the Bendix when it became apparent there was no time to adequately prepare for the race.[4] The P-39 and F-5G eventually flew in the Sohio Trophy Race. As a consequence, the Ortman-Mighton team became the first to enter three unlimiteds in any race program.

In retrospect, Earl didn't punish his racer during the two lap Thompson qualification trial; however, his speed belied the capability of N65453. Five of the twelve entries in the Thompson race that year were North American P-51 *Mustangs*. Certainly one of the competing P-51s was demonstrably faster. Ron Freeman's *Mustang*, piloted by George Welch, qualified in excess of 394 miles per hour. Other entries enjoying a significant speed advantage included Tex Johnston's highly modified P-39 "Corbra II" and Charley Tucker's severely clipped-wing Bell P-63C-5. Tony LeVier flew his P-38L through the time trial at a speed some thirty

miles per hour faster than Ortman, thus placing him fourth in the starting line. Ultimately the speed of LeVier's and Ortman's racers were comparable. The more favorable starting position enjoyed by Tony apparently paid dividends.

The Thompson Trophy Race was the final event on Labor Day, Monday, September 2, 1946. Just before the race, Earl confided to Sep that he would be "lucky to finish in the money." As Sep later recounted, "Earl and I were both poor boys. We didn't have any business screwin' around up there in Cleveland. Cleland and Johnston and most of the others had money and an aircraft company behind them." But the Thompson race, initiated with a tense racehorse start of twelve powerful airplanes, was a punishing nerve-jangling 300 mile test of speed, skill, and endurance. The Ortman-Mighton team possessed two of the three needed attributes. Ortman was a skilled, experienced pilot and the unmodified *Merlin* engine was durable. With moderately good speed, Earl's race 2 could be expected to give others in the Thompson a bit of competition.

As the race unfolded, two of the contenders fell by the

Race pilot Dale Fulton stands along side of his Mustang for a publicity photograph taken in Los Angeles in late August, 1946. Photo Credit: NAA via Birch Matthews

Bob Swanson smiles for the camera and well he should. He was, at the eleventh hour, able to obtain and qualify a replacement P-51 and, somewhat to his surprise, placed fifth in the Thompson race. Photo Credit: Bob Burke Photographers

wayside early in the race. Charley Tucker dropped out with landing gear problems in the first lap and George Welch had engine problems in the second lap. From ninth position on the starting line, Earl pushed ahead of four other racers to gain third place during the first lap. Powering the *Merlin* engine along at an estimated 3000 revolutions per minute and 67 inches of manifold pressure, Earl trailed only Tex Johnston and Tony LeVier. The *Mustang* performed flawlessly. Earl flew a skillful race, no doubt drawing upon his years of pylon flying experience. With Sep Mighton and Jack Kuepfin stationed on the field in front of the grandstands and Earl's French-Canadian wife, Maryette Ortman, watching nervously from the reserved section of the spectator seats, race 2 eventually crossed the finish line in third place with an average speed of 367.625 miles per hour.

Earl led all *Mustangs* across the finish line. He flew an extra lap as a precaution against a pylon cut, zoomed for altitude, and circled into the landing pattern at Cleveland Municipal Airport. Sep Mighton was elated. "Third place is as good as first to me," he shouted to Earl when the racer pulled to a stop on the apron in front of the grandstands. And for Earl Ortman, who had earlier misgivings about his

ability to ever finish in the money, third place in the premier 1946 Thompson Trophy Race was undoubtedly very acceptable too. It was a credible performance for a couple of "poor boys."

Post-war pylon racing continued at Cleveland for three more years. But Earl Ortman's long quest for the elusive Thompson Trophy ended with the 1946 race. The Ortman-Mighton team was disbanded. Sep Mighton returned to his Tulsa business interests. He sold all three of his aircraft and contented himself with being a spectator during subsequent National Air Races. The Ortman-Mighton *Mustang* raced again, but under new colors. The aircraft was purchased by Northwest Airlines pilot William Fairbrother, who continued to fly N65453 through 1949.

Evolution of the *Mustang* as a racing aircraft continued during the Cleveland years. For most, the search for ever faster race speeds centered on developing more power out of the *Merlin* engines as opposed to any significant aerodynamic modifications. Higher sustained power settings were sought by employing supercharging, antidetonant injection and various exotic fuel mixtures. Numerous engine driven supercharger configurations were tried, boosting

Although it was unplanned, Bob Swanson brought two Mustangs to the 1946 races at Cleveland. He crash-landed the first one, resulting in extensive damage, although he was unhurt. This led to a frantic search for a replacement P-51. Photo Credit: Liang-O'Leary Collection

Woody Edmonson brought an Allison-powered P-51A Mustang to the 1947 National Air Races. He managed a third place in the Kendall Trophy Race but disaster struck later during the Thompson race. The Allison engine quit during the eleventh lap and Woody crash landed, damaging the aircraft. Photo Credit: Warren Bodie

William Fairbrother purchased the Mustang flown in 1946 by Earl Ortman and arrived at the 1947 air races with a new paint scheme and race number. Photo Credit: Warren Bodie

Merlin manifold pressures to between 80 to 90 inches of mercury, some 25 to 30 percent above military ratings. Antidetonant injection became the norm. Most entrants either concocted their own fuel blends or accepted racing fuels provided by Standard Oil of Ohio (Sohio) or Shell Oil Company. Whatever fuel was selected, the objective was to prohibit detonation and pre-ignition phenomena which was prevalent at increased power settings.

As engine revolutions and manifold pressure increased, thermal loads imposed on fixed capacity cooling radiators became higher. Consequently, *Merlins* were operated at extreme engine coolant and oil temperatures. In the best of situations, these extreme temperatures caused exit doors on the *Mustang* belly scoops to remain wide open for maximum cooling airflow, with a consequent penalty in aerodynamic drag. All too frequently, however, redline temperature operation resulted in disaster. During the 1947 races, two instances of connecting rod structural failures were reported. Main bearings suffered a similar fate that year. By 1948, the list of problems expanded to include a broken oil cooler, a supercharger impeller failure, and ruptured oil lines. With *Merlins* running at higher and higher speeds, engine driven accessories such as oil and coolant pumps ran at speeds exceeding design margins. More failures followed. *Merlin* reliability and durability predictably suffered the cumulative effects of greater power output. Unfortunately, augmented cooling capacities, refined subsystem designs, and *Merlin* structural modifications to cope with the extreme demands of dramatically higher power levels would await another era of unlimited class racing. *Merlin* engine performance never reached its potential during the Thompson races.

Drastic modification of the P-51 airframe was avoided during the late forties, except for two notable exceptions. These exceptions were, of course, Anson Johnson's and Bill Odom's entries in the 1949 races.[5] Anson had won the Thompson in 1948, flying a comparatively stock *Mustang* and inheriting victory when faster competitors were forced out of the race for various reasons. Most racing entrants were reluctant to aerodynamically modify the *Mustang*. Conventional wisdom inhibited them from performing surgical alterations to the airframe. This reluctance was no doubt influenced by North American Aviation's response to inquiries regarding airframe changes. The corporate reply suggested that the P-51 was already a thoroughly optimized design, a response no doubt influenced by concerns over liability and an inherent pride in their product. In any event, only the most adventurous altered the *Mustang's* configuration during this era.

The last of the great Thompson Trophy Races in 1949 ultimately proved only a starting point in the evolution of the *Mustang* as a racing machine. Over two decades would elapse before an effective blend of increased *Merlin* power and refined airframe aerodynamics yielded the necessary winning formula.

There is historical need to provide an epilogue to the four post-war years of Cleveland air racing. It has been suggested by a number of writers that the tragic crash of Bill Odom during the 1949 Thompson Trophy race caused cancellation of the 1950 National Air Races.[6] Indeed, it has been suggested as the only reason for the demise of the Thompson Trophy Race and what we now call unlimited class racing. There were editorials in the news media as well as trade journals questioning the need for air racing. The City of Berea, Ohio, was prepared to obtain a legal injunction to prevent racing in their air space. There were questions regarding pilot qualifications for such racing and, of course, there were calls for more safety.

A review of past records clearly shows that plans for a Labor Day Weekend race program was scheduled for 1950 at Cleveland airport. It was recognized that the course had to be re-routed to avoid Berea's air space. This resulted in a course lengthened to twenty miles. By December 1949, permission was secured from all affected communities to use this course and the National Aeronautics Association was so notified.

In 1950 the National Aeronautics Association gave the Air Foundation, the air race sponsoring group, a new five year sanction to conduct the races. Planning for the 1950 event included a critique of prior racing years. In reviewing problems, including the Odom crash and the diminishing supply of surplus military aircraft, it was decided that air racing with ex-military aircraft would be discontinued. On March 30, 1950, Air Foundation president Fred Crawford released these findings to the public. No more Thompson, Bendix, Sohio, or Tinnerman races! The 190 cubic inch, engine-powered Midget Classes would be continued. Air race management was also considering a custom-built class, with engines between 300 and 500 cubic inch displacement. The only large plane races would be for the military jet powered aircraft. However, in June 1950, Secretary of Defense, Louis Johnson, announced there would be no military aircraft or personnel participation in civilian air shows. Any such demonstrations would be limited to Armed Forces Day. Coincident with this, the Korean War erupted. Crawford then announced cancellation of the 1950 air races because of the loss of military participation. At the same time Crawford indicated the 1951 races would be held in May at Cleveland and there would be jet races for the Bendix and the Thompson.

Benjamin T. Franklin, general manager of the Air Foundation, stated in the early part of 1951 that because the

Paul Penrose flew this beautiful bronze-colored P-51D, called "Wraith," at the 1947 Cleveland races. Probably the fastest Mustang at Cleveland, the racer was plagued with problems and was forced out of the Thompson race in lap six. Photo Credit: Dusty Carter Collection

Woody Edmonson returned to the 1948 races with yet a third P-51. This red and white racer was named "City of Lynchburg, VA III." Photo Credit: Pete Bowers

William Fairbrother returned to Cleveland in 1948 with race 21. The only apparent change in this classic profile view was the installation of a tank aft of the pilot's seat, probably for antidetonant injection fluid. Photo Credit: Emil Strasser

"bomber plant" at Cleveland airport was being converted to tank production for the Korean War, the airport was no longer a viable site for the races and they were being canceled. The grandstands were dismantled and donated to a local university. The increased air traffic, continuing tank production, and large-scale local land development made it obvious there was no way a suitable race course could be established to bring "big time" air racing back to Cleveland.

There have been several races at Cleveland's Burke Lakefront Airport embracing the little Formula One, Formula Vee and sport biplane racers, but they were never on the scale of any races held at Cleveland Airport. The city had indeed been the home of closed-course racing through the golden years of 1929 through 1939, and interest rekindled in this fastest motor sport during the immediate post-war years of 1946 to 1949. The legacy of the Cleveland races may be found today at the long running Reno National Championship Air Races, which owes its success to the fact that it was patterned after the classic that Cliff and Phil Henderson developed!

Notes

1. The course was shortened to a fifteen mile circuit for following years.
2. Ironically, a highly modified P-39Q-10-BE Bell *Airacobra*, flown by Bell test pilot Tex Johnston, would win the coveted Thompson Trophy that first post-war year.
3. The task of preparing three aircraft for the races overwhelmed the small Ortman-Mighton team. Only the Mustang received significant attention. Earl eventually withdrew from the Bendix race when it became obvious that necessary modifications could not be made to both the F-5G and the P-51 in the limited time available. Consequently, all three aircraft were entered in the pylon events. The P-39 and F-5G were lightened to some extent, waxed, and entered the races in essentially stock configuration.
4. In addition to his duties at Spartan, Earl became a member of the contest committee for the pylon races. This responsibility consumed more than a week of time, including two trips to Cleveland.
5. Anson had won the Thompson in 1948, flying a comparatively stock *Mustang* and inheriting victory when faster competitors were forced out of the race for various reasons.
6. The story of Bill Odom's infamous crash and the highly modified *Mustang* racer he was flying is related in Chapter Nine and Appendix B.

Woody Edmonson bends around the home pylon during the 1948 Thompson Trophy Race. Engine problems forced him out of the race during the fourteenth lap. Photo Credit: Emil Strasser

Home pylon at Cleveland was also the scatter pylon for racehorse starts. This 1948 photograph shows an example of this exciting but dangerous method of beginning an air race. Photo Credit: Robert E. Burke

Race 37 was back at Cleveland in 1948. It was now owned by J.D. Reed and carried the nickname "Jay Dee." The pilot this year was Chuck Walling. Photo Credit: Emil Strasser

James Hanon brought this pretty and clean P-51A to Cleveland for the 1949 National Air Races. With an Allison engine, and a basically stock airframe, it was no match for the more powerful racers. Photo Credit: Liang-O'Leary Collection

This A-36A version of the Mustang appeared at the 1948 races and was sponsored by the Essex Wire Corp. The air scoop on this aircraft was enlarged somewhat over the stock configuration. In addition, the framing for the cockpit canopy and windscreen have been reinforced. Photo Credit: Liang-O'Leary Collection

Chapter Six
MODERN AIR RACING: 1964 - PRESENT

Modern air racing began in September 1964, when a Cleveland-style race program was held at Sky Ranch Airport, a few miles east of Reno. The Reno National Championship Air Races have continued uninterrupted since then, making it the longest continuous event of its kind in the world. While Cleveland may be considered home of air racing's golden years, Reno, Nevada, certainly became the home of modern air racing. Reno is where some of the newer

race pilots tried their wings before going on to capture international speed records. The first was Darryl Greenamyer, who brought the world piston engine speed record back to the United States in 1969. Ten years later, Steve Hinton, in the highly modified *Red Baron Mustang*, exceeded Greenamyer's mark. In 1983, Frank Taylor set a new record for the 15 kilometer course, piloting another *Mustang* called *Dago Red*. More recently still, Lyle Shelton ran his F8F-2

Mustangs usually dominate the entry list at Reno. This view looks west toward the mountains in the unlimited pit area and six Mustangs are visible. Photo Credit: Birch Matthews

Bearcat through the timing traps and took the record away from Hinton.

Air racing at Reno was a catalyst for other race programs across the United States and one in Canada. Following the lead of Reno, Los Angeles, California, had two multi-class races in 1965 and 1966, held at Fox Field near Lancaster in northern Los Angeles County. Las Vegas, Nevada, had two races scheduled for 1965, one in August and the other in September. A cross-country race, called the P-51 Tournament, was held at East Alton, Illinois, in May of 1971. The success of racing over Reno's desert caused other promoters to create a long, one thousand mile race. The first such race was held in November of 1970 at Kern County Airport Number 7, Mojave, California. The race was repeated in 1971 as well as a similar race in San Diego in July of that year. A full blown multi-class race was held at Cape May, New Jersey in June of 1971, but two unfortunate mid-air collisions in the T-6 racing class marred that new program. Nineteen seventy-three saw the beginning of the California National Air Races, originally called the California Air Classic, held in October at the Mojave site. That race program continued through 1979 before ceasing. Homestead, Florida, was the scene for yet another race in March, 1979. This affair was promoted by race pilot Don Whittington and his brothers. The only unlimited race outside the United States was the Canadian International Air Races program held at the Canadian Forces Base in Moose Jaw, Saskatchewan, in June 1984. In 1985, Bill Destefani of Bakersfield, California, managed to promote an unlimited race at Minter Field outside of Shafter, California. Two more unlimited races were held in Texas and Colorado during 1989.

The National Air Races of the 1930s were managed and directed by the energetic Henderson brothers, Cliff and Phil. Those races enjoyed support of both the city of Cleveland and local businesses associated with aviation. In the post-war period at Cleveland, the Henderson brothers were no longer involved, having retired in 1939. There were others, however, who had worked the pre-war races, including Ben Franklin. Some of the same Cleveland businessmen were still active. Fred Crawford of Thompson Products, Inc., remained a driving force behind the races. Support also came from members of the Cleveland Chamber of Commerce. In 1946, these people formed the Air Foundation organization which promoted the races.

The Reno air races started differently, although the program was certainly patterned after the historic Cleveland events. Bill Stead was the spark behind the Reno events. Bill was a member of the Stead ranching family and had gained some fame in the sport of hydroplane racing. He was National Champion in 1958 and 1959. When he retired from

Chuck Lyford's Bardahl-sponsored, white Mustang racer was a 1965 Reno entrant. Although the racer used a highly tuned racing Merlin, the airframe was basically stock at this point. Photo Credit: Bob Pauley

active participation in boat racing, he became manager of Bill Harrah's (Harrah's Casino) hydroplane racing team. During this period, Stead rekindled his interest in air racing. He traveled to Cleveland and met with Ben Franklin to discuss the possibilities of introducing racing in Reno.

By 1963, Stead was convinced air racing could be made viable again. There were still any number of World War II fighters and trainers in the hands of civilian owners and pilots. He felt sure that enough of them could be persuaded to compete in a race program if he could promote the necessary resources and facilities. To achieve his dream, he formed a group of about ten Reno businessmen. Some he had known in college and others were local business acquaintances. The group was certainly inexperienced in matters relating to air racing. They did possess abilities, though, with respect to organization, finance, promotion, and management. Air racing is entertainment and businessmen in Reno understand this fine art.

Nineteen sixty-four was the Centennial Celebration of Statehood for Nevada. Bill Stead saw an opportunity to use the centennial as a vehicle to promote a national championship air race. It would be a part of the state celebration plans. September had long been "air race month" in Cleveland, and September was a slow tourist month in Reno. So, promoting a race program during September drew the applause of local Reno businesses. Stead made all of the pieces fit. The races were on!

The race site would be Sky Ranch, a few miles east of Reno on Highway 33, a road that carried vacationers and fishermen to nearby Pyramid Lake. It was really nothing but raw Nevada desert, but the location was easily accessible to Reno's accommodations and night life. The sagebrush was

Bob Hoover has started the unlimited racing class virtually every race at Reno and around the country. Here Hoover lifts off in front of the home pylon on his way to another race start. Photo Credit: Birch Matthews

cleared and two runways installed. These were nothing more than vintage World War II steel matting laid out on the desert floor. The runways resembled wartime combat air-fields. Pylons were erected to define the race courses and grandstands built for spectators across the road from the runways. Highway 33 ran directly through the race site and all traffic had to be stopped during a race. When the wind blew, the dust was almost intolerable. One racer was disqualified because he refused to take off or land on such primitive facilities.[1]

The program included events for small midget race planes, a stock Stearman class of World War II training biplanes and, of course, the big ex-military fighters. Bill Stead and Bob Downey of the Professional Race Pilots Association (PRPA) also inaugurated a sport biplane class of racers. Defining race classes and timing requirements for these events was done by Stead's old hydroplane racing friends. Because big racing hydroplanes powered by Allison or *Merlin* aircraft engines were called unlimited class boats, it was natural that the big ex-fighters would become the "unlimited class" of air racing. Today, this is the official title of a class that in years past was called "Thompson Trophy Racers."

A problem arose when timing officials adopted the

Opposite: The first two years of Reno air racing took place at Sky Ranch airport, literally a strip carved out of the Nevada desert. In 1966, the races moved to the recently deactivated Stead Air Force Base, north of Reno. This 1981 aerial view shows the ramp area and pits used by the unlimiteds and T-6 class racers. The grandstands are to the upper right. The facilities are excellent. Photo Credit: Neal Nurmi

Lyford's P-51 is seen here at Stead Field in 1967. By this time, the airframe had been cleaned up with clipped wings and horizontal stabilizer. A nitrous oxide system was employed for added bursts of speed. Photo Credit: Dusty Carter

Dave Allender flew this pretty D model Mustang at Reno during the 1967 races. The airplane later became Howie Keefe's well known "Miss America." Photo Credit: Dusty Carter

hydroplane point system for the air racers. In hydroplane racing, points are given for finish positions in each heat race, and the boat with the highest number of points is the ultimate winner. As a consequence, the winning boat is not necessarily the fastest. The late Bob Love handily won the final race of the 1964 program. He was not declared the 1964 champion because his point accumulation was not the highest at the conclusion of the races. The system was unsatisfactory for pilots and spectators alike, and was never used after this first year. One racing feature initiated at Reno which is still with us today is the "air start."

Historically, air races were begun with what was called a race horse start. And that's what it resembled. Airplanes were lined up abreast as in horse racing and when the starter's flag dropped, the race was on. Pilots released brakes and opened throttles wide. Everyone made a mad dash for the first pylon. It was a dangerous beginning to an already risky sport. Bill Stead, Bob Hoover, and others reviewed the race horse technique and decided to abandon that method in favor of an air start. The air start has been used ever since for all unlimited races and more recently, for the T-6 race class.

Russ Schleeh in the "Maytag Mustang" and Frank Sanders prepare to takeoff at the 1966 Lancaster, California races. Photo Credit: Dusty Carter

Bob Abrams acquired this P-51D and brought it to Reno in 1965. The all-red airframe featured clipped wings and the wing to fuselage fillet was completely removed. He experienced engine problems at Reno but was back two weeks later at the Las Vegas International Air Race. Photo Credit: Al Chute

Abrams was killed at Las Vegas in the modified P-51 when he stalled on final approach after leaving a heat race with mechanical problems. Photo Credit: Bob Lawson

E.D. Weiner was one of the early Reno race pilots who worked to keep the unlimited class going. E.D. is pictured here with his pylon racer at Long Beach, California, before a test flight. Note the absence of a dorsal fin on the vertical tail. This modification did not last long. Lateral stability suffered and the dorsal was replaced. Photo Credit: Hal Loomis

Air starts use a pace plane that orbits an area away from the race site. Racers form up off the right wing of the pace plane in a line abreast. The fastest qualifier is adjacent to the pace plane. The remaining racers take up a formation to the right, based upon descending qualification speed. When the pace plane pilot is satisfied with the formation, he leads the flight into a shallow descent toward the race course. When the pace plane pilot has the formation, he radios: "Gentlemen, you have a race!" The pace plane then pulls up sharply to clear the race course and the racers are underway. Bob Hoover, flying his bright yellow M*ustang*, perfected the air start and has started almost every unlimited race since 1964.

In 1967, E.D. Weiner experimented with a striking zebra paint scheme on his pylon racer. A year later, he reverted to his familiar checkerboard design. Photo Credit: Hal Loomis

The unlimited race class got off to a modest start in 1964. Only seven ex-fighters arrived for the races. There was limited publicity before the races. Some of the entrants were not aware of the race program until a few weeks before the event. None of the unlimited entrants had ever participated in pylon racing. They were all rookies. Four P-51 *Mustangs* and three F8F-2 *Bearcats* (one was owned by Bill Stead) made up the total field of unlimiteds. Over the years, the field of unlimited entrants at Reno has grown. Twenty-five to thirty planes entered in the unlimited class is not unusual. The 1964 Reno races were a tentative beginning to modern air racing. But it was enough. The races were scheduled again for the following September at Sky Ranch.

In 1966, the race site moved to Stead Air Force Base, some twelve miles northwest of Reno along U.S. Highway 395. During the war this facility was known as Reno Army Air Base. It was renamed Stead Air Force Base after the war, in honor of Bill's brother, Croston, who perished in a P-51 accident while flying with the Nevada Air National Guard. The airfield now belongs to Washoe County and is known as the Stead Facility.

Howie Keefe and "Miss America" were a familiar team at many races. In this 1970 photograph, his crew chief performs an engine run on the ramp at Reno. Photo Credit: Birch Matthews

Mustangs dominated entry lists at Reno and the other unlimited competitions around the country. Most appeared relatively stock, although their cowlings enclosed racing engines. Perhaps typical of the early Reno race *Mustangs* was E.D. Weiner's pylon racer, race number 49. E.D. was an ex-military pilot who flew a variety of aircraft, including fighters. He spent quite a bit of his military time ferrying planes all over the country. E.D. would have loved to have flown in the Thompson races after the war. His finances at that time just wouldn't allow participation. Three thousand, five hundred dollars for a surplus P-51 was a lot money in those days. To that one had to add the cost of preparing a racer and supporting a crew during the races. It was beyond Weiner's means. His racing career would wait another twenty-nine years.

E.D. Weiner truly was one of the personalities that helped get a second generation of free-for-all pylon racing established. Based in Long Beach, California, Weiner owned two *Mustangs*. One he set up for cross-country racing, and the other for pylon events. He was the first of the new generation unlimited class racers to enter two airplanes. Weiner always sported unusual or spectacular paint schemes on his aircraft. He believed that color and design on a racer was as much a part of the sport as a highly tuned engine.

For the first year or two, Weiner's closed-course *Mustang* flew a bronze paint scheme with white trim. The race number was 14, the same as his transcon P-51. This changed

Bearcat pilot Walt Ohlrich (left) and Mustang racer Howie Keefe (right) compare notes on their most recent heat race at Reno during 1969. Photo Credit: Birch Matthews

Photographer Chuck Aro captured this Mustang cockpit by the late afternoon sunlight of the Nevada desert. Photo Credit: Chuck Aro

Earl Ketchen flew this black Mustang racer named "Habu" at the 1982 Reno races. Note the decorated clipped wing tips and accompanying aileron fences to minimize spanwise flow. Photo Credit: Neal Nurmi

Pilot John Wright goes over the numbers on runway eight at Reno during the 1977 races. This essentially stock, metallic blue P-51D was a frequent entrant at Reno for several years. Photo Credit: Jim Larsen

Photographer Bob Lawson captured the characteristic Mustang profile at dusk over the Las Vegas desert. Photo Credit: Bob Lawson

to race number 49 very early in 1966. In 1967, E.D. repainted race 49 with a striking black and white zebra motif. It was, without a doubt, the most unusual design scheme ever to appear on an unlimited racer. From 1968 on, both of his aircraft sported checkerboard paint schemes. The cross-country P-51 was black and white, while the pylon racer was black and yellow. Characteristic of E.D., he spent considerable time concerning himself with the layout detail of the checkerboard pattern. He wanted to achieve a balance and proportion the squares over the entire fuselage length. It was worth the effort. His aircraft always attracted attention and the geometric effect of the checkerboard paint

scheme was aesthetically pleasing.

A successful, self-made businessman dealing in surplus electronics, E.D. appointed the cockpit of his racer with the latest devices. Enunciator lights gave prompt warning if any engine operating parameter was going critical. He felt the lights simplified a pilot's cockpit tasks in the midst of a fast, demanding race. Weiner's P-51 went through a modest modification program. He never made structural changes that couldn't readily be restored to a stock *Mustang* configuration. Fit and finish of the aerodynamic surfaces on E.D.'s airplane were always superb. And all of his aircraft were constantly hangered and maintained. When

This photograph illustrates the five-bladed propeller used on the Whittington H model P-51. Photo Credit: Birch Matthews

In 1983, The Whittington Brothers brought this rare P-51H to Reno. This profile view shows the subtle differences between this late version of the Mustang and the ubiquitous P-51D. Photo Credit: Neal Nurmi

Mike Loening was a popular unlimited class racer during the late 1960s. His P-51D is shown here on the ramp at Reno in 1968. Photo Credit: Birch Matthews

John Crocker in race 6 and "Clay" Klabo in race 85 fly formation over the flatlands of Homestead, Florida, during the 1979 Miami races. Photo Credit: Ron Burda

Race pilot Chuck Hall and engine expert Dwight Thorne discuss the results of a 1980 flight at the Reno races. Photo Credit: Neal Nurmi

Greenamyer appeared at Reno with modified wing tips, Weiner was one of several *Mustang* pilots to adopt the idea. Wing tip assemblies on his pylon racer were removed at the production break and replaced with new aluminum sheet stock tips. There was nothing scientific about the tip design. They were simply made to look like what could be seen on other airplanes. E.D. wondered out loud one evening at a party if these "new wing tip designs were doing me any good?" Because Weiner was willing to carefully experiment, it was suggested he run some tuft tests or even generate smoke at the wing tips to make the flow visible. In the end, he concluded that sufficient roll control existed and he retained the new wing tips.

The horizontal stabilizer was also clipped, reducing the span by fifteen inches. No attempt was made to fashion contoured tips for the stabilizer. The ends of the structure were capped with flat sheet stock. At about the same time, E.D. also had the dorsal fin on the vertical stabilizer removed. The fin was replaced by a small aluminum fillet. This modification didn't last long. Weiner flew the airplane and decided that directional stability suffered without the dorsal. It was soon refitted to the racer. Aside from the aerodynamic features cited, E.D's *Mustang* was

equippedwith a dash 9 *Merlin* and utilized antidetonant injection. A P-51H Aeroproducts propeller converted engine horsepower into thrust.

There were others during those early Reno years that helped rebuild the sport of unlimited class air racing. Some, such as Lyle Shelton and Chuck Hall, are still competing at Reno. Others like Clay Lacy, Darryl Greenamyer, Ben Hall, and Chuck Lyford, to mention only a few, no longer race. Of all the early *Mustang* drivers, perhaps Chuck Lyford had the most energetic racer. Lyford could always be counted upon to give Darryl Greenamyer and his *Bearcat* a run for the money. His airplane was painted solid white with orange markings, trimmed in black. This stunning P-51 first raced around the pylons in 1964 with Korean War ace Bob Love at the controls. The plane was sponsored by Bardahl, makers of fuel additives. After that first year of closed-course racing, Chuck Lyford flew the airplane whenever it raced. The name of the plane changed to "Challenger," a reflection of the competition between Lyford and Darryl Greenamyer.

In his book *Air Racers*, Jim Larsen recounts the modifications to Lyford's beautiful *Mustang*, "Principle efforts were concerned with producing a maximum performance engine. Engine expert Dwight Thorn, built up a potent

Automobile dealer Scott Smith of Orlando, Florida, fielded this exceptionally clean P-51D, race 04, at the Miami races of 1979. The aircraft was later sold and became known as "Habu." Photo Credit: Birch Matthews

"Lou IV" is a beautifully finished Mustang owned by Tom Kelly. The airframe is stock and the racer frequently qualifies for the silver or bronze competition at Reno. Photo Credit: Birch Matthews

Merlin V-1650-9 (engine) and installed a P-51H Aeroproducts propeller. The airframe was subjected to a thorough clean up campaign, which included the removal and refairing of the wing gun ports. All protruding bolts and screws were replaced with flathead countersunk equivalents. The exterior surfaces were given a special covering of epoxy paint and polished smooth."

"A unique auxiliary cooling system was installed in the underwing scoop. A spray bar, located just forward of the radiator face, was fed by water pumped from tanks built into the wing gun bays. During high speed flight conditions requiring maximum engine performance aspirated water was directed over the radiator core to provide additional cooling."[2] A year later, Lyford's *Mustang* was equipped with nitrous oxide injection. Indeed, Chuck Lyford was the first of the *Mustang* pilots to use many of the innovations found on current championship P-51 racers.

At this writing, the Reno National Championship Air Races have been run twenty-seven years. In almost three decades, the complexion and sophistication of the races has changed dramatically. From humble beginnings in a dusty airstrip in the Nevada desert, the races have evolved into a multi-faceted program in a Stead airport facility which has been improved almost yearly. Thornton Audrain was a member of the original Reno Air Race Association (RARA) group and has served in some capacity ever since. In January 1987, Thornton retired from the accounting profession to become Executive Director of RARA, the only full-time, paid position in the organization. At a race meeting in the spring of 1987, he spoke of some of the changes that have occurred. Budget for the first race in 1964 was $133,000, compared to $2,000,000 in 1987. Prize money in 1964 was $31,000. By 1987, the total purse had grown to $450,000. Insurance covering spectators and participants was a modest $6,000 in the beginning. Now it is a major expense, reaching a whopping $230,000 in 1987. Some 2,000 volunteers now assist with the Reno race program every year. In cooperation with Washoe County, the county and RARA now own nineteen square miles around Stead Facility. Land acquisition assures that air racing will be held at Reno for a long time to come.

Safety is a primary concern each year at the Reno races. Restrictions for contestants and crowd control have evolved over the years. When racing started at Stead, unlimiteds

Photographer Chuck Aro froze Mickey Rupp on takeoff at Reno. The aircraft sports clipped wings and a highly tuned Merlin.
Photo Credit: Chuck Aro

This picturesque scene is a frequent one in September at Reno as two Mustangs warm up prior to qualification time trials. Photo Credit: Birch Matthews

Pete Regina owned this rare P-51B which appeared at Reno in 1982. Skip Holm flew the airplane. This was the first B model Mustang to race since the National Air Races in Cleveland during the late 1940s. Photo Credit: Birch Matthews

Veteran race pilot Jimmy Leeward winds "Cloud Dancer" around a pylon at Reno. Photo Credit: Chuck Aro

In 1984, an unlimited class air race was held in Moose Jaw, Canada. Neal Nurmi caught Rick Brickert and Earl Ketchen leading the pack in the Gold Race passing home pylon. Photo Credit: Neal Nurmi

were parked in two lines along the pit area. Pilots could start engines and taxi into and out of the pit area. This was acceptable when the number of unlimiteds was relatively small and comparably few people were allowed into the pits. As crowd size increased and the unlimited entries grew, changes were made. Aircraft parking was compacted to accommodate the large number of airplanes participating in the races. More airplanes on the ramp meant more race crews. RARA initiated the sale of pit passes for spectators as a means to increase revenues. As a result of these factors, safety regulations were changed. Engines could no longer be started up in the pit area. All aircraft are towed out of the pits to designated areas on the Reno ramp before engines are started.

Pilots flying at Reno adhere to a demarcation known as the "dead line" which separates the racers from the spectators. For the unlimited class this distance is one thousand feet.

The home stretch of the race course in front of the pit and grandstand areas is about 1300 feet from the spectators. Aircraft crossing the deadline must be at or above one thousand feet altitude. Failure to adhere to this rule results in the pilot being disqualified.

Through the Reno Air Race Association, the National Championship Air Races are a permanent institution in Reno, much like the Indianapolis 500 race in Indiana. The air races attract the largest weekend attendance of any Reno event, including top performers in the entertainment field. The championship air races are probably far beyond even the most imaginative dreams of the late Bill Stead.

Notes

1. One of the racing rules required participating racers to takeoff and land at the race site. This was done to accommodate television coverage of the races.
2. Larsen, Jim, *Air Racers*, American Air Museum, Inc., Kirkland, WA, 1971, p. 50.

Wiley Sanders Truck Lines, Inc. sponsors this fast P-51D racer named "Georgia Mae." The aircraft is just leaving the ramp area for a heat race at Reno. Photo Credit: Birch Matthews

Chapter Seven
MORE THAN ONE GHOST

One of the more popular and highly modified *Mustangs* racing today carries United States civil registration N79111. Until recently, it was believed that this *Mustang* was the oldest racing P-51 in existence, for N79111 first appeared on the scene in 1946. The story really started in 1945, when two Hammond, Indiana, friends of many years decided they were, ". . . gonna get us an airplane after the war and we're going to fly it in the Thompson." The two were Steve Beville and Bruce Raymond. At the time, Beville was a captain on active duty with the Army Air Force. Much of his service

time was spent ferrying aircraft around the United States and overseas. As a consequence, he had the opportunity to fly a wide variety of military aircraft. He knew with certainty that the fighter he wanted for the Thompson was the North American P-51 *Mustang*. His military experience told him that this was the airplane to race.

Bruce Raymond had already returned to civilian life. He had purchased about a half dozen BT-13s for refurbishment and resale. With the two friends committed to acquiring a *Mustang*, Beville went to Washington D.C., to visit the War

After the war, Steve Beville and Bruce Raymond decided to go racing at Cleveland in a Mustang. The result was the "Galloping Ghost," named after football star, Red Grange. Photo Credit: Warren Bodie

Emil Strasser captured the "Ghost" in full profile and all alone at the 1948 National Air Races. Photo Credit: Emil Strasser

Assets Administration. Beville convinced a Colonel working there to reserve a P-51 from the hundreds in storage at Walnut Ridge, Arkansas, until he could fly down and take possession. This occurred about two weeks later when Beville and Raymond flew to Walnut Ridge in one of the BT-13s. There were literally hundreds of *Mustangs* on the field and the two men spent the better part of two days trying to choose which one to buy. They finally settled on a D model with a dash 3 *Merlin*, and went to the local War Assets office to make the purchase. In the end, the local War Assets official talked them into another P-51D, sitting outside on the ramp. This one had a new dash 7 *Merlin*. The

Mustang was fresh from the Army Air Force Training Command and total time on the airframe was less than 1000 hours. Before leaving Walnut Ridge, the two aspiring race pilots talked the War Assets people into a new coolant pump for the engine (the old one was leaking slightly), a new battery, and two wing tanks. The pair took title to the airplane on 11 July. It carried Army Air Force serial number 44-15651, a detail we shall return to later in the story. Bruce Raymond flew the *Mustang* back to Hammond while Steve Beville went about getting his discharge from the Air Force.

Preparations for the 1946 races were minimal because there was little time for work on the plane. The *Mustang* was

With towbar in place, the "Galloping Ghost" awaits a tug at the 1948 races. Photo Credit: Liang-O'Leary Collection

Pete Bowers photographed the "Galloping Ghost" on the starting line for the Thompson Trophy Race in 1949. The racer never finished lower than fourth place in any race over the four years of unlimited class racing at Cleveland. Photo Credit: Pete Bowers

Early in race week at Cleveland, race 77 underwent maintenance on the cockpit canopy in a hangar on the east side of Cleveland airport. Photo Credit: Birch Matthews

Rolls-Royce is a name synonymous with the North American Aviation Mustang. Their emblem is an elegant symbol of their products. Photo Credit: Rolls-Royce Ltd.

This Jim Larsen photograph illustrates a racing Merlin engine being lifted from its shipping crate for installation in a Mustang racer. Photo Credit: Jim Larsen

The engine compartment on a Mustang is tightly packed. This view illustrates the motor mount which is fabricated from aluminum components as opposed to more traditional steel weldments on many aircraft of that era. Photo Credit: Jim Larsen

This is Gunther Balz's beautiful silver P-51 racer undergoing an engine test prior to the 1972 races. The exhaust stacks are inverted for testing. Photo Credit: Jim Larsen

"Strega" is the fastest P-51 Mustang racing today. This is a typical scene in the Reno unlimited pit area during race week as work on the Merlin engine seems unending. Photo Credit: Neal Nurmi

The Maytag Mustang was unique in the duel fuel system developed for racing. For takeoff and landing, regular aviation gas was used. During a race, methanol would be employed. Unfortunately, the Merlin failed during a test flight and the system was never used. Photo Credit: Dusty Carter

The National Air Races had become a tradition each September in Cleveland, Ohio. This emblem for the 1949 races would mark the end of these events due to Bill Odom's fatal crash and the coming Korean War. Photo Credit: Dusty Carter Collection

Right: Established in 1930, the Thompson Trophy became symbolic with high speed pylon racing. In 1946, two trophies were fashioned. The one shown here was for the "R" Division awarded to pilots winning the Thompson reciprocating engine race. Photo Credit: TRW, Inc.

Fifteen years after the last Thompson race for piston engine airplanes, Bill Stead resurrected pylon racing for what is now called the unlimited class of aircraft. The year was 1964, and the host site was Reno, Nevada. Photo Credit: National Championship Air Races

Race 37 became a familiar entrant at Cleveland all four years of the post-war National Air Races. This rare 1949 color photograph shows J.D. Reed's entrant uncowled between events sitting in an area reserved for the Thompson class racers. Photo Credit: Fred Buehl

Another familiar sight at Cleveland after the war was the Mustang entry of Steve Beville and Bruce Raymond. The racer was named "Galloping Ghost" and consistently placed in the money each year. Photo Credit: Fred Buehl

The graceful lines of this Allison-powered P-51A Mustang were recorded by photographer Fred Buehl at the 1949 Cleveland races. Flown by James Hannon, the racer was forced out of the Tinnerman Race during the seventh lap. Photo Credit: Fred Buehl

For three years, Wilson Newhall ran a Bell P-63C-5 Kingcobra at the National Air Races. In 1949, Newhall appeared with a P-51 Mustang and placed seventh in the Thompson at 372 mph. Photo Credit: Fred Buehl

William Fairbrother bought Earl Ortman's 1946 Mustang racer and campaigned this aircraft through 1949. Note the revised lower cowling beneath the engine to accommodate a Merlin 225 low altitude engine installation in 1949. Photo Credit: Fred Buehl

In 1966, the races were moved to Stead Field about ten miles north of Reno on highway 395. Over the years, this race site has been constantly improved. As a consequence, the races draw over 150,000 people each year. Photo Credit: Birch Matthews

E.D. Weiner was one of a handful of early unlimited class pilots to enter the Reno races. His 1964 pylon racer was licensed N335J and was photographed in this illustration at Long Beach, California, after the races. Photo Credit: Birch Matthews

E.D. Weiner's race 49 flew again at Reno in 1966. One propeller blade was painted red for optical effects. The green tank aft of the pilot contained antidetonant injection fluid. Photo Credit: Birch Matthews

Chuck Hall first flew race 5 at Reno in 1966. The aircraft went on to become "The Red Baron" racer some years later. Pictured here, the aircraft was being towed out for a photographic session before the 1966 races. Photo Credit: Birch Matthews

E.D. Weiner flew his Mustangs regularly and even used them for business trips. This flight shot was taken off the coast of Southern California, near E.D.'s home base at Long Beach in May, 1967. Photo Credit: Tom Piedmont

Right: A unique 1000 mile pylon race was held in 1970, at the Kern County Airport located in Mojave, California. Upwards of twenty aircraft would fly the course at the same time and most would make pit stops to refuel. In the foreground of this ramp photograph is George Perez's stock P-51D, one of the contestants. Photo Credit: Birch Matthews

Another unlimited racer of the early years at Reno was Mike Loening, shown here with his famous father, Grover Loening. Photo Credit: Birch Matthews

In 1970, Clay Lacy became the first Mustang pilot to capture the gold championship race at Reno. Like E.D. Weiner, Clay was one of the first pylon racers helping to re-establish unlimited air racing in 1964. Photo Credit: Tom Piedmont

The late Bob Love straps in for a test flight at Reno. Love raced this highly modified P-51D for a few years before restoring the airframe to stock condition. This photograph was taken at Reno before the 1973 races. Photo Credit: Birch Matthews

Jimmy Leeward taxis across the Reno ramp for takeoff on runway 26 for a qualification flight before the races. Named "Cloud Dancer," the aircraft incorporated clipped wings and horizontal stabilizer, a modified canopy and racing Merlin engine. Photo Credit: Birch Matthews

What would become the "Red Baron" in later years began its racing career in 1966. The airplane was owned and flown by Chuck Hall. Photo Credit: Birch Matthews

In 1967, Hall's racer was refinished but remained externally a stock P-51D Mustang. Again, Chuck Hall was the pilot at Reno. Photo Credit: Dusty Carter

In 1968, E.D. Weiner evaluated the flying qualities of his pylon racer without the traditional dorsal fin of a D model Mustang. This rare photograph shows the appearance of the P-51 during this short period before the fin was reinstalled. Photo Credit: Hal Loomis

Gunther Balz bought race 5 and flew it to victory in the 1972 Reno race program. Once again, the racer had been thoroughly prepared including an outstanding Merlin engine. Photo Credit: Dusty Carter

Race 5 next went to Ed Browning who quickly established the "Red Baron" racing team composed of the Mustang and a North American T-6 racer. The "Baron" raced at Mojave and Reno in 1974. In this photograph, it is shown during a deadstick landing at Kern County Airport in Mojave, California. Photo Credit: Dusty Carter

Steve Hinton, fresh from his record setting speed run, brought the "Red Baron" to Reno in September, 1979. In the championship race, engine failure caused Steve to crash land the racer at the finish of the race. Hinton survived but there was not much left of the once mighty "Red Baron." Photo Credit: Dusty Carter

In August, 1979, Steve Hinton set the three kilometer speed record for piston engine airplanes flying the "Red Baron" at 499 mph. The racer is seen here on the three kilometer course at Tonapah, Nevada. Photo Credit: Bruce Treadway

By 1977, the "Red Baron" was extensively modified and equipped with a Rolls-Royce Griffon engine. It was flown at Reno this year by Darryl Greenamyer. Photo Credit: Dusty Carter

Race 5 was again modified and refinished for the 1969 races. During a qualifying attempt, Chuck Hall's Merlin broke resulting in an emergency deadstick landing. Results of the broken engine are seen in this illustration. Photo Credit: Dusty Carter

stripped of every non-essential piece of equipment and military gear. After this was done, the partners spent every available hour smoothing the wing. Putty was applied to cover dimples in the laminar airfoil wing surface. Several coats of primer were sprayed on the wing and sanded smooth. The finish coat was a light grey color. After it was dry, the paint was rubbed down. In Steve Beville's words, "... the wing was slick. A wipe cloth dropped on the upper surface near the cockpit would slide down to the ground." The rest of the airframe was buffed until the aluminum was bright and shiny. The airplane was christened the *Galloping Ghost*, after the famous football player, Red Grange. Beville and Raymond applied for racing credentials and were able to get race number 77, the same number Grange carried on his football jersey. They were ready for the races. A coin toss was made to determine which pilot would fly and Bruce Raymond won. He went on to capture fourth place in the

Thompson race of 1946.

Both men knew they would have to get more power out of the *Merlin* if they were to be competitive in 1947. The answer appeared to be the addition of a water injection system.[1] They knew a man who ran the aircraft shop at Hammond Technical High School. The school had a P-47 fuselage, complete with an R-2800 engine equipped with a water injection system. Their friend removed the system and presented it as a gift. An acquaintance at Indiana Air Service, located in South Bend, was familiar with injection systems and agreed to do the engineering necessary to adapt the apparatus to the *Merlin*. The *Mustang* was flown to Indiana Air Service for the installation. Bendix was also located in South Bend and agreed to make the necessary modifications to the carburetor. Tanks for the liquid were installed in the wing gun bay compartments and Beville recalls that they carried about 80 gallons. The other change

Markings on the "Galloping Ghost" changed very little over the four years of racing at Cleveland. The aircraft is seen here during the 1949 races. Photo Credit: Birch Matthews

made to the aircraft involved deactivating the automatic boost (manifold pressure) device. With this inoperative, the engine could be run at manifold pressures higher than 67 inches. With water injection, it was possible to pull 80 inches of mercury manifold pressure, a significant increase.

It was Steve Beville's turn to fly the *Galloping Ghost* in the 1947 races. And fly he did. He won the first race he entered, the Kendall Trophy Race for P-51 *Mustangs*. Racing again in the Thompson Trophy, Steve finished fourth behind Cook Cleland and Dick Becker in their large, powerful Goodyear F2Gs and Jay Demming, ex-Bell test pilot, flying the 1946 champion Bell P-39Q racer. It was a wild race. Thirteen aircraft started the Thompson and only six finished. Beville remembers Cook Cleland moving ahead of him "like a freight train passing a bum." His *Mustang* was no match for the big Pratt & Whitney R-4360-powered F2G. It was still a good racing season for the *Galloping Ghost* and the partners returned to Hammond to await another year of racing.

The racer sat outside during the cold Indiana winter. The two men didn't have the money to afford a hangar. This proved to be a problem in 1948. The water injection system developed corrosion and this resulted in erratic operation during the races. In spite of this, Bruce Raymond won the Tinnerman Trophy Race, placed fourth in the Sohio race, and wound up second in the Thompson. As in the previous year, the Thompson was once again an adventure. Only three aircraft crossed the finish line. Anson Johnson won the race when all the fastest racers dropped out. Raymond didn't know what position he had gained until after landing. After shutting down his engine, a man came over and said, ". . . you're second." "You're kidding," Bruce replied. It came as a big, but welcome surprise to Bruce Raymond.

With the money received from the 1948 races, Raymond and Beville paid to have the plane hangered over the winter. When warm weather arrived, the two overhauled the water injection system to eliminate the corrosion problems. The only other change involved installing dash 9 *Merlin* heads and banks to the dash 7 engine together with grinding the valves and installing new piston rings. With these changes, the aircraft was entered in the 1949 races. It was again Steve Beville's turn to fly. He managed a fourth place finish in both the Sohio and Thompson Trophy races. In looking back upon the racing career of the *Galloping Ghost*, Steve Beville was justifiably proud of the performance of the *Mustang* that he and Bruce Raymond achieved. In his own words, the airplane, ". . . finished every race it was entered and finished in the money every race."

Raymond and Beville parted company with the *Galloping Ghost* the following year. In the spring of 1950, race pilot Jack Hardwick suddenly appeared in Hammond with an offer to purchase the P-51. After some haggling, the two partners agreed to the sale and Hardwick strapped on a parachute, climbed into N79111 and flew away.

At this point, the history of *Mustang* N79111 takes a mysterious turn. The original aircraft was seen as late as 1952 at Hayward, California. At about this time, a number of *Mustangs* were sold and shipped overseas. *Mustang* historian, Dick Phillips, invoked the "Freedom of Information Act" seeking government records associated with a number of P-51s that departed United States civil aviation records during this era. He uncovered details concerning Israeli purchasing agents who were actively buying P-51 *Mustangs* for eventual use by the Israeli Defense Forces. The *Galloping Ghost* was one of many *Mustangs* exported to Israel. The fate of this aircraft with the Israeli Air Force is unknown.[2]

In 1956, according to Dick Phillip's research, A P51D with Army Air Force serial number 44-15651 – identical to the *Galloping Ghost* serial number – was sold at auction to cover a mechanics lien. Was this the original airplane of the 1946-1949 era? In all probability it was not. Israeli agents used N79111 and other civil registrations a number of different times, according to Phillips. It was a matter of convenience in moving the aircraft about and preparing paperwork for eventual export.

In 1960, Cliff Cummins of Ontario, California, acquired the aircraft carrying license registration N79111. By 1969, he was campaigning this *Mustang* at a number of races. It would go on to an interesting and often exciting career of its own. At the time, everyone assumed that the Galloping Ghost had returned to air racing. But, it seems there was more than one Ghost . . .

In 1969, Cliff Cummins brought his *Mustang* to Reno. By now, the airplane had a new name, *Miss Candace*, and a new race number, 69. Cliff finished in fourth place in the championship race. The myth of *Galloping Ghost* was perpetuated. Beville and Raymond had never finished lower than fourth position in the races of the late 1940s. In 1970, Cummins arrived at Reno with the first of a series of modifications this *Mustang* would undergo. The wing span was shortened by removing the tip assemblies. Modified tips and a new lower profile canopy were installed. A *Bearcat* propeller replaced the stock *Mustang* unit. Cummins managed to post the ninth fastest qualifying time at a speed of 357 miles per hour. During race Heat 1A, Cliff experienced an engine problem, forcing him to make a dead stick landing. He made a wheels up, belly landing in Lemon Valley to the east of Stead Airport. The landing did major damage to the racer and it was eventually trucked back to Southern California into Frank Sander's hangar at Long Beach Airport.

What was thought to be the old "Galloping Ghost" reappeared at the 1969 Reno races. The pilot and owner was Cliff Cummins. Cliff retained the polished aluminum look of the "Ghost" as well as the N79111 registration number. Photo Credit: Liang-O'Leary Collection

In 1970, Cliff returned to Reno with clipped wings and a lower profile canopy. The aircraft was named "Miss Candace," one of several names the racer would wear over the years. Photo Credit: Liang-O'Leary Collection

The crash landing at Reno literally tore the belly scoop from the fuselage. The engine mount was bent and the propeller mangled. A decision was made to further modify the racer during the rebuilding process. Because the belly scoop was damaged beyond repair, a new unit was made. The P-51D radiators were reworked to provide coolant inlet and outlet fittings on the upper surface of the radiator assembly. This eliminated all plumbing on the bottom of the radiator. The oil cooler was replaced by a P-51H heat exchanger and located near the oil tank. The belly scoop inlet was made from a Lockheed Constellation oil cooler scoop, reworked to proper size. The result was a scoop inlet about ten percent smaller than a stock *Mustang* doghouse. The profile contour of the new scoop design changed significantly. Revision of the cooling radiator systems reduced the depth of the scoop below the fuselage. The belly scoop external shape was re-faired to extend aft of the fuselage break. Topside, the forward fuselage was reworked to accept an even smaller cockpit bubble canopy. Fuselage skin and formers above the longeron were removed in the

"Miss Candace" and Cliff Cummins ran out of luck at Reno during a 1970 race and the aircraft was bellied in on the desert floor. As can be seen, damage was significant but the airplane would be rebuilt. Photo Credit: Liang-O'Leary Collection

After the accident in 1970, "Miss Candace" was rebuilt, and further modified in the process. This 1972 photograph shows the new shallow belly scoop and minuscule cockpit canopy. Photo Credit: Liang-O'Leary Collection

vicinity of the cockpit. New formers and skins were fabricated to the diminished bubble canopy and cockpit cover assembly. In the reconstruction process, additional weight was removed and the finished racer had an empty weight of about 6500 pounds.

Cummins reappeared at Reno in 1972, where he won first place in the Medallion race at a speed of 367 miles per hour. He then took the racer to the Miami Air Races in 1973, and placed fifth at a speed of 354 miles per hour. He did much better at Reno in 1973, where he placed second in the Championship Race at 417 miles per hour. The following year, Cliff Cummins didn't fair well. In the second unlimited heat race, his engine developed problems that forced him out in the second lap. The racer sat out the rest of the Reno meet. The first Unlimited race of 1975 was the California Air Classic, and Cummins won the final event at a speed of 422 miles an hour. Unfortunately, a burned piston put Cliff out of the Reno championship race the following September. The airplane was temporarily repaired at Reno and flown back to Chino, California. The racer was thoroughly serviced and the engine rebuilt, employing special connecting rods purchased in England. The new rods were supposed to be capable of higher stress levels. While Cummins was flying from California to Reno, one of the expensive connecting rods failed, forcing Cliff to land at Bishop, California, high in the Sierra Mountains in central California. *Miss Candace* was out of the 1976 competition.

Cliff was back at Reno in 1977. He qualified third fastest in the unlimited field, thus assuring himself a place in the championship race. As this final race got underway, it was apparent that Cummins was out to win. He pushed

hard to keep *Miss Candace* in the running against Darryl Greenamyer, who was flying the *Red Baron*, and Don Whittington, in *Precious Metal*. Cummins stayed with the leaders as the race progressed. His pit crew started to become excited with the situation developing. The racer seemed to be running without trouble. When he took the checkered flag a cheer went up from Cliff's crew. He had finished the race with no problems. They then noticed *Miss Candace* going flat out around the course on a "safety lap." A stream of white smoke began trailing the racer. Mayday! It was another broken engine, but this time Cliff made a successful forced landing. Cliff had won third place at more than 424 miles per hour. It was the highest speed he ever achieved with N79111, and yet it only garnered third place. The competition at Reno was becoming fierce.

Unlimited class racing is a very expensive proposition. This is even more true if one tries to win the championship. To offset some of the expense, Cliff Cummins obtained sponsorship from the Circus-Circus Hotel and Casino in Reno and Las Vegas, Nevada. Things must have looked more promising at that point. Before the races began, publicity photographs were taken with the *Mustang* sitting in front of the grandstands. The aircraft gleamed in the sunlight. Cliff was off to a good start. He qualified the racer at just over 400 miles an hour. This was good enough for a place in the 1978 championship race. He was the second top qualifier behind only the *Red Baron* at 427 miles per hour. However, bad luck seemed to be ever lurking near *Miss Candace* and Cliff Cummins. In the very first heat race Cliff dropped out after a couple of laps, with burned valves inside the *Merlin*. *Miss Candace* sat somewhat forlornly on the

Cliff Cummins continued to race "Miss Candace" for several more years. The aircraft is seen here coming in from a practice run at Reno in 1977. Photo Credit: Neal Nurmi

ground for the remainder of race week.

Apparently this most recent setback was the last straw. In 1979, Cliff sold *Miss Candace* to Dennis Schoenfelder and Dave Zeuschel. The aircraft was sold again by Zeuschel and Schoenfelder to Wiley Sanders of Troy, Alabama. With new ownership came a new name for the venerable racer. It was now called *Jeannie*. Sanders engaged Zeuschel of Sylmar, California, to rework the racer for the 1979 race season. Zeuschel owned his own company, Zeuschel Racing Engines, which specialized in *Merlin*, Allison, and *Griffon* engine rebuilding. Dave was also an accomplished pilot and established himself in the field of warbird reconstruction and restoration.

When the airplane arrived at Zeuschel's shop it weighed 6700 pounds, some 200 more than when first built up by Frank Sanders. Some of the weight increase was due to an accumulation of dirt, oil and grease in relatively inaccessible cavities in the aft fuselage. However, most of the increase came from the addition of such things as an in-flight windshield clearing system. This was probably installed by Cliff Cummins after experiencing a number of engine failures which often left the cockpit canopy covered with oil film. The windshield washer was a bit complicated, using a pressurized solvent tank located in the aft fuselage together with associated lines, valves, and switches to complete the system. When Zeuschel reworked the airplane this apparatus was removed. Dave went through the veteran racer in great detail with a goal of reducing the weight to a minimum. He changed the stainless steel coolant and fuel lines to aluminum. The existing radio was removed and replaced by a light weight radio system that met racing requirements. All existing systems and instruments were reviewed and removed or replaced by lighter components where feasible. When the airplane was ready to fly it weighed 6100 lbs. Six hundred pounds of empty airframe weight was removed during the rework process.

The airplane was flown in the 1979 Reno contest by "Mac" McClain, who was previously the pilot for the *Red Baron*. As it turned out, the 1979 race season was not very kind to the Wiley Sanders racing team. Electrical troubles and engine problems plagued the *Mustang*. On his first qualifying attempt, McClain racked up a speed of almost 447 miles per hour to make it the top Reno unlimited qualifier. Mac took *Jeannie* to first place in the initial heat race. In the second heat race, Mac didn't complete the first lap. Because of his qualifying speed, Mac still retained the

The plan view of race 69 may be seen in this photo taken in 1978. The air racer was sponsored by Circus-Circus Hotel and Casino that year. Photo Credit: Colin Aro

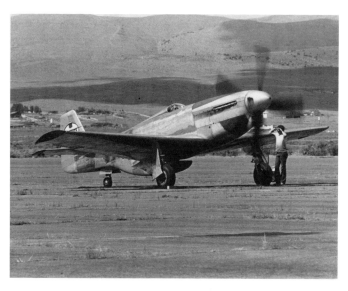

Wiley Sanders purchased race 69 from Cliff Cummins and campaigned the aircraft as "Jeannie." In this 1980 photograph, the engine is run up by Dave Zeuschel. Photo Credit: Neal Nurmi

pole position for the championship race. When Sunday afternoon arrived, the racers launched and formed on the pace plane. Just as the race started, Mac pulled *Jeannie* up sharply and declared a Mayday. He brought the very modified *Mustang* down safely while the rest of the racers were on the back side of the course. It was another disappointing finish for N79111.

Although it didn't seem like it at the start, the 1980 Reno races would mark a dramatic turn around for *Jeannie*. The races were scheduled for September 12 through 14 with qualification time trials starting on the ninth. On Friday, September 5, Dave Zeuschel took off from Van Nuys

Airport in Southern California, to put a little time in *Jeannie* before flying the racer to Reno. Zeuschel wanted to be on hand for an early qualification run. The Van Nuys take-off was late Friday afternoon; it was to be a short flight. It turned out to be a little shorter than expected. A few miles from the airport the engine failed completely. Dave set *Jeannie* down in a corn field. The ensuing landing badly damaged the racer. The prop was bent and twisted and the special low profile belly scoop was gone. The engine was torn loose from its mount. The landing gear doors were ripped off. It appeared that once again N79111 would be out of the running.

The aircraft was severely damaged and the deadline for arrival at Reno was noon Wednesday, just four and one-half days away. The P-51 was trucked back to Zeuschel's hangar and Saturday morning the crew examined the wreckage. By noon they had decided it was possible to get the airplane repaired and ready to fly to the races in time to qualify. Saturday afternoon, work began. The telephone lines hummed as the search for replacement parts was mounted. By Sunday, parts started arriving at the Van Nuys hangar. A P-51 dog house (belly scoop assembly) had been located and was on its way. The existing radiator installation was removed to make way for a standard assembly. When the belly scoop arrived it was a disappointment. The basic structure was so badly oxidized and damaged and required rather extensive structural repair. A dedicated crew literally worked around the clock.

Meanwhile, word of the accident to *Jeannie* reached Reno. Officials removed race 69 from the entry list on Wednesday morning, September 10th. Racing rules at Reno stipulate that all entries must be at the race site no later than noon on Wednesday of race week. About one-half hour before the deadline, a silver P-51 flew over the main runway at Stead. It was *Jeannie*. People on the ground were stunned and few at first recognized the racer. When Mac McLain landed and taxied up to the pits to shut down, a huge cheer went up. It seemed impossible that the badly damaged racer had been repaired and flown to Reno before the deadline. But there it sat, ready to race.

The racer had an unkempt and crazy quilt appearance due to the haste of the repair work and the borrowed hardware from many sources. Some parts of the plane were painted and some were not. There was a bit of black paint here and olive drab there. But the machine was complete and had made the deadline for arrival. The racer was then pushed into the pit area and preparations were made to qualify. In addition there was a crew put to the task of polishing the airplane to make it appear bright and shiny as it had once been. McClain qualified the racer at a bit over 396 miles per hour, thus becoming the sixth fastest qualifier, which in itself was a bit amazing. The climax of the Reno event was the championship race. At the very start of the race Mac jumped into the lead, flying a low, tight course. John Crocker in race 6 was close on his tail, with Don Whittington right behind in third place. Mac maintained his lead throughout the race and took the checkered flag with a speed of 433 miles an hour. It was a new closed-course record. The previous record was set by Darryl Greenamyer in 1977, when he flew the *Griffon*-powered *Red Baron* at just over 430 miles per hour. What a finale to the 1980 Reno National Championship races. An airplane scratched earlier in the week because of a major crash came back to win, setting a new record in the process.

Jeannie was flown back to Van Nuys to put some of the racing refinements back in place and make the plane competitive for the 1981 season. The borrowed stock belly scoop and radiators were once again removed. New systems were installed so that a low profile belly scoop could be used. By summer, the racer was nearing completion. However, unknown to all but a few, Mac McLain was terminally ill. He would not race again. Owner Wiley Sanders obtained the services of Lockheed test pilot "Skip" Holm for the 1981 season. Skip Holm and *Jeannie* were ready for the Reno races. In qualifying the racer, Holm set a new course record of 450.085 miles per hour. Holm was a rookie at Reno that year but his performance was veteran to say the least. His circuit of the race course was low and precise. In the Championship Race, Skip took the lead from his pole position and flew the eight laps in front of the pack. He finished with a speed of over 431 miles an hour. It was a second straight win in the gold championship race at Reno for N79111.

Fortune was not so kind the following year. *Jeannie* and Skip Holm returned to Reno in 1982, with a goal of taking the championship for the third consecutive time. It was not to be. During qualification, the propeller governor failed, putting *Jeannie* out of competition. Disappointed but undaunted, the owner and crew set out to make even more changes to N79111. This time, the wing span was further reduced to a diminutive 28 feet, 11 inches.

This would be the shortest span ever employed with a racing *Mustang*. Approximately nineteen inches were removed from the already short wing. Some thought was given to an even shorter span, but Zeuschel decided the aileron area was becoming marginal and this idea was abandoned. As the modified airplane was nearing completion, Wiley Sanders decided to sell the racer to Jimmy Leeward of Ocala, Florida.

Jimmy is a real estate developer in Florida and no stranger to air racing. His air racing career began years earlier, flying formula class midget racers. At Reno, Jimmy

Just before the 1980 races, "Jeannie" suffered a crash landing. A hasty rebuild ensued and the plane arrived just before the deadline for entries. Miraculously, Mac McClain went on to win the championship race that year. Photo Credit: Neal Nurmi

had raced a modestly modified *Mustang* called *Cloud Dancer*. After racing *Dancer* for several years he decided to obtain a highly modified racer, capable of championship performance. Leeward made another change to the airframe. He replaced the small bubble canopy with a new, slightly larger, but well-designed assembly that faired into the dorsal fin. The shiny aluminum racer was renamed *Specter* and carried racing number X (roman numeral 10). In 1946, the first N79111 was called *Galloping Ghost*, and thirty-seven years later an apparition of the "Ghost" returned as the *Specter*. But problems haunted the airplane in 1983. During qualifying, the official timer never saw Jimmy rock the wings, signaling that he was ready to run his qualification lap. Leeward flew a good, fast qualifying lap in vain. The time was not recorded. He did manage to qualify his other P-51, *Cloud Dancer*, and when its turn came up to race Jimmy brought *Specter* out. In the bronze consolation race on Sunday, Leeward flew *Specter* even though it was not qualified. It was a show. There is no record of *Specter's* performance in the 1983 race. For 1983, anyway, the airplane was aptly named.

When N79111 appeared at Reno in 1984 it carried a new airplane number. Race number 44 had replaced roman numeral ten. The flashy red and yellow paint scheme had been removed and the name was changed from *Specter* to *Leeward Air Ranch Special*. The racer was now polished aluminum with blue numbers. It had posted a qualifying speed of 425 miles per hour. It did not finish the two heat races it was flown in, but did manage to finish fourth in the Championship Race with a speed of 407 miles an hour. This was somewhat better than the 1983 season, but still not what was anticipated.

In succeeding years, Jimmy had mixed results with the racer. When the racer appeared in 1985, it was still named the *Leeward Air Ranch Special*. It was painted a brilliant yellow with red trim. It qualified well, but engine problems again plagued pilot and crew. In 1986, Leeward brought both of his *Mustangs* to Reno. Jimmy flew the "Special" and his twenty-four year old son, Dirk, flew *Cloud Dancer*. It was the first time that both a father and son had competed in the unlimited class. Succeeding years brought further frustrations. In 1988, Jimmy qualified at a very fast 457 miles per hour. But trouble and potential disaster lurked just ahead in the form of Heat 3A of the Saturday unlimited races. The race was successfully launched but at the end of lap three, Don Whittington, in *Precious Metal*, declared a Mayday and landed safely. On lap four, three airplanes were forced out of the race: Scott Sherman in race 84; John Maloney in race 1; and Lyle Shelton in race 77. All three pilots declared their intention to land on runway 32. Sherman and Maloney got down safely but the situation was chaotic. Lyle Shelton was set up on his final approach when Jimmy Leeward's engine just quit. He lined up for runway 32 only to discover to his dismay that a fuel truck was parked in the middle of the strip. He next saw a dirt road, headed for it, and

again discovered serious problems. There were two helicopters and about six people directly ahead of his path. After touching down, Jimmy hit the brakes hard three times. The third time he caught the propeller tips as the racer nosed down a little too much. Jimmy was down and he was safe and he was extremely mad. Once again, the racer was out of competition.

Jimmy was back in 1989, flying with an engine borrowed from John Sandberg. He qualified at a slow 376 miles per hour and really didn't compete, although he started one of the heat races. The racer didn't appear at the 1990 races. In spite of all the problems, Leeward's airplane is one of the premier *Mustang* racers.

_____

Notes

1. The system is more formally known as antidetonant injection, or ADI, and consists of fifty percent mixture of water and alcohol.
2. Information about N79111 was graciously provided by Dick Phillips in private communications, dated 10, June 1991, as the final manuscript was being prepared. The authors are grateful for his timely input.

Jimmy Leeward eventually settled on a bright yellow paint scheme and race number 9 for his airplane. The racer is seen here just after arriving in Reno for the 1989 races. Photo Credit: Birch Matthews

Wiley Sanders sold N79111 to Jimmy Leeward who renamed the racer "Specter." The name was apt because this was not really the old "Galloping Ghost" airframe. The original P-51 was sold to the Israelis after the 1949 National Air Races. Photo Credit: Birch Matthews

Leeward is seen here banking around a pylon during a 1983 race at Reno. The severely clipped wingspan is evident in this picture. Photo Credit: Chuck Aro

Chapter Eight
A MODERN "RED BARON"

By 1917, during the First World War, Baron Manfred von Richtofen was already a legend among both German and Allied forces for his exploits as a fighter pilot. He was called the *Red Baron* and the Fokker Triplane he flew was painted blood red. A modern *Red Baron* appeared on the racing scene in the early 1970s when a Mustang racing team was formed to compete in pylon races and eventually go after the world piston engine, three kilometer, speed record. In racing circles, this new *Red Baron* would become something of a legend also, reaching both the pinnacle of success and ultimately a disastrous ending.

The story of the *Red Baron* Racing Team's P-51 racer began in Dallas, Texas. On June 25, 1945, P-51D-25-NT, Army Air Force serial number 44-84961 rolled off the assembly line at North American Aviation's Dallas facility. The fighter never went overseas to combat. It was flown directly from the factory to a storage facility at Kelly Field, Texas. In 1947, it was drawn from storage and went into service with Air National Guard units in California and Wyoming. From there the fighter saw service with the Tactical Air Command and later the Air Defense Command. The military career of this *Mustang* ended with the 169th Fighter Interceptor Squadron of the Illinois Air National Guard stationed at O'Hare Airport in Chicago.

In 1956, The P-51 was flown to McClellan Air Force Base at Sacramento, California, and once again placed in storage. Two years later, the aircraft left Air Force inventory when it was sold to Capitol Airways of Nashville, Tennessee. In civilian hands, the *Mustang* received registration N7715C. When Capitol acquired the P-51 it had a little over 1200 flying hours. In July 1964, a partnership of Charles Willis, Frank Lynott, and Charles "Chuck" Hall acquired the *Mustang*. The airplane first appeared at the Reno air races in 1966, when the event moved to Stead Field. Hall flew the stock black and red trimmed P-51D to a sixth place finish in the consolation race after qualifying at a slow speed of 284 miles per hour. A year later, Lynott and Willis lost interest in the aircraft and Chuck Hall became sole owner. The P-51 returned to Reno in 1967, with a new green and grey paint scheme, reminiscent of a World War II *Mustang*. Other than general airframe cleanup, the only noticeable difference was the installation of a P-51H Aeroproducts propeller. Chuck Hall managed a fourth place finish in the final race that year.

The airplane was back again in 1968, this time with more extensive modifications. The wing span had been shortened and new tips contours fitted, designed by Jim Larsen. The entire wing was smoothed and surfaced with

What would become the "Red Baron" racer began life as a stock P-51D Mustang, owned and raced by Chuck Hall. It first appeared at Reno in 1966. Photo Credit: Birch Matthews

Chuck Hall's racer was painted black with red trim when it first raced. It is seen here sitting in the unlimited pit parking area at Reno in 1966. Photo Credit: Liang-O'Leary Collection

By 1968, race 5 had been refinished in dark green and silver. Chuck named the racer "Miss R.J." and added clipped wings to the airframe. Photo Credit: Liang-O'Leary Collection

Under the supervision of Jim Larsen, "Miss R.J." was extensively modified and wore a new white and crimson trim color scheme in 1969. Photo Credit: Birch Matthews

Race 5 sits on the ramp at Reno in 1970, while the crew checks the engine during a test run. Photo Credit: Birch Matthews

flexible fiberglass covering. Crew Chief, Al Raines, fashioned and installed a finely tuned Rolls-Royce *Merlin* V-1650-9 engine. The racer was now named *Miss R.J.* Changes to the airframe and the new engine combined to make the *Mustang* very fast. Chuck Hall posted the highest qualifying speed at Reno that year. After a fascinating duel with Darryl Greenamyer in the final event, Chuck's propeller governor broke a seal on the last lap of the race. Losing power and virtually blinded by the leaking hydraulic oil on his windscreen, Hall managed to limp across the finish line in third position, later changed to second. This occurred because the second place finisher, Clay Lacy, was tagged for a pylon cut, resulting in a position penalty.

Further modifications were made to the airframe in 1969. The standard P-51 canopy and windshield were removed and a low profile canopy and windshield, ingeniously derived from a stock P-51D canopy, were installed. The top section of the fuselage from the canopy aft was faired to the vertical tail, using aluminum frames and foamed-in-place plastic worked to a smooth continuous contour. The plastic material was next covered with fiber-

glass for strength and to obtain a hard outer surface. The completed fairing gave the *Mustang* a unique image. The overall design was completed with the installation of a sharply pointed spinner. The airplane looked like a racer. The paint scheme was all white with tangerine trim, giving it a very striking appearance. During Hall's first attempt to qualify, the *Merlin* broke a piston causing him to make a forced landing. The broken part was one of a set of high compression pistons installed in the *Merlin* for racing. Although the disabled racer was down safely, it looked like the 1969 season was over.

The other participating race pilots decided to waive the qualification requirement and let Hall start as an extra in the forthcoming consolation race. He had to place at least third in this race to reach the championship event. The last piece of cowling was being installed when the rest of the aircraft taxied out for takeoff. The repaired engine started with no difficulty and Hall was able to take off and start the race. He placed second in the consolation race, thus earning a spot in the final event. The championship race included the record holding F8F-2 Grumman *Bearcat*, flown by Darryl

Greenamyer; Lyle Shelton's *Bearcat*, and three modified P-51s. From the beginning it was Greenamyer's race, and he eventually lapped the entire field to set a new closed-course record just over 412 miles per hour. Chuck Hall was second, flying with a stock engine. It was a remarkable comeback.

The 1970 Reno race constituted another year of engine problems, frustrating Hall and preventing *Miss R.J.* from qualifying or racing. The inaugural California 1000 was run in October, that same year. It was, as the name implied, a 1000 mile race. Hall and his crew had about one month to get *Miss R.J.* ready for the longest pylon race ever attempted. A racing engine was installed and fuel capacity increased. The latter was done by using the antidetonant tanks for fuel instead of water. The long distance of this unique race virtually eliminated running the *Merlin* at high manifold pressures, requiring the use of antidetonant injection. Hall started in fifth position when the race began. He was able to complete only twenty of the scheduled sixty-six lap race when a cam shaft broke. *Miss R.J.* was down again.

After the California 1000, Chuck Hall put the racer up for sale. Gunther Balz of Kalamazoo, Michigan, had been racing a rare Grumman F8F-1 and apparently had no desire to modify the *Bearcat* into a competitive racing machine. When Hall made his aircraft available, Balz bought the *Mustang* and brought it to Reno in 1971. There appeared to be no changes in the racer except for a paint scheme. Balz had the racer painted a silver color and named his new airplane the *Roto Finish Special*. During his first heat, the plastic rudder trim tab blew off. A trim tab was borrowed from another P-51 and the "Special" was ready for the Championship race. Balz ran against Greenamyer and his *Bearcat*, Shelton in his Wright R-3350-powered F8F-2, and Sherm Cooper in his big Hawker Sea Fury, all with engines having displacements twice the volume of the *Merlin*. The winning speed for the race was 413.987 miles per hour, and Balz finished fourth at 412.101 miles an hour. It was an excellent showing for the rookie pilot and his *Mustang*.

Balz arrived at Reno in 1972, dedicated to winning the championship race. Greenamyer had been suspended from racing due to race violations in 1971. Dick Laidley was flying Greenamyer's *Bearcat* and Lyle Shelton was back with his big unlimited. Gunther's race 5 *Mustang* had been groomed for this meet by Jim Larsen, who made the aerodynamic modifications. Jim had designed prior modifications for the airplane when Chuck Hall was the owner. Jack Hovey rebuilt the engine and Dwight Thorn was now crew chief. During the heat race on Friday, a large section of fiberglass fairing aft of the cockpit peeled off. This was repaired and Gunther was ready for the main event on Sunday. As the championship race got underway it was apparent that Balz and his crew had the machine running very smoothly. Near the end of the race, Balz increased manifold pressure, picked up speed, and won. When the timing sheets were compiled, Gunther had set another new course record of 416.160 miles per hour breaking Greenamyer's record by over two miles an hour. Race 5 had performed flawlessly.

Race 5 appeared at the next Reno race where it was flown by John Wright, a local Reno pilot. Wright flew to a qualifying speed of just over 410 miles an hour, assuring himself of a spot in the championship race. But, this was Lyle Shelton's year as he put the *Bearcat* around the Reno course flashing by the finish line at better than 428 miles per hour. John Wright came in at third place, with a speed of 407 miles an hour. Shortly after the 1973 Reno race, the airplane was sold to Jack Sliker, who entered it in the Mojave, California, race a few weeks later. Sliker qualified and eventually placed fourth in the championship event.

The racer was sold again, this time to Ed Browning, owner of the Red Baron Flying Service in Idaho. Browning engaged Roy McClain to fly the P-51 as well as a North American T-6 class racer. The combination formed the *Red Baron* Racing Team. Race 5 received a new, all-red paint scheme and was renamed *Red Baron*. Ed Browning entered the team in the 1974 Reno races. McClain put the racer into the final gold championship race with little trouble. In the second lap of this final gold class race, McClain declared a Mayday when the engine backfired, blowing away a portion of the air induction system and the lower cowling as well. Browning's first outing with the *Mustang* was a disappointment. A few weeks later the team entered the *Red Baron* in the Mojave race program in Southern California. Their fortunes changed dramatically. The championship race turned into a contest between Lyle Shelton and Mac McLain virtually from the start. Mac tailed Shelton lap after lap, remaining tantalizingly close to the big *Bearcat*. As the two racers entered home stretch on the last lap, Mac lowered the nose of the sleek red racer and passed Shelton just as they crossed the finish line. The finish was so close Shelton thought he had won the race. This first win by the *Red Baron* would not be the last. The airplane would become faster still.

After the Mojave victory, the airplane was flown to Chino, California, for major rework in the Aero Sport hangar. Browning and a team of experts were planning to pull the *Merlin* and install the much larger Rolls-Royce *Griffon* engine, which was equipped with contra-rotating propellers. The *Griffon* has a displacement of 2239 cubic inches, identical to the Rolls-Royce R engine which powered the Supermarine S6B racer of Schneider Trophy fame. The crew at Aero Sport was augmented by engine expert Randy Scoville, together with Lockheed engineers Pete

Chuck Hall sold the racer to Gunther Balz; Gunther appeared at Reno in 1971 where the racer had an all-silver finish. Race 5 number was retained throughout the life of this racing Mustang. Photo Credit: Birch Matthews

Gunther Balz called the racer "Roto Finish Special." It was beautifully prepared and finished during the 1972 Reno races when it won the championship race. Photo Credit: Liang-O'Leary Collection

A section of the fiberglass overlay on the fuselage of Race 5 tore away during one flight at Reno in 1972. Gunther landed safely and the damage was quickly repaired. Photo Credit: Bruce Treadway

Law and Bruce Boland. The *Red Baron* was in for major surgery. The top of the fuselage was removed and replaced with a well-designed, low profile canopy which faired into a new vertical fin. At the same time, all the foam plastic and fiberglass applied over the years was removed with a resultant weight savings of several pounds. The vertical fin height was retained but the surface area was increased by fifteen percent for improved lateral stability. The front of the fuselage was disassembled and the firewall moved aft a foot and a half. The *Merlin* engine mounts were strengthened and modified to accept a *Griffon* powerplant. The heavier *Griffon* was installed aft of the normal position for a *Merlin* for reasons of aircraft balance. This posed a problem, however. With the *Griffon* moved aft, there was insufficient room for the updraft carburetor on this engine. To overcome this situation, the supercharger housing was rotated 180 degrees, thus placing the carburetor mounting flange facing upward. A down draft carburetor from a P&W R-2800 engine was mated to the repositioned mounting flange. A long intake duct was fabricated and installed topside to

Pilot Mac McLain poses by the tail of the "Red Baron" during an appearance at Reno. Photo Credit: John Tegler

In 1973, the Race 5 first appeared as the "Red Baron." This photograph was taken at Chino Airport, where the conversion work was done. Photo Credit: John Tegler

When the airframe was converted to accept a Rolls-Royce Griffon engine, the appearance of the Mustang changed drastically. This photograph was take at Chino Airport in 1975, shortly after the modifications were completed. Photo Credit: S.W. Addis

"Red Baron" pilot Steve Hinton received the congratulations of Jimmy Doolittle after winning the championship race of the Mojave, California air races. Photo Credit: Neal Nurmi

deliver ram air to the carburetor.

Work continued and the reconfigured racer was ready for flight testing by spring of 1975. Flight testing quickly revealed a need for more lateral stability. Additional vertical tail surface was added, increasing the fin height about a foot. The racer was now ready for another race at Mojave, California. Because of the extensive and distinctive changes to the airframe, it was unofficially redesignated as an RB-51.

At the Mojave race Mac McClain qualified the *Red Baron* at 401 miles an hour, only to be exceeded in qualification speed by both Greenamyer and Shelton in their *Bearcat's*. McClain did not have much time in the RB-51. The additional power of the *Griffon* as well as the counter-rotating propellers caused unfamiliar flying qualities in the airplane that disturbed McClain. After qualifying, it was decided to add more vertical surface in the form of a fin installed just behind the tail wheel door opening. This five square foot surface seemed to improve handling, although it was only a temporary measure to get through the race. During the final

event, McClain pulled out of the race after a couple of laps when he discovered he couldn't latch the canopy into a locked position. Air loads were lifting the canopy off the tracks and the possibility existed that the entire assembly would depart the airframe. The new unlimited was out of the race. The rest of that summer was spent testing and tuning the airplane for the Reno race in September. The airplane arrived at Reno with a new ventral fin that was much more pleasing in appearance than the temporary installation used at Mojave. McClain qualified the RB-51 at 407 miles per hour, while Greenamyer, returning after his one year suspension, set a new qualifying record of 435 miles per hour. In the championship race the *Red Baron* placed second with a speed of 427 miles an hour. Lyle Shelton won the race at 430 miles per hour. Greenamyer missed the main event when his propeller governor failed during his takeoff roll.

The Mojave races were held again in June the following year and McClain was top qualifier. The number of racers fielded for this meet were limited and most of the aircraft were stock or nearly so. Because of this, the championship race was not worth running the risk of breaking an engine. Consequently, the speeds were more modest than usual, with the *Red Baron* winning at 407 miles per hour. In September racing buffs converged on Reno, bringing some new names to the unlimited class. Early in the week Mac had flown the *Red Baron* to a qualifying speed of 436 miles an hour. It was a very good speed, but Don Whittington, in a P-51, would top that with a speed of almost 439 miles per hour to establish yet another course record. Ken Burnstein's old racer, *Foxy Lady*, in the hands of new owner John Crocker, also qualified at 436 miles per hour. With Don Whittington's *Precious Metal* and Crocker's *Sumthin' Else* in the championship with Mac, it promised to be a very exciting race. Unfortunately, Whittington blew an engine and had to replace it before the Sunday race. The new engine didn't survive and Don Whittington was out of the race. Crocker's racer was running flawlessly but John had trouble keeping inside the course and he was later disqualified. The *Red Baron* was out after a few laps with a gear failure in the blower section of the engine. All three top qualifiers were out of the main event! It was another disappointment for the *Red Baron* Racing Team.

Nineteen seventy-seven saw a new pilot in the *Red Baron* cockpit. Darryl Greenamyer donated his world record holding *Bearcat* to the National Air and Space Museum and was looking for a ride at Reno. The *Red Baron* again appeared slightly different from years past. The ventral fin was removed and the wings were painted snow white with *Red Baron* stylishly emblazoned on the top and bottom surfaces. Darryl qualified the racer with a relatively slow speed of 385 miles per hour. It was good enough to get him in the

As the "Red Baron" banks around a pylon at Reno, the markings are clearly evident. At this point, the wings had been repainted white and the aircraft was sponsored by Michelob Light. Photo Credit: Jim Larsen

championship race, which he proceeded to win at yet another course record of 430.703 miles per hour. The bugs were being removed from the RB-51 and it was beginning to reveal its potential.

A third pilot flew the racer in 1978. This was Steve Hinton, who had been performing a good measure of the RB-51 test flights. He was top qualifier at Reno with a speed of 427 miles per hour. This year, the Reno meet was beset with bad weather. On the day of the championship race, it became a cold, windy, and snowy; the race program was virtually canceled. They did run a shortened Unlimited Championship Race, with Hinton winning at just over 415 miles per hour. Steve also flew the RB-51 in the Mojave races during October, where he was again top qualifier. Like

Reno, the final race day at Mojave was plagued with bad weather. It was very windy, causing many problems with the various events. Nonetheless, Steve Hinton drove the RB-51 to yet another victory in the final race. Because of the weather, his speed was a slow 371 miles an hour.

Homestead, Florida was the site of the first championship race of 1979. This was the International Air Race put on by the Whittington Brothers. Once again, Steve rolled the RB-51 to victory. The next race at Mojave belonged to the *Red Baron* team as well. It was a remarkable string of wins. In August the *Red Baron* was taken to Tonapah, Nevada for an assault on the world three kilometer speed record, then held by Darryl Greenamyer in his F8F-2 *Bearcat*. The existing record was 482.462 miles per hour, set ten years earlier on August 26, 1969. The first attempt at the record was on August 9, but cool temperatures and turbulence held the average speed for four passes over the measured course down to 480 miles per hour, well below the existing mark. The next morning Hinton took the *Red Baron* onto the course but aborted the run because of excessive engine vibration. The big Rolls-Royce *Griffon* engine had thrown a rod through the crankcase. A new engine was installed during the night and some engine "slow time" flights were made the next day, August 11. These flights were plagued by excessive oil loss so the next night was spent locating the source of leakage and making repairs. At noon on August 12, the *Red Baron* took off from Tonapah and headed for the 3 kilometer course set up on Mud Lake. Observers noted the tail wheel door was open, but Hinton pushed the RB-51 through four passes gaining a speed of 489.251 miles per hour, good enough for a new record even with the added drag of the open tail wheel door. The door was repaired, and at 10:41 a.m. the next day the RB-51 was rolled out once more in an attempt to better the 489 mark. Again, a rough running engine aborted the record attempt. This time it was a bad spark plug.

With time running out for use of the course and the 500 miles per hour mark still illusive, a last attempt was made on August 14. Hinton and the *Red Baron* were off at 8:42 in the morning. The air temperature was only 68 degrees, well below the hoped for 100 degrees. Steve made yet another four passes over the course. This time, everything worked and a new record was established. Hinton and the *Red Baron* had traveled an average speed of 499.018 miles per

hour. The *Red Baron* Teams's roll continued. Next stop: Reno.

At last, winning ways for old N7715C seemed firmly established, and the meet at Reno would be one more layer of icing on the cake. Future plans called for another assault on the three kilometer record to finally push the speed over 500 miles per hour. It was not to be. The *Red Baron* suffered minor problems throughout the week and the competition looked tough. John Crocker's P-51 was running better than it ever had. Mac McClain was back again flying Cliff Cummins old racer and had set the top qualifying mark at 447 miles per hour. Hinton was next at 442 miles per hour, followed by Crocker at 433 miles per hour. This was a very fast trio of P-51 racers! The championship got underway on a picture perfect day, with McClain dropping out before the start. As the racers came across the start line, Crocker was in first place, with Hinton a close second. The entire race was run with the airplanes in their starting positions throughout; Crocker flashed across the finish line only seconds ahead of Hinton. But, Steve was in trouble. Coming down the home stretch in front of the pit area and then the grandstands, the sound of the engine and propeller was sickening. Everyone knew there was a serious problem occurring with the racer. Airspeed was bleeding off rapidly as the propeller blades swung into flat pitch, immediately becoming a large air brake. Steve swung the dying racer right and then rolled left, trying in vain to set up for an emergency landing on Stead runway 32. He couldn't make it. The RB-51 came down beyond the east end of the airport in Lemon Valley. The land falls off sharply just east of the runway and the crash landing couldn't be seen by the crowd. What could be seen was a large fireball erupting from the scene of the accident site. This made no difference to Steve's crew in the pits. They scrambled onto a truck and raced to the crash site. Steve had survived the crash, although he was seriously injured. What probably saved his life was the fact that after the RB-51 hit an outcropping of rock in Lemon Valley the wings were torn off, thus dissipating some of the kinetic energy as the airplane hit the ground. The fireball witnessed by the crowd was one of the wing tanks exploding after it was torn from the fuselage. Steve Hinton was evacuated from the crash site by helicopter to a local hospital where he recovered not only to fly again, but successfully race once more.

At rest in the Reno pit area. This picture of Race 5 illustrates the enlarged vertical tail surfaces required to improve directional stability with the Griffon engine. Photo Credit: Chuck Aro

Chuck Aro photographed the "Red Baron" minutes before the stricken racer crash landed in Lemon Valley, east of the Reno-Stead airport, at the end of the championship race in 1979. Steve Hinton escaped with serious injuries. Photo Credit: Chuck Aro

In 1948, J.D. Reed created this unique racing Mustang by removing the belly scoop and relocating the cooling radiators to the wing tips. This photograph was taken in Los Angeles on the ramp next to the North American Aviation plant. Photo Credit: Dusty Carter Collection

Part III
Stable of Thoroughbreds

Out of perhaps one hundred or so Mustang's that have been used over the years for racing, only a very few stand out as true thoroughbreds. These aircraft are unique because of the innovative engineering modifications applied to airframes, engines, and supporting systems.

They are exceptionally light weight and aerodynamically clean. Phenomenal performance levels have been attained by each of these special few racing Mustangs. Some went on to establish new national and international speed records. In each instance, these racers were the creation of individuals, not large corporations in the field of aviation.

Succeeding chapters in this section relate the stories of four prominent racing Mustang's. The first Mustang chronicled was known as Foxy Lady, when owned by the late Ken Burnstine. Aerodynamically, it was the creation of engineer Jim Larsen. When Ken was killed in an airplane accident, John Crocker bought the racer and renamed it Somthin' Else. John has campaigned the racer ever since. The next P-51 was initially owned and raced by Garry Levitz who called his racer Precious Metal. Indianapolis 500 auto racer and pilot, Don Whittington, bought this Mustang and for one year called it Miss Florida III. Don subsequently reverted to the Precious Metal identity, which was probably appropriate based upon the amount of money both men must have expended on this racer over the years.

The last two Mustangs portrayed might be considered second or even third generation racing conversions. Both were built up in the early 1980s. Bill DeStefani of Bakersfield, California, was involved with both airplanes, first Dago Red with Frank Taylor and later by himself with Strega. Both aircraft are champions and represent perhaps the ultimate degree of engineering refinement in Merlin-powered Mustang racers. Indeed, Strega is the fastest P-51 in the world. During the 1991 Reno races, Bill Destefani flew this airplane to second place in the championship race at an average speed of just under 479 miles an hour!

A great deal of engineering, craftsmanship, labor, and yes, money, has been poured into these racing machines. Each is the product of almost continual refinement and this process is ongoing year by year. The men who created these and all of the thoroughbred Mustang racers push the engineering art. They are aided by new methods and materials, miniaturized electronics, and sophisticated techniques which keep forty-five year old engines and airframes racing.

The authors once asked Lockheed engineer Bruce Boland just how long these World War II aircraft could be kept running, especially in the harsh environment of pylon racing. Our preconceived thought was that availability of Merlin engines would soon become the limiting factor which eventually would ground racing Mustangs. Bruce pointed out that many more Merlins were built than P-51 airframes. Replacement engines and spares were needed during the war. It was no doubt more efficient to pull an engine and replace it with a new one after so many combat hours, and for this reason thousands of engines were manufactured. In addition, Merlin production continued after the war as Rolls-Royce attempted to penetrate the commercial airline engine market. Coupled with sufficient residual stocks of engines and remanufactured or newly manufactured components, there is no critical shortage of Merlin powerplants. Over the years, of course, as stocks decrease, the price of a racing Merlin has increased substantially. If you have a hundred thousand or more, you too can buy a racing engine designed to help you get to the winner's circle.

It was Bruce Boland's opinion that fatigue of critical airframe components would ultimately put the racing Mustangs on the ground for good. Racing aircraft are essentially single point designs. That is, they are created for one purpose, which is namely to perform at maximum speed around a pylon course for very short durations. For instance, the gold championship Reno race consumes about ten minutes of high-speed flight, together with perhaps another fifteen minutes during the air start process. Landings after a race are accomplished rapidly. Most pilots carry a minimum fuel allotment onboard to reduce the gross weight of their airplanes. As a consequence, engines are briefly allowed to cool down at altitude before the recovery process begins. This scenario results in a high ratio of landings versus actual flight time. Repeated landings induce stress concentrations, which after a time contributes to metal fatigue that leads to structural failure. This failure mechanism can be avoided by periodic inspection and replacement of critical assemblies and castings. This is a very expensive process and in the end may someday cause many warbirds to drop by the wayside. On the other hand, the meticulous care and attention to detail given championship racing machines will insure their participation in the fastest motor sport in the world for some time to come.

Chapter Nine
THE GELDING

In the sport of horse racing it is accepted practice to surgically modify stallions (known as geldings) to improve their performance as racers. A somewhat analogous approach has been tried on the *Mustang* to produce a superior racing airplane. Most racing P-51 modifications typically involve a reduction in wing span, use of a much smaller, lower profile cockpit canopy, general cleanup of wing fillets and aerodynamic surfaces, and the application of very smooth surface finishes, especially on the wings. However, three P-51 racers have had radical surgery. In that never-ending racing fraternity quest for more speed, another severe airframe modification has been tried. This was the removal of the *Mustang* belly scoop housing the engine cooling radiators. The intent was to further reduce aerodynamic drag associated with this fuselage appendage on the P-51. Cooling systems in the scoop were relocated in varying fashion to the wings. Three racers have tried this tactic. The very first was in 1948; this was J.D. Reed's beautiful P-51C named after the popular music score, *Beguine*.

To tell the story, let us figuratively "begin (with) the *Beguine*." This airplane has become one of the most controversial racers of modern times, due to its unusual configuration, the secrecy of its origin, the popularity of its pilot and, last but not least, the tragically spectacular crash that brought an end to the airplane, its famous pilot, a mother, and her small child.

The story of *Beguine* begins with a brief history of its owner, the late J.D. Reed of Houston, Texas. Reed, known to his friends as "J.D.," learned to fly in 1926 from a small airfield near Houston. Today this land is part of the campus of Rice University. During the 1930s, J.D. did some air racing with a Monocoupe 110, powered by a 180 horsepower Warner engine. It was during this time that J.D. met Walter Beech, founder of Beech Aircraft Corporation. The two became life-long friends.

During this same era, J.D. was a member of the National Guard. He and twenty-eight other National Guard officers built a flying field that is now Houston's Hobby Airport. This group of Air Guard officers subsequently prevailed

"Beguine" crash landed during a 1948 ferry flight to Cleveland for the races. Returned to Houston, the racer was rebuilt and repainted. Photo Credit: Dusty Carter Collection

Pilot Paul Penrose poses in the cockpit of the 1948 racer called "Beguine." Paul conducted the test flights for the new racer. Photo Credit: Dusty Carter Collection

upon the Army Air Corps to ship them a World War I hanger, then in storage at Wright Field in Ohio. In 1936 the hanger was completed and the airport firmly established. J.D. started a fixed-based operation at this field, becoming a distributor for Fairchild, Howard and Beech airplanes. During World War II, Reed was a pilot with the Pan American Airways aircraft ferrying program. At the cessation of hostilities, J.D. reopened his Houston operation and became one of the largest distributors for Beechcraft airplanes.

J.D. Reed desired to go racing again when this sport returned to Cleveland after the war. In 1947, he fielded two entrants, both were Lockheed P-38 Lightnings. One carried license NX25Y and is still racing today. Reed's P-38s didn't fare well in the pylon events and following the 1947 racing season he purchased a P-51D racer called *Wraith* (Scottish for "ghost") from Ron Freeman of Santa Monica, California. Ron had entered *Wraith* in the 1946 races and George Welch, the pilot, set the highest qualifying speed that year at 395 miles an hour. Freeman again entered the racer in 1947, with Paul Penrose as pilot, and *Wraith* again did very well. J.D. Reed was impressed with the performance of the airplane. Furthermore, he was greatly impressed with how well the racer was prepared and maintained. By the end of 1947, Freeman – a West Coast representative for Packard's license-built Rolls-Royce engines during the war – was more than willing to part with the racer. The airplane developed fuel feed system problems and was expensive to

race and maintain. As a consequence, J.D. purchased the airplane for $5000. He also bought the fuel flow problems.

After the 1947 Cleveland races, Reed and Walter Beech discussed possibilities of preparing a more competitive racer for the next year. Beech considered the P-51B and C model airplanes a better basis for a racer than the P-51D and suggested Reed acquire such a machine if he were indeed ready to go racing again. In June, 1948, J.D. located a C model *Mustang* owned by Frank J. Abel of Wichita Falls, Texas. J.D. traded a Beech Bonanza for the P-51C which was located at Sheppard Field, Texas. Originally, this aircraft was one of 464 suplus military aircraft purchased for $70 thousand on 19 February 1946, by a Paul Mantz partnership consisting of Mantz, J.W. Heath and L.B. Hapgood.[1] The partnership subsequently sold this particular P-51C aircraft to Frank Abel in late July 1947.[2] The *Mustang* apparently saw little or no use until J.D. bought the fighter on 10 July 1948.

The P-51C was intact but had not been run, much less flown, in a long time. When J.D. and his crew journeyed to Wichita Falls to pick up the airplane, they found the propeller was essentially frozen in place from disuse – it would not budge. Reed's crew pulled the spark plugs and squirted a dose of Marvel Mystery Oil penetrant into each cylinder then rocked the propeller back and forth. This process was repeated until the propeller could be rotated a bit. Eventually they were able to pull the propeller through several revolutions. In the end, they added Mystery Oil penetrant to both engine oil and fuel. When the engine finally started it smoked furiously for several minutes blowing out months of residue and excess Marvel Mystery Oil. This was the humble beginning of what was to become the *Beguine* racer.

When the crew finally got the engine running, J.D. called Paul Penrose in Los Angeles and asked him to ferry his airplane to the West Coast for modifications. When asked why Penrose, J.D. responded, "I hired Penrose because he beat me at Cleveland and Miami and I thought he was a damn good pilot."

When first acquired, the airplane was all grey and carried civil registration N4845N. After J.D. took title to the *Mustang*, he applied for a race number, eventually obtaining number seven. The racer was ferried to Los Angeles about the middle of June, 1948. During an interview, Reed was asked why the aircraft was sent to Los Angeles for modification. This question prompted a story of secrecy and conspiracy between J.D. and his long time friend, Walter Beech.

Walter's wife, Olive Anne Beech, was a strong willed business women. She was against Walter having anything to do with air racing. She felt that racing was a risky affair and not at all consistent with promoting safe, private flying.

The wing tip pods on "Beguine" were fashioned from tip tanks used on the North American FJ1 Fury jet fighter. Photo Credit: Dusty Carter Collection, Bob Bailey Photo

Olive Anne was aware of Walter's close friendship with J.D. and his involvement in racing. In reality, the entire concept of the *Beguine* was the product of Walter Beech's fertile mind. But Walter had no wish to reveal a racing involvement to his wife, so the two friends decided to have modifications performed as far away as possible from Olive Anne, Beech Aircraft, Inc., and the midwest in general. Besides, Los Angeles was the home of the P-51. There would be a lot of knowledgeable people nearby for consultation. J.D. had sworn secrecy to Walter so that Olive Anne would never know her husband was again engaged in the sport of air racing. Ultimately, Reed did reveal the conspiracy in 1987.

The airplane was flown to Los Angeles International Airport and put into the Airesearch Corporation hangar near the southwest corner of the airport. The Airesearch facility modified many business aircraft, so the necessary equipment and talent for major airframe alterations were readily available. Construction of Reed's P-51C into a major contender for the Thompson Trophy Race began in June, 1948. It was not a formal project of Airesearch. Rather, management simply supplied floor space for the modification work. Personnel performing the work were off-duty Airesearch and North American Aviation employees, including Ed Horkey. For instance, North American engineers instrumental in designing the NA-73, forerunner of the P-51, provided analytical support to the project. Airesearch engineering provided expertise on the cooling systems and made a recommendation to use aluminum oil heat exchangers (radiators) designed for the R-4360 engine installation on Boeing's B-50 bomber. For the *Beguine* project, these B-50 heat exchangers were used for removing heat from the engine coolant and for the supercharger intercooler. A P-51H oil heat exchanger replaced the stock P-51C unit. This unit was mounted in front of the oil tank.

Shaping of the wing tip radiator cowling or pod was an important part of this design approach. Time to design and refine such a pod was not available. Project engineers

selected the North American FJ-1 "Fury" fuel tip tank for the *Beguine* wing pod installation. Here was an available component that was well-designed and had been flight and wind tunnel tested. Conveniently, the diameter of the tank was slightly larger than the B-50 radiators, so no change to the outer structure was required.

The tank shell was modified to form a cowling, or pod, around the radiators. The forward opening was framed in a laminated mahogany ring to form a smooth inlet lip. A streamlined strut was installed vertically at the inlet to relieve hoop tension loads on the wood ring and to provide a leading edge for a flow splitter that ran aft to the face of the heat exchanger. The splitter dividing the inlet air flow into two equal volumes was added after the first flight. Cooling problems were encountered during the flight and it was determined that uneven flow distibution was occuring in the divergent entrance section leading to the radiator face. Ed Horkey was instrumental in defining and resolving this particular problem.

The pod exit was formed by riveting the internal duct directly to the outer fairing, forming a knife edge. Two B-50 oil heat exchangers were used as engine coolant radiators in each wing tip pod. Unlike the conventional *Mustang* belly scoop, there was no method of varying airflow through the pod duct. Pod inlet and exit areas were of fixed geometry. Existing P-51 cooling system lines were intercepted near the cockpit area and rerouted through the wings to the new radiation locations.

The wing tip radiator pod concept was Beech's idea and according to J.D. Reed, "Walter determined that such an installation would result in little or zero drag. Walter designed the installation so the left wing was six inches longer than the right wing. He gave me all the technical reasons why this was necessary but all that technical stuff was over my head since I'm only a pilot and not an engineer." The possibility that this highly unusual modification was made has added to the legend of *Beguine*. Rumors about the wing geometry appear to have begun at the races in 1949. Some said there

Cooling water is sprayed into the pod-mounted radiators during an engine test run in Los Angeles in 1948. With the radiators located outside of the propeller arc, ground cooling was non-existent. Photo Credit: Dusty Carter Collection

was as much as an eighteen inch difference between the left and right wings. Even Reed's own statements on this subject have varied with time.

The only physical evidence relative to the wing panels in existence today are full front view photographs of the airplane taken in 1948. Two of these were analyzed during the research for this chapter and the inescapable conclusion is that the wings were symmetrical when the airplane was first modified in 1948. This was subsequently verified by Ed Horkey during an interview at the 1991 Reno Championship Air Races. Ed provided aerodynamic engineering support for the *Beguine* project during the initial modification effort. He stated emphatically that the panels were identical in span and that persistent rumors of an unsymmetrical wing planform were incorrect.

Further support for a symmetrical planform occured during an interview with Virgil Thompson of Fresno, California, who revealed details of the 1948 airframe modifications. Virgil was "shop supervisor" for *Beguine* modifications, as well as a member of North American Aviation's field service group. He was very familiar with the P-51 and had done most of the work on Ron Freeman's

"Beguine" sits in profile on the east side of Cleveland Airport, ready for an engine test. The musical score from "Begin the Beguine" was on both the fuselage and tip pods. The color was dark green, apparently with a clear lacquer overcoat. The finish was immaculate. Photo Credit: Dusty Carter Collection

Wraith. During the *Beguine* modification process, Virgil recalled that, ". . . we installed the radiators directly to the end of the front and rear spars." He had no recollection of further work on the spars to shorten one of the wings. In essence, the wing tip was removed at the production break to gain access to the ends of the wing spars.

If the wing panels were not dissimilar when the plane was first built for racing, were they altered in 1949? There was a forced landing in 1948, and the airplane was repaired before the 1949 races. During a second interview, J.D. Reed said, ". . . we never touched the wing tip pods (in 1949). They were left as they were built in Los Angeles."[1] This was recently confirmed by pilot Ken Cooley who conducted all of the test flying on the 1949 version of *Beguine* in preparation

for the National Air Races.

Beguine was also equipped at this time with an antidetonant injection system to permit higher engine manifold pressures (more horsepower) during a race. This system injected a mixture of water and methanol into the induction system at the pilot's discretion. Water-methanol tanks for this system were fabricated of aluminum to fit into the wing gun bays. Pumps, plumbing and controls were added to complete the system.

Race modifications were completed around the middle of August, some four months after Paul Penrose brought the airplane to Los Angeles. The engine was run for the first time on Thursday, 19 August. It was run again on Friday and the paint scheme finished the following day. A North

American staff photographer, Buzz Holland, took pictures of the new airplane on Sunday, August 22, at the North American facility on the airport. The airplane was now painted dark green with the musical score from "Begin the Beguine" emblazoned on the fuselage sides in a golden yellow color. According to Virgil Thompson, the primary color of the airplane, ". . . was about like the British racing green used on the MG sports car."

Virgil Thompson, Bill Goff, and Paul Penrose made engine runs on Sunday and again on Monday morning. That Monday, Paul Penrose lifted off the runway at Los Angeles International for the first flight of *Beguine*. The flight was shortened when Penrose experienced aileron vibrations, preventing much in the way of high speed testing. When Paul Penrose landed, *Beguine* was hangered and Virgil Thompson went through the entire control system and could not find one item that was out of specification.

North American engineers were called in for consultation. The story that follows is J.D. Reed's account. "When Penrose discovered aileron vibration, the engineers thought it was airflow interference between the pod and aileron, but some lady engineer from North American looked at the problem and told them to re-balance the aileron. They did, the problem went away and the airplane flew great. The lady really saved the airplane." That "lady" no doubt was Rose Lund, a premier engineer in the field of flutter and vibration. Rose had saved more than one North American airplane. While the ailerons were being reworked, Penrose left for the National Air Races in Cleveland where he was to test fly and qualify a Goodyear racer, designed and built by Art Chester. *Beguine* would not be ready in time for him to ferry the aircraft to Cleveland and also qualify the little racer. Penrose called on a friend of his, Joe Roger Howard, to fly *Beguine* and verify the aileron rework. This was done on 26 August. Time was running out.

After the test flight, Howard was to fly *Beguine* to Phoenix, Arizona, where the crew would again check the airplane. Howard made the flight to Phoenix and fuel consumption was calculated for that portion of the trip. From the calculations, fuel requirements from Phoenix to Cleveland were estimated. Power settings and flight profiles were provided to Howard. Reed's crew then departed for Cleveland in a private twin-engined Beechcraft. Joe Howard lifted *Beguine* off the runway at Phoenix and headed east. When the estimated time for his arrival in Cleveland came, there was no sign of Howard or *Beguine*. Time passed nervously for the crew until J.D. got a call from Anthony, Kansas. Howard had run out of fuel and bellied *Beguine* into a freshly plowed field. The date was September 2, 1948. According to a local weekly newspaper, the racer, ". . . crash landed one-half mile east of Attica (Kansas) – about 11:00

a.m. on September 2. There was small damage to the plane and no injury to Joe R. Howard. According to the pilot the ship had been checked and it would use 67 gallons per hour but it actually used about 89 gallons per hour."[4] The Thompson race was scheduled four days after the forced landing. There was not enough time to recover and repair the racer. J.D. was not a happy man! He fired Penrose over the Joe Howard fiasco saying, ". . . Penrose was hired to fly my airplane and no one else. When Howard belly landed in Kansas I fired Penrose." A new propeller and engine were sent to Kansas and the airplane was subsequently flown back to Texas by Marlin Jacobs, one of J.D.'s staff.

Around this time, a story was released regarding the paint scheme on this new racer. It was named Beguine by J.D.'s wife, Jackie, because "Begin the Beguine" was her favorite song. When the airplane was painted in Los Angeles, a local artist, Ted Grohs, painted a portion of this Cole Porter musical score on the sides of the fuselage. A story carried by Associated Press and United Press International stated that, "Mr. Patrillo, head of the American Society of Composers, Authors and Publishers (ASCAP) was bringing action against the owner of *Beguine* until a royalty was paid for use of the musical score." J.D. Reed replied, ". . . hell, nobody in the music business is going to tell me I can't fly my airplane." The story went on to tell of a confrontation between these two men until someone thought to check with ASCAP president Patrillo. It turned out that Patrillo never heard of the conflict, the airplane, or Reed. J.D. had planted the story and gained some publicity for his new racer.

After *Beguine* was safely back at Reed's facility in Houston, it underwent a number of additional changes.

All of the coolant and oil lines from the engine to the radiators were removed and replaced with larger diameter lines to improve the flow of fluids in the cooling cycle. In the original modification, the quantity of antidetonant fluid had been limited to the aluminum tanks in the wing gun bays. It was believed that some forty more gallons of this fluid would be required for the Thompson Trophy Race. Therefore, a small tank was made to fit under the pilot's seat to provide more water-methanol capacity. The new tank installation had one drawback. In a stock P-51C, the pilot's seat could be raised and lowered to accommodate differences in physical stature of the pilot. The height of this new fuselage tank, however, prevented the seat from being lowered.

While revisions to *Beguine* were in progress, Kenneth C. Cooley approached J.D. about flying the racer. Ken was an ex-military pilot with time in P-51s. After the war, he completed his college degree and went to work in Houston for one of the oil companies. Ken continued to regularly fly P-51s with the Texas Air National Guard. He convinced

J.D. to give him a shot at flying the airplane, and when the 1949 modifications were complete, Ken proceeded with the test work. Ken was of average height and flying *Beguine* with an elevated pilots' seat to accomodate the newly installed water tank beneath it was not a problem. So in a sense, the aircraft cockpit was tailored to a specific pilot. During flight testing, Ken Cooley discovered the canopy was opening a bit so a new, considerably strengthened canopy was made to prevent deflection. The redesigned canopy did not open like the original military version. Ingress and egress could only be achieved by crawling through the side panels. In a flight emergency the entire canopy assembly, except the windscreen, could be jettisoned as a unit.

J.D. was quite unhappy with the 1948 paint job applied in Los Angeles. There had not been enough time in 1948 to put a super finish on the airplane before the races. When the airplane reached Houston after the accident, it was overall green with markings in a golden yellow. Registration numbers were painted in block style. J.D. Reed's crew repainted the airplane in a very dark green lacquer.[4] Fuselage trim remained the golden yellow color. A portion of the *Beguine* musical score was added to the side of the wing tip pods, similar to what was already on the fuselage. This trim was in yellow, also. The registration numbers and racing number on the wing were painted white, using a more rounded style of lettering. The final finish was very glossy and appeared to have several coats of clear lacquer applied over the color coat. J.D. recalled it as "a beautiful emerald green."

In his quest for maximum performance, J.D. located a special propeller made by Hamilton Standard for the P-51H program. The propeller was part of a series of new designs being developed for high-speed aircraft. This particular propeller had flown on a North American P-82 test aircraft, but the blade design never went into production. Reed bought the four blades at $2500 each and had them installed on *Jay Dee*, his other P-51D *Mustang*. This aircraft was used to evaluate performance with the new propeller. "*Jay Dee* was a little faster with that prop," Reed recalled.

One of the goals for the *Beguine* was an assault on the world speed record for propeller-driven aircraft. At that time, the record was held by Germany's Fritz Wendell, flying a highly modified Messerschmitt aircraft.[5] Toward this goal, Reed set up a measured one mile course at LaPort, Texas. Apparently this "course" led some in later years to conclude that Reed had established a duplicate of the Cleveland race course on which to test *Beguine*. This belief tended to somehow reinforce the idea that an asymmetric wing was used and proven on this so-called course. Ken Cooley flew the course in a simulated timing run and was unofficially clocked at "just over 500 miles per hour." Once

Shortly before the 1949 National Air Races, J.D. Reed sold the beautiful "Beguine" racer to Floyd Odlum, Jackie Cochran's husband. The new pilot was Bill Odom, shown here with J.D. and Walter Beech. Photo Credit: Dusty Carter Collection

again, there appears to be no surviving documentation of this flight and certainly no official claim to a new record was ever established. One can safely speculate the actual speed was considerably under 500 mph.[6]

Beguine was now basically ready for the 1949 National Air Races. The group support truck was loaded with a spare prop, spare engine, and the necessary parts and tools to keep a racer in the air. A couple of weeks before the races were to start, J.D. received a call from Walter Beech. Reed related the conversation: "J.D., I have a fellow here that would like to fly *Beguine* at Cleveland," Beech said. "Walter, I can't do that. My boys are ready to go and they've worked hard all year to get the plane ready," Reed responded. But Walter Beech persisted. "Well, this chap is Bill Odom and he has done a lot of good things for me." Bill Odom had recently set point-to-point records flying a Beechcraft Bonanza, obviously of great significance to Beech because it was one of his products. J.D. was not swayed. "Walter, I can't change pilots now!" Walter Beech countered with, "Odom says he has someone to buy the airplane. That would get us both out of the picture." His reference was to the problem of keeping Olive Anne Beech away from knowledge of Walter's engagement in air racing. Responding to an inquiry about whether Odom really had financial backing to buy the racer, Beech responded with, ". . . yeah, it's Jackie Cochran. Floyd (Odlum, Jackie's husband) will be down to see you." As predicted, Floyd Odlum arrived in Houston with his checkbook. He was ready to deal. He looked over *Beguine* and the accompanying support equipment that went with the airplane. What he saw apparently was acceptable, for he promptly wrote out a check for approximately $100,000. This was a great deal of money in 1949; however, Floyd Odlum was a very wealthy industrialist and apparently

Jackie Cochran wishes Bill Odom luck in this publicity shot. Note that Jackie has removed her shoes to protect the near perfect finish of the racer. Photo Credit: Robert E. Burke Studios

Below: J.D. Reed originally planned to field two racers for 1949. "Beguine" is in the foreground and "Jay Dee" sits in the back. In the end, "Jay Dee" was the only plane Reed entered in the Thompson. Photo Credit: Bob Bailey

willing to indulge his wife's strong passion in high-speed airplanes.

Just a few days before the 1949 races, *Beguine* was in the hands of a new owner, Jackie Cochran. Because women were prohibited from flying in the Thompson Trophy Race, Jackie selected Bill Odom as her pilot. It was a fateful decision. William P. Odom was a tall, slim, ex-military pilot who had carved a name for himself after the war with long distance record-making flights. He became very prominent in April 1947, when he broke Howard Hughes' 1938 around-the-world record flight. The final connection between *Beguine* and J.D. Reed was a cable to the National Aeronautics Association on 22 August 1949, canceling his sport flying license for *Beguine*. The aircraft now belonged to Jackie Cochran.

Selling *Beguine* was a blow to the entire crew at the J.D. Reed Company. No doubt there was resentment. Walter Beech put a lot of pressure on J.D. to sell the racer. Reed was one of the largest distributors of Beech aircraft in the country

This pre-race flight shot illustrates the markings carried by "Beguine." This picture was taken over Houston, Texas, with pilot Ken Cooley at the controls. The racer was doomed to a fatal crash during the 1949 Thompson Trophy Race. Photo Credit: Dusty Carter Collection, Bob Bailey Photo

and had a long standing friendship with Walter. And there was the pressure of hiding the fact that Beech was once again involved in air racing, of which Olive Anne strongly disapproved. J.D. was sworn to secrecy and couldn't tell his pilot or crew or anyone else of Walter Beech's role in the airplane or the sale.

When the airplane went to Cleveland, J.D. Reed supplied the service crew for the racer. This was part of the agreement. Saturday, September 3, Odom flew *Beguine* to victory in the Sohio race. According to Reed, "Odom flew a sloppy race and when Walter and I talked to him after he landed he appeared to be shaken a bit. When he was questioned he said he was all right, but he seemed to have been jostled around the cockpit a little." The cockpit area had been modified with an extra tank under the seat, preventing any adjustment to a lower position. The situation was satisfactory for Ken Cooley; however, it must have

been uncomfortable for Odom. Bill was a tall man. He took most of the padding out of his helmet just to get into the cockpit. After some discussion with Odom about the Thompson Race, J.D. offered to let him fly *Jay Dee* and have Cooley fly *Beguine*. The other *Mustang* had a conventional canopy and cockpit configuration which was a lot more suited to Odom's physical frame. In addition, J.D. offered to let Odom retain any winnings. As Reed later recalled, "Odom said no one flies that airplane but me!"

Bill Odom had limited experience in fighter aircraft and virtually none as a race pilot. Perhaps understanding this, Jackie Cochran brought in support for him in the person of Bennie Howard. Howard was well respected for his career in designing, building, and racing various aircraft before World War II. In preparation for the 1949 assignment from Jackie, Bennie had a DC-3 equipped with radios. He proposed to sit in the Douglas transport during the Thompson race and coach Odom as the race progressed. He would also inform Bill as to his position at the end of each lap. Howard also briefed Odom on take-off procedures as well as advising him on a race strategy. Odom listened but no one is sure how much he absorbed. At take-off Odom either ignored Howard's advice or never understood what he was told. *Beguine* nearly got away from him but he did back off on the power and got the racer straightened out. He was back in the pack during the race horse start. At the end of the first lap Odom had moved well up on the field into third place. Passing the home pylon for the start of lap two, Bill Odom rolled left. He continued his turn far too long and was headed inside the race course. He lost his bearing on the location of pylon two. Sensing his mistake, Odom reversed the controls and rolled back to the right to get on the course. Without hesitation, the airplane continued to roll right into an inverted position. The nose of the *Mustang* dropped and the racer plunged into a single family house in the Cleveland suburb of Berea, Ohio. The airplane exploded and burned on impact, killing Bill Odom as well as a woman and her small child. It was a phenomenal tragedy.

Witnesses to the accident reported various accounts of what took place. For the most part, these were not much more than impressions. There were a few expert witnesses who consistently cited the overturned pylon, right roll correction and almost simultaneous rotation into an inverted position. The entire sequence of events occurred in probably less than sixty seconds. What happened in those sixty seconds? It is extremely doubtful that anyone will ever know for sure.[7]

Notes

1. Bill of sale from the War Assets Administration to the Mantz partnership dated 19 February 1946. This document was part of the records file on P-51 N4845N.
2. Civil Aeronautics Administration (CAA) registration papers indicate the Army Air Force serial number to be 42-103757 making the aircraft a P-51C-5.
3. *The Anthony Republican*, 9 September 1948.
4. The color was equivalent to Ditzler Paint & Lacquer Company No. 43848.
5. Fritz Wendel piloted the Messerschmitt Me 209 VI to the world's speed record of 469 miles per hour on 26 April 1939.
6. See Appendix B.
7. The pilot, the airplane, and the accident are examined in more detail in Appendix B.

Anson Johnson posed with his well-engineered Mustang racer in this rare 1949 color photograph taken after the races at the north end of Cleveland Airport. Johnson was forced out of the 1949 Thompson when special exhaust stacks started to fail structurally due to high exhaust gas temperatures. Photo Credit: Birch Matthews Collection

The third Mustang to race without a belly scoop was "Stilleto." Like Anson Johnson's airplane, the radiators were buried in the wings. Wing leading edge inlets for the cooling radiators are evident in this 1984 Reno photograph. Photo Credit: Al Hansen

Ken Burnstine raced this gaudy P-51 Mustang at Reno in 1974. Author John Tegler relates that the designs and colors were developed by Ken and a friend while verifying the attributes of an excellent bottle of scotch. Photo Credit: Dusty Carter

Bill Odom's beautiful emerald green "Beguine" racer is towed in front of the grandstands at Cleveland for the start of the fatal 1949 Thompson Trophy Race. Originally built in 1948, this was the first Mustang to have the belly scoop removed and the cooling radiators relocated. Photo Credit: Fred Buehl

Burnstine bought a second Mustang which he had modified extensively for air racing. Airframe refinements were the product of Jim Larsen's engineering. The artistic addition to the side of the fuselage was strictly Ken Burnstine's. Photo Credit: Dusty Carter

Another Mustang racer in natural finish is Wiley Sander's "Georgia Mae." The airframe is modestly modified and carries a Dave Zeuschel engine up front in this photograph. The pilot is John Putman. Photo Credit: Dusty Carter

Cliff Cummins brought a racer named "Miss Candace" to most of the pylon races for many years. The aircraft was modified repeatedly and evolved into a very fast Mustang. The racer is shown here at Reno in 1974. Photo Credit: Dusty Carter

Cummins sold his racer to Wiley Sanders. The aircraft was renamed "Jeannie" and won the 1981 Reno championship. The racer is seen here rounding a pylon with Skip Holm at the controls. Photo Credit: Dusty Carter

On his way to the "office," Cliff Cummins approaches "Miss Candace" for a morning test flight at Reno in 1974. Photo Credit: Dusty Carter

Engine failure forced Cliff Cummins into an unplanned belly landing in Lemon Valley, east of Stead Field. The stock belly scoop was torn off during the wheels up landing. As a consequence, when the racer was rebuilt, a new more shallow scoop was fashioned to reduce drag. Photo Credit: Gerry Liang

"Dago Red" sits at rest in the pits at Reno. The racer possesses one of the prettiest paint schemes of any airplane currently racing. Photo Credit: Chuck Aro

"Strega" sits quietly in the Reno unlimited pit area in the late after-noon Reno sun. This Mustang is absolutely the fastest P-51 now flying. Bill Destefani won the 1987 Reno championship at 452 mph and place second in 1991 at 478 mph. Photo Credit: Chuck Aro

The most recent owner of "Jeannie" is Jimmy Leeward of Florida. Jimmy bought the racer and renamed it "The Leeward Air Ranch Special" after his real estate development in Ocala, Florida. Photo Credit: Chuck Aro

John Sandberg's custom built unlimited racer "Tsunami" may be an example of what unlimited class air racing will see in the not too distant future. "Tsunami's" heritage can in part be traced to the P-51 Mustang. Photo Credit: Neal Nurmi

When Bill Destefani decided to compete for the "gold" at Reno, he and Frank Taylor created "Dago Red." This much modified P-51 captured the Reno championship race in 1982 with Ron Hevle at the controls. Photo Credit: Birch Matthews

John Crocker bought Burnstine's Mustang and raced the aircraft for many years. The racer received a more sedate paint scheme and continued refinement. In 1979, John won the Reno gold championship race with this Mustang. Photo Credit: Dusty Carter

Don Whittington of Fort Lauderdale, raced this beautiful Mustang equipped with an extended vertical fin for several years. Don always bent the throttle all the way and in the process, expended several Merlin engines. The aircraft was appropriately named "Precious Metal." Photo Credit: Dusty Carter

When Bill Destefani sold "Dago Red," he immediately set about creating yet another outstanding racer. Bill called this airplane "Strega." It is seen here shortly after it was finished. Photo Credit: Dusty Carter Collection

The slim lines of Stilleto are seen to advantage in this profile shot. Race 84 was flown by Skip Holm in this 1984 version. Photo Credit: Birch Matthews

Chapter Ten
MORE GELDINGS

Anson Johnson's Race #45. Anson Johnson won the 1948 Thompson Trophy Race flying a relatively stock, dark blue P-51D, carrying license N13Y and racing number 45. The airplane captured the Thompson not because of its inherent speed but because it possessed the durability and reliability to finish, other faster racers having dropped by the wayside with various problems. With prize money in hand, Anson Johnson set out to add the third ingredient, speed.

When Johnson arrived for the 1949 races, he was flying a strikingly modified airplane which, like Bill Odom's *Beguine*, was devoid of the trademark *Mustang* belly scoop. Although the belly scoop was absent, there the similarity between Anson's racer and *Beguine* ended. Johnson relocated the cooling radiators in his aircraft to the wings, where the gun bays had been. Although his airplane was aerodynamically cleaner and lighter than *Beguine*, it failed to get

Anson Johnson first raced at Cleveland in 1947 when he brought this dark blue stock Mustang to the National Air Races. Race 45 carried a yellow pin striping down the side of the fuselage that first year. Photo Credit: Liang-O'Leary Collection

Later in the week, the race number was applied to Anson Johnson's P-51D. The 1947 pin striping was absent in 1948. Note the re-contoured lower engine cowling to accommodate the updraft carburetor on the dash 225 Merlin engine. Photo Credits: Liang-O'Leary Collection

Anson returned to Cleveland in 1948, with a Merlin dash 225 engine installed. When it first arrived, the airplane was without markings or trim. Here, the racer is being pushed into a hangar on the east side of the Cleveland Airport before the races. Photo Credit: Birch Matthews Collection

Classic view of Johnson's 1948 trophy winner. The coolant door on the aft end of the belly scoop is wide open. Spray bar cooling augmentation was unknown in the early years of unlimited racing at Cleveland. Photo Credit: Warren Bodie

the news media's attention, perhaps due to the quiet, unassuming way of Tennessean Anson Johnson.

Johnson's story actually began two years earlier in 1947, when he bought a P-51D from Di Ponti Aviation in Minneapolis. The airplane previously belonged to Woody Edmundson, who flew it as race number 42 in the 1946 National Air Races. Woody finished seventh that first year of the post-war Nationals. When Anson Johnson acquired the racer in July 1947, the aircraft had been relicensed N13Y. He bought the plane and promptly took off from Minneapolis. While flying his new possession from Minneapolis to his base of operations in Florida, Johnson encountered engine problems caused by a set of bad magnetos. He was forced to land at an abandoned World War II airfield in Georgia. At the time, there was only one person on the field with a Piper J-3 Cub. To Anson's amazement, this individual knew the whereabouts of a batch of magnetos left behind at the field when the military departed. With new

magnetos plus spares, Johnson got N13Y going again and the rest of the trip to Florida was uneventful.

Johnson was first bitten by the racing "bug" after flying a Bell P-39 *Airacobra* at the 1947 Miami Air Races in January. Armed with his own P-51, he was "goin' racin'" at Cleveland in September. His experience that first year at Cleveland was more dismal than Edmundson's had been. Johnson completed only five laps in the Kendall Trophy race before being forced out. So ended his first shot at major air racing. Back in Miami, Johnson took stock of his racer. He decided there must be a better engine than the Packard-built *Merlin* V-1650-3 that was presently in his *Mustang*. After reviewing what engines were available, he settled on a *Merlin* 225. This engine, also built by Packard, was used in Canadian-built DeHavilland Mosquito bombers. It is basically a low altitude *Merlin*. The supercharger is a single stage, two speed blower with no aftercooler. The dash 225 engine is lighter and some six inches shorter than the V-

1650-3, yet produces a bit more power at low altitudes. Carburetor relocation on the dash 225 engine (relative to the dash 3, dash 7 or dash 9 engines) required modification of the lower engine cowling. The change produced a slight deviation from the otherwise smooth contour of the standard P-51 nose section. The gun bays were reworked to provide tankage for one hundred gallons of antidetonant fluid. The racer was repainted a glossy, dark blue. The wings had previously been shortened for the 1947 races and remained unchanged for 1948. Johnson was ready to race.

Ten racers lined up for the 1948 Thompson Trophy race: two F2G Corsairs, two P-63s, a P-39, and five *Mustang*s. The F2Gs were favored and Chuck Brown's modified P-39 would certainly be in contention. Johnson's plan was to fly his race and let the really hot racers set a torrid pace that perhaps might take a toll in the form of broken engines. That is exactly what happened, and Anson Johnson finished the race getting the checkered flag and first place. With a few dollars in his pocket, he was off to make a real racer of N13Y.

Back in Miami, Johnson sought the help of J.D. Crane, National Airlines Vice President for engineering. Since Johnson was a senior pilot with National, it was a fortuitous and natural team. They retained the *Merlin* 225; however, major alterations were made to the airframe. The nose was refaired to eliminate the distinctive *Mustang* chin inlet for the air induction system. A small carburetor air scoop was located further aft on the lower engine cowling near the carburetor, thus eliminating a long air induction duct. The inlet was a more advanced design that incorporated boundary layer bleed to assure a good ram air condition. This modification resulted in a somewhat sleeker nose than the original P-51. The belly scoop was removed and coolant radiators relocated in what had been the wing gun bays and previously housed the antidetonant injection fluid. With coolant radiators thus relocated, the antidetonant fluid tankage had to be relocated into a fuselage tank behind the pilot's seat. Standard P-51 coolant radiators were too large to fit into the wing, but it was discovered that P-39 radiators would fit if cut in two and laid side by side. Inlets were cut into the wing leading edge and large openings made in the front spar to permit air flow into the radiators. The spar was modified by additional cap material and post type supports to maintain wing structural integrity. The coolant air exit consisted of a smooth ramp out over the rear spar with a moveable door or flap on the trailing upper wing surface to provide a measure of control of the exit air flow. This door was extremely simple and indicative of the innovative nature of the designer. It was simply the upper wing skin with slots cut on either side to form a tab. A ground adjustable actuator was attached at the trailing edge of this tab and the door was opened or

Anson Johnson won the 1948 Thompson Trophy Race when faster competitors dropped out. He is shown here receiving the Thompson Trophy from three-time Thompson winner, Roscoe Turner. Photo Credit: Emil Strasser

closed by merely bending the wing skin. No hinges were required. Unlike *Beguine*, the cooling system on Johnson's racer allowed control over the volume of airflow through the radiators. The exit doors were manually adjusted on the ground until sufficient flow was achieved to cool the engine. In this way, drag was minimized. From this perspective, Johnson's racer exhibited a more sophisticated design approach. Other changes in race 45 included a reduction in propeller diameter by removing six inches from the tip of each blade and the installation of special exhaust stacks to provide a net increase in thrust. The airplane was refinished in an overall yellow paint scheme.

When the flag dropped, signaling the start of the 1949 Thompson Trophy Race, Anson Johnson immediately encountered problems. Once airborne, Anson found that his landing gear would not fully retract. This was later attributed to problems associated with a second accumulator installed in the hydraulic system to facilitate more rapid retraction of the landing gear, a technique previously used by Tex Johnston in the 1946 Thompson race.[1] Anson lowered his speed and recycled the gear several times before he got full retraction. With the gear up and the airplane clean, Johnson opened the throttle on the *Merlin* and for the next several laps he turned speeds well in excess of 400 miles per hour. In the ninth lap he began to hear thumps along the fuselage and smoke started to enter the cockpit. Johnson pulled out of the race. Upon landing, he discovered the source of the smoke and thumping. The special exhaust stacks had failed, and as they broke off they bounced along the fuselage. The smoke was from the engine exhaust seeping into the fuselage. The aborted ending to the 1949 Thompson race was a major disappointment to Anson Johnson and his crew.

With all the excellent work in preparing a first class racer for the Thompson going for naught, plans were made to prepare the *Mustang* for an assault on the world's absolute speed record for piston engine airplanes. The airframe was thoroughly serviced and the engine brought to maximum potential for a record attempt. The airplane was refinished in a glossy blue paint and carried the logos of sponsors for the speed run. On June 6, 1952, a course was set at Key Biscane, Florida. A briefing was given to the press before the official attempt at a new speed record. On the previous day, Johnson had flown the course on a familiarization run

and he had briefly pushed the racer past an indicated 500 mile per hour mark. The official timing run was scheduled for 5:30 a.m. on June 6, but timing gear set up delayed the flight several hours and Johnson did not get airborne until after 9:00 a.m. His first pass was clocked at 510 mph, the second at 503 mph, but on the third pass the engine started to overheat and Johnson aborted the attempt. The next day things went better and a total of eight passes were completed. Bad luck haunted Johnson again. The camera at the south end of the course failed and the timing system recorded the four best passes at 435 mph, no where near the existing record.

The engine was removed from N13Y and sent for overhaul after the stress of the record attempt. Somehow the *Merlin* 225 was "lost" and a dash 9 engine was received as a replacement. There was no way N13Y would be as fast with this engine as with the 225. The record attempt was abandoned and Anson Johnson eventually parted with the racer in September 1959. After that, the airplane was re-

Anson Johnson completely modified race 45 for the 1949 season. The belly scoop was removed and the radiators relocated into the wings. Leading edge inlets were cut into the wings for cooling air entry. Photo Credit: Liang-O'Leary Collection

registered as N502 and subsequently changed hands several times. In August 1972, the New England Air Museum, in Connecticut, obtained the airframe for eventual restoration to its racing configuration and exhibit. Anson Johnson's airplane was a beautifully prepared and well-engineered racing *Mustang* that, unfortunately, never reached the glory it deserved.

Race#84 - "Stilleto." In 1984, a distinctive, new *Mustang* racer appeared at Reno. Not since 1949 had a P-51 been so extensively modified! The familiar trademark of the *Mustang* was gone. The belly scoop had once again been removed. The new racer was a creation of the late Dave Zeuschel, Sun Valley, California. Well known as an expert on Rolls-Royce engines, Zeuschel also built the record breaking *Mustang* named *Jeannie*. Dave built the new racer out of parts and assemblies from a number of different *Mustangs*. It carries the serial number and registration from one of those that had previously raced, N332.

From its inception this race plane project was focused on weight reduction. Each part of the airframe was disassembled to nothing but frames, stringers, skins, and components. When again assembled, only those parts absolutely necessary to make a racing craft were utilized. Careful attention was given in the fabrication of every bracket, clip, fitting, and component to obtain the lightest weight possible consistent with strength requirements. Some parts were fabricated from magnesium to take advantage of the lighter weight of this metal. The entire manual trim tab system was removed and replaced by an electrically operated system. This change eliminated cables, pulleys, pulley brackets, and cable guides located throughout the airplane. The electrically operated system consisted of a small trim motor at each tab, as well as wiring to the power source and control switches in the cockpit. Although this system caused some problems in operation, it saved weight and was simpler to service. The airplane had a minimal electrical system. For this reason, engine starting is accomplished by ground support equip-

Johnson's crew works on his racer in front of the race hangars at Cleveland Airport. The aircraft was painted bright yellow for the 1949 race. Photo Credit: Harry Gann

Race 45 is towed in front of the grandstands at Cleveland prior to the races. The clean lines of this modification are readily seen in this photograph. Photo Credit: Bruce Fraites Collection

Anson Johnson sits in the cockpit of his racer, waiting for the start of the 1949 Thompson race. The dark stripe on the left wing is the exit area for the wing-mounted radiator. Photo Credit: Liang-O'Leary Collection

Anson Johnson was forced out of the 1949 Thompson when exhaust stacks overheated and burned off. The airplane was returned to Florida and preparations made for an assault on the world three kilometer speed record. Photo Credit: Liang-O'Leary Collection

This profile photograph illustrates the small updraft carburetor air intake on the bottom of the engine cowl, just ahead of the wing leading edge. Photo Credit: Liang-O'Leary Collection

ment, the starter having been removed.

The landing gear is representative of the intensive approach to weight saving. The struts were completely disassembled and internal steel parts were replaced with aluminum where possible. The struts were centerless ground, and tapered to remove weight. Parts of the strut were rifle bored. The result was a twenty-three pound saving on each strut. The standard P-51 wheels, brakes, and tires were replaced with lighter P-63 units with simultaneous improved braking.

The wing span was shortened to 28 feet, 11 inches, giving the racer a rather dramatic appearance. The wings were modified to provide for internal installation of engine coolant and supercharger aftercooler radiators. P-51H radiators are employed by disassembling the radiator unit into its three elements. The left wing houses two of these elements for coolant and the right wing houses the aftercooler

radiator. Slotted inlets are fashioned into the wing leading edges with the heated air from the radiators departing through slots in the wing upper skin surface. Various slot designs have been used to reduce drag and turbulence caused by the heated air. One design was considered that would have allowed the heated air to exit through the trailing edge of the wing, but the cost of this modification was considered prohibitive.

With the change in location of the radiators and a reduced airframe weight, it became clear that further modifications were required to achieve a proper airplane balance. The pilot's seat was moved aft approximately twenty inches, limited only by the location of the existing control system assembly. In addition, a P-51H heat exchanger for oil cooling was relocated aft of the cockpit. When the airplane was completed it was set up on scales to locate the center of gravity. At this point, the fifty-five pound, nickel

Details of the carburetor inlet scoop on Johnson's racer are clearly seen in this photograph. The recess above the upper edge of the scoop was a boundary layer bleed provision. Photo Credit: Liang-O'Leary Collection

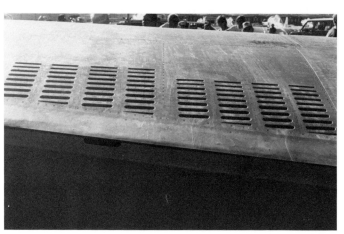

Louvers were used in 1984 to allow cooling air to exit from the wing-mounted radiators of Race 84. These were later changed in geometry to improve air flow. Photo Credit: Chuck Aro

Weight reduction was paramount in Dave Zeuschel's rebuild of race 84. Lightning holes were drilled in the landing gear doors and wheel covers to take every last ounce of weight out of the airframe. Photo Credit: Chuck Aro

The third Mustang to race with the belly scoop removed was the product of Dave Zeuschel. The aircraft is shown here at the 1984 Reno races. The racer was named "Stilleto." Photo Credit: Birch Matthews

cadmium battery was positioned to achieve the necessary center of gravity location.

Fuel is carried in the right wing, antidetonant fluid in the left wing, and spray bar water in the fuselage. Fuel capacity is 135 gallons, with 110 gallons in a bladder tank in the fuel bay, plus 25 gallons in a siamese tank outboard of the aftercooler radiator. The siamese tank is connected to the main tank through tube-like extensions of the outer tank running along the front and rear spars. The fuel filler fitting is outboard. Antidetonant fluid capacity is 110 gallons. P-51 vane-type, submerged fuel pumps have been replaced with positive displacement submerged pumps used on F-86 aircraft.

When *Stilleto* first appeared at Reno it had a smaller diameter propeller. The standard P-51D hub was used with blades from a North American T-28 to give a diameter of 10 feet, 2 inches; the stock diameter is one foot larger. The purpose of the smaller diameter is to keep the propeller tips from reaching supersonic velocity at higher engine speeds. Engineers consulting with Zeuschel recommended the small diameter propeller, but Dave Zeuschel was not convinced that supersonic tip speeds had much effect on performance.

The larger diameter stock propeller has been run on *Stilleto* with no appreciable change in performance.

The as-built empty weight of *Stilleto* was 5800 pounds. This is believed to be the lightest racing *Mustang* ever built. Even though the wing of the racer was drastically shortened by eight feet, relative to a stock P-51 the *Stilleto* wing loading remains reasonable at 28.40 pounds per square foot, which is slightly less than a stock P-51D at 29.57 pounds per square foot.

Skip Holm flew *Stilleto* from its first flight through the 1986 race season. During the 1984 Reno championship race, Skip set a new course record for the Gold Race at 437.62 miles an hour. All the effort that had gone into the design and rebuild of the racer had paid off. In the 1985 Bakersfield race, Skip Holm and Ron Hevle fought for first place until *Stilleto's Merlin* engine temperature rose too high, forcing Skip into a Mayday and a dead stick landing. The bad luck experienced during the Bakersfield competition followed *Stilleto* to Reno in 1985. Once again, the racer did not finish.

Alan Preston, owner of *Stilleto*, obtained sponsorship for the racer in 1985 and again in 1986 from Color Tile Inc.

Skip Holm turns a pylon on his way to victory in the 1984 championship Reno air race. The drastically clipped wings are apparent in this picture. Photo Credit: Neal Nurmi

Race pilot Skip Holm flew "Stilleto" in the 1984 Reno races. He is shown here in a low pass over Stead Airfield. Photo Credit: Neal Nurmi

In 1986, Stilleto was sponsored by Color Tile and, together with the sponsor's logo, was painted all white. In this unusual view, the underside details of the racer are visible. Photo Credit: Neal Nurmi

In fact, Color Tile used the airplane in its contemporary television commercials. Reno 1986 brought new problems for *Stilleto*. During preparation for a qualifying run, the electric trim motor on the rudder tab malfunctioned, causing the tab to go full over in one direction. The resulting force tore off the tab and damaged the top portion of the rudder. Skip was running at a pretty high speed when this occurred. As the airplane bled off speed, Skip lowered the landing gear. When the gear first popped out of the wing, high speed air entered the lightening holes and tore the landing gear fairing cover from the airplane. A quick landing was made with no further damage. In the championship race Skip Holm led for five laps when he lost an oil breather line, forcing him out of the race. After the 1986 season, Alan Preston put *Stilleto* up for sale. Shortly before the 1987 Reno races, the airplane was sold to Dennis Sherman of Fort Lauderdale, Florida. Sherman is not a newcomer to Reno racing. In 1964, Sherman Aircraft of Fort Wayne, Indiana, fielded a midget racer, "Little Gem", that had previously been raced by designer/builder Jim Miller. Bob Porter flew Sherman's "Little Gem" to victory that year. Sherman sold the midget to the late Bob Downey and then dropped out of air racing. Now residing in Florida, Sherman re-entered air racing in a big way with the purchase of *Stilleto*. Dennis' son, Scott Sherman, who is an airline pilot, qualified *Stilleto* at a very respectable 439 miles an hour and went on to fly *Stilleto* to near the 400 mile an hour mark in several heat races at Reno. *Stilleto* is an extremely fast airplane. How fast is yet to be demonstrated.

In reviewing the three gelded *Mustangs*, there are some observations worth noting. *Beguine*, with all its attention by the media and latter day historians, was actually not much better than a well-prepared, modestly modified P-51D. It

allegedly exceeded 500 miles per hour in an unofficial speed run, but this is very questionable in the absence of any official timing and documentation. *Beguine* had more frontal area than a stock P-51C, by some 2.2 square feet. It had more projected plan area by over seven square feet and it undoubtedly had more surface area than a stock P-51C. All of this additional area translates into drag. Because of the large tip pods and the big circular radiators, the weight of *Beguine* was some 6800 pounds, only 200 pounds lighter than an empty military P-51C.

Johnson's Race #45 did have less frontal and surface area than a stock P-51D and probably weighed around 6400 pounds. It also was reportedly clocked at over 500 miles per hour, a speed questionable in light of more recent records achieved by Steve Hinton in the RB-51 *Red Baron* and the Grumman F8F *Bearcats* of Darryl Greenamyer and Lyle Shelton. Dave Zeuschel commented on the 500 miles per hour claims by comparing a speed run made with the racing *Mustang*, *Jeannie*, at Edwards Air Force Base, California. As Dave says, "We took *Jeannie* out to Edwards Air Force Base for a speed check. The airplane was in prime racing condition. We had a freeze during the night (before the speed run) and the morning temperatures were pretty cool (he did not recall the true temperature). We ran *Jeannie* over the course several times and the very best we could do was 468 miles per hour. I am not sure those other guys ever reached 500 miles per hour."

Notes

1. Johnston flew a modified Bell P-39 *Airacobra*. On this airplane, the landing gear retraction system was electrical and Johnston's crew increased the electrical voltage from 24 to 36 volts as a means of increasing the speed of the gear retraction.

Zeuschel modified the racer to have leading edge intakes for the radiators buried in the wings. When this 1984 picture was taken, the finish was natural aluminum. Photo Credit: Chuck Aro

Chapter Eleven
IMPROVING THE BREED

Preceding chapters considered three different *Mustangs* that were aerodynamically altered rather severely in an attempt to improve on the original design and achieve ever higher speeds. In each instance, the objective was to reduce frontal drag and skin friction by eliminating the belly scoop. All three airplanes incorporated *Merlin* engines tailored to the race course: Anson Johnson's Thompson Trophy racer, the *Beguine* racer and Dave Zeuschel's *Stilleto*. The *Stilleto* racer went a step further in refinement by incorporating a dedicated weight reduction program as yet unmatched by any other *Mustang* entrant. Interestingly, none of these "gelding" racers succeeded to the ultimate goal of establishing a world speed record in the three kilometer category for piston engine aircraft. The possibilities for *Stilleto* are still open as it remains an active racing machine. The only *Mustang* to capture a three kilometer world speed record employed the traditional approach of using more horsepower, through installation of a Rolls-Royce *Griffon*. Again, the versatility of the basic *Mustang* design is underlined in that the *Red Baron* team was able to install the much larger *Griffon* engine with what actually amounted to relatively moderate airframe alterations.

The succeeding narrative looks at another approach to gearing the *Mustang* for championship racing and the winner's circle. In each of the following instances, the basic general arrangement of the *Mustang* has been retained. Structural surgery was applied but in a more traditional or conventional manner. In other words, wingspans were shortened and canopy and belly scoop profiles reduced. However, the overall approach is one of refined improvements and utilization of newer technology in the form of subsystems, electronics, and materials. In all subsequent *Mustangs* reviewed, the *Merlin* engine was retained, albeit in highly tuned form. All have been highly successful in closed-course racing at Reno and other locations over the years. In a real sense, these aircraft represent the consummate *Mustang* with respect to closed-course racing speed.

Miss Foxy Lady. The white and blue *Mustang*, currently being raced by John Crocker, at one time belonged to the late Ken Burnstine. Burnstine was a flamboyant entrepreneur from Ft. Lauderdale. The ex-marine first appeared at the 1973 Reno National Championship Air Races with a near stock P-51D. The airplane attracted a great deal of attention because of its paint scheme. It was a conglomeration of colors with military insignia of the United States Air Force

superimposed, creating a psychedelic visual assault. It looked as though it had been painted by a committee after a hard night of celebration! The race entry for the airplane listed it as a P-51 with registration N69QF, race number 33 and the name "Quick Finger"; however, when the airplane appeared on the ramp it carried a more sedate and socially acceptable name, "Miss Susie Q." The outrageous color scheme and the original name fit the colorful Burnstine who seemed to have an endless supply of tee shirts, each carrying a provocative or suggestive message. Behind all of this flash was a good race pilot, even though he was a rookie at that point in time. He placed third in the 1973 Reno Silver, or Consolation, race; this whet his appetite for more serious racing. Shortly after the 1973 season, Burnstine engaged Jim Larsen to build up a new, all-out racer for the 1974 campaign. Burnstine bought a P-51D-30 registered N6321T. It had previously served with the Royal Canadian Air Force. The modifications were made at Chino Airport in the late Leroy Penhall's hanger.

Larsen designed a new upper fuselage and low profile canopy that replaced the existing structure above the upper longerons of the forward fuselage assembly. The cockpit cover was hinged at a single aft point and could be jettisoned in an emergency. The instrument panel was new and tailored for racing. It employed a unique method of alerting the pilot to "out of limit" conditions for various systems. The panel was designed around standard instruments with panel lighting that would glow red when a particular system was reaching an over limit condition, much the same as the red lights on automobile panels. The "red" condition could then be evaluated by the pilot, using the instruments to determine what action was necessary. The rest of the airplane was modified in a conventional manner with the wing tip assemblies removed, ailerons shortened, special wing tips added, weight removed, and a racing engine and supporting systems installed. The standard P-51 propeller spinner gave way to a new sharply pointed spinner, similar to one Larsen had used earlier on Chuck Hall's racer.

The airplane was flight tested at Chino, California, then ferried to Reno. The registration was changed to N70QF and race number 34 assigned. The low canopy, short wings, pointed spinner, and black paint scheme gave the racer an ominous appearance as it sat alone on the ramp at Reno for nearly a week before the races began. The racer was christened *Miss Foxy Lady* and Ken Burnstine was ready to race.

Ken Burnstine first appeared on the racing circuit with a D model Mustang named "Miss Suzie Q." It had perhaps the wildest paint scheme combination ever seen on any airplane. Photo Credit: Chuck Aro

When it first appeared at Reno, Burnstine's newly finished racer was all black and presented a sinister appearance. The trim lines of the Mustang are quite evident. Photo Credit: Dusty Carter Collection

Ken adorned his black racer with race number 34 and a shapely nude. Correspondingly, the airplane was named "Miss Foxy Lady." Photo Credit: Chuck Aro

Burnstine lifts off at Reno for the 1973 races, passing the familiar home pylon. Photo Credit: Birch Matthews

Early during the qualification period at Reno, Burnstine employed a local sign painter to decorate his new machine. The decorations consisted of the airplane name, special wing tip designs done in gold leaf with red trim, a very large race number on each side of the fuselage painted gold with white trim, and a large, almost life-size, titian haired, nearly nude, reclining foxy lady! One was reminded of the classic bar room nude, so fashionable at one point in our history. The crew wore black outfits that were soon abandoned in the heat of the Reno desert. Unfortunately, during qualifying *Miss Foxy Lady* backfired, blowing off the lower cowling and induction system, putting the airplane out of competition in its initial appearance. Burnstine went on to win the 1974 Reno Championship race with his other P-51, race number 33. After the Reno races, *Miss Foxy Lady* was entered in the October classic at Mojave, California, where Ken flew to a fifth place in the championship race at a speed of 352 miles per hour.

After the Mojave race, *Miss Foxy Lady* was returned to Chino where Bruce Goessling was engaged to make further modifications to the aircraft. The outward appearance of race 34 was altered with the addition of long, graceful fillets at the wing to fuselage juncture. The airframe received a new paint scheme of overall white. The freshly refinished aircraft was entered in the 1975 California National Air Races held in June at Mojave. The all-white racer simply carried its race number and name and was devoid of other markings. The painting of the titian haired nude was gone. In spite of the refinements and new finish, Burnstine did not do as well as expected, coming in sixth in the time trials at 374 miles per hour and seventh in the Championship Race at 356 miles an hour. When *Miss Foxy Lady* appeared at the 1975 Reno event it was unchanged in appearance. Once again, Burnstine secured the services of a local artist who adorned the flanks of the racer with a pixie blonde in a blue string bikini. While taking photographs of the newly painted racer, Burnstine approached Dusty Carter saying, "... What do you think of the new white paint job?" Dusty replied, "What's the reason for the change? Getting rid of the black hat villain image?" Ken Burnstein replied, "Somethin' like that. Don't ya' think the blonde has more class?" So much for class. The 1975 Reno race was the last for Burnstine. He turned in a very competitive 421 miles per hour qualifying speed, but encountered problems with the induction system which kept him out of the main event. Ken died in a crash in race 33 before the 1976 Mojave race. Race 34 was sold out

Once bitten by the racing bug, Burnstine decided to build a first class racer. Jim Larsen designed the aerodynamic modifications for this racer, seen here at Chino Airport during re-construction. Photo Credit: Jim Larsen

A year later, the black hat image was gone from "Miss Foxy Lady." Burnstine had repainted the racer all white. Photo Credit: Les Aro

of Burnstine's estate to John Crocker of San Mateo, California.

Sumthin' Else. John Crocker's first change to his new racer was a change in registration number, with N51VC replacing Burnstine's N70QF and race 6 replacing race 34. This may have been done to distance Crocker from the past history of the racer and its owner, Ken Burnstine. At the time of Burnstine's fatal accident he was under subpoena to appear in Federal Court to testify in a Florida drug smuggling operation.

The paint scheme was also changed. The bikini clad blond was removed and replaced by a conservative single blue stripe that covered the propeller spinner and tapered aft to the tail. Crocker engaged Jack Hovey to do the engine work and prepare the racer for the 1976 Reno classic. Hovey did an excellent job and Crocker qualified in second spot at 437 miles per hour. Top qualifying went to Don Whittington in a P-51 with a new course record of 439 miles per hour. With a great qualifying speed under his belt, Crocker was set to take the championship race the first time out with his new racer. On Sunday, September 12, the main event was run. Whittington's hot *Mustang* had engine problems and dropped out. Crocker, at the head of the pack, stretched his lead and flashed over the finish line way ahead of three stock *Mustangs* and one sick Bearcat. Victory? Not quite. Crocker's new airplane had a very small, tight-fitting canopy. Visibility was limited. Crocker flew outside the "deadline," or safety zone established by the race committee in conjunction with the Federal Aviation Aeronautics Administration. John was disqualified and his timing was never officially released. However, the sleek, white racer flew in excess of 427 miles per hour for the race. It was simultaneously a grand performance and rather bitter disappointment.

Following Reno, the racer was returned to the San Fransisco Bay area for further refinements. Long time air race activist, Jack Sweeney, designed an innovative antidetonant fluid control system for John Crocker's *Mustang* during this period. The objective was to control the engine induction air temperature automatically to a desired temperature and relieve the pilot of one more burden. Jack relates that, ". . . a water injection servo, working in conjunction with a fast response temperature tranducer monitoring engine induction air temperature in the carburetor, and a modified valve metering the water mixture to the carburetor controlled the injection rate." As the transducer sensed a higher induction temperature, due say to a power application, this signal was fed to the servo control unit which commanded the metering valve motor to make a proportional adjustment in water flow. The desired induction air temperature could be set between 136 and 183 degrees Fahrenheit.

According to Jack Sweeney: "The system really did an excellent job as long as all components were intact. Proper cooling was provided throughout the range of engine power settings and response to temperature changes was very rapid. The problem was that any failure would result either in full water on (in which case the engine would "sneeze" or worse) unless caught immediately by the pilot. I was particularly concerned about the "full on" type of failure during takeoff." The temperature transducer was the weak link in the system. Operating life could vary between one flight and a couple of years. In the end, Jack convinced John Crocker to switch to a widely used system designed by Pete Law. Even though Jack's system was eventually abandoned, it illustrates some of the innovative concepts employed in unlimited air racing.

Crocker has flown in nearly all unlimited races since he acquired his racer. The 1979 Reno Championship Race was the highlight of his career with *"Sumpthin' Else."* At the very start of this race, Crocker moved into the lead with Steve Hinton in the record-holding *Red Baron* in hot pursuit. John

John Crocker bought "Miss Foxy Lady" from the Burnstine estate and refinished it to his own tastes. The racer was re-christened "Sumthin' Else." Photo Credit: Birch Matthews

was able to maintain his lead and went on to win the Championship Race only seconds ahead of the ailing Red Baron, which was destined to crash only moments later. While the race was marred by the crash, it truly was a championship contest and John Crocker earned his victory every inch of the way.

Precious Metal. Gary Levitz, a member of the Levitz Furniture business family, began his unlimited class racing career by flying his Lockheed P-38 in the 1970 California 1000 at Mojave, California. The following year he participated in the one thousand mile race held in San Diego, California, known as the United States Cup Race. He began racing at Reno in the 1972 Reno National Championship Races, flying the same P-38 he had used in the long distance 1000 mile races. After several years of competing against *Mustang* racers and always finishing behind, he acquired a P-51D and engaged Ralph Payne of Scottsdale, Arizona, to prepare it for racing.

The first race for Levitz's new *Mustang*, now called *Precious Metal*, was at Mojave in June, 1975. Gary qualified race 81 at 370 miles an hour and went on to place fifth in the championship race at 356 miles an hour. By the time *Precious Metal* appeared at Reno in September, 1975, Payne had installed a low profile windshield and canopy acquired from Tony D'Allesandro of Reno, Nevada. D'Allesandro had modified a P-51D for racing, with the intent of entering

John Crocker poses beside "Sumthin' Else" at Reno. The white aircraft was trimmed in a light metallic blue stripe down the fuselage. Photo Credit: Birch Matthews

the 1973 Reno event. The modifications consisted of the specially built, lowered windshield and canopy, clipped wings, and the installation of an Allison V-1710 in place of the *Merlin* V-1650. The airplane never raced and was eventually converted back to a stock P-51D. With the new canopy and a little more time to improve engine performance, Gary's qualifying speed rose to 409 miles per hour in 1975. In the championship race, Levitz flew beyond the "deadline" and, like John Crocker, was promptly disqualified.

Sensing that part of the problem of flying outside the deadline boundary might be directional stability, Ralph Payne acquired a vertical tail from a P-51H and installed it on *Precious Metal*. In addition, he removed the wing tip assemblies, cut off the ailerons accordingly, installed special wing tips, and added new long, sweeping wing fillets. Race 81 arrived at Mojave sporting these modifications in June, 1976. Levitz proceeded to qualify at 386 miles per hour and placed a respectable second in the championship race at 376 miles an hour.

After the Mojave race, Gary Levitz sold *Precious Metal* to Don Whittington of Ft. Lauderdale, Florida. The Whittington brothers, Don and Bill, were accomplished, top level race car drivers in road racing as well as Indy car racing. With the acquisition of *Precious Metal*, they were embracing a new and even faster motor sport.

Don appeared at the 1976 Reno races with his new racer renamed *Miss Florida III*. He was assigned race 09. The rookie air race pilot quickly established himself as a real contender by qualifying at a new course record of 439 miles per hour. But the qualifying speed record was costly. During the run the highly tuned *Merlin* backfired at the end of the time trial and essentially destroyed itself. Whittington brought the wounded bird in without difficulty and his crew immediately set about installing a new engine. Early Sunday morning, Whittington took *Miss Florida III* up to "slow time" the newly installed *Merlin*. The hour or so flight was just not enough time to loosen up the engine and it failed during the championship race, denying Whittington a win or even a finish in his rookie year of air racing.

Don returned to Reno for the 1977 event with race 09 unchanged from 1976, except that it had reverted to its

For several years, Don Whittington raced this beautiful P-51, which was modified for racing. This profile photograph shows the extended vertical fin and the sweeping wing fillets of this clipped wing racer. Photo Credit: Birch Matthews

Don taxies "Precious Metal" out for a trial run at Reno. The racer was always highly polished and made a striking appearance. Photo Credit: Birch Matthews

"Precious Metal" is towed back into the Reno pits after a heat race. Don had a clean, low profile canopy installed on race 09. Photo Credit: Birch Matthews

In 1988, Don Whittington brought another highly modified P-51 to the Reno races, which was also called "Precious Metal." This was the second Mustang to be equipped with a Rolls-Royce Griffon engine. Photo Credit: Neal Nurmi

original name of *Precious Metal*. With the engine failures, the racer was aptly named. Whittington qualified in the number two spot at 399 miles per hour, somewhat off of his 1976 performance but with an intact racing engine. *Precious Metal* ran the championship race in second place to finish at 398 miles an hour behind Darryl Greenamyer, who set a new course record of 431 miles an hour flying the *Red Baron*. Not a bad showing for a second year race pilot. However, the show was not over. Since the championship race is the last event of the race meet, the first, second, and third place finishers are taxied before the crowded grandstands at the conclusion of the race so the pilots may receive accolades from the spectators. The *Red Baron* was the first to taxi in and park, causing well wishers on the ramp to surge toward the winning aircraft. A ramp official sought to clear the area for Whittington and Cliff Cummins to park their second and third place racers. The official borrowed a new Datsun belonging to Air Race Director, Jerry Duty, and drove into proximity of the post-race parking area. His choice of a parking spot was ill conceived and directly in the path of Whittington's racer. Before anyone could stop the action, the big eleven foot diameter propeller of Whittington's racer sliced up the new Datsun. It was never known if second place money went for a new car for Jerry Duty.

Whittington continued to race *Precious Metal* – seemingly without any appreciable changes – through the 1983 season, missing only the 1979 and 1980 Reno events. The airplane consistently performed near the 400 mile per hour mark, placing second behind the *Red Baron* in most races.

Dago Red. This was the first of two *Mustangs* modified by Bill Destefani. Destefani is the owner of a farming operation known as "Flying Tigers Farms," located in Bakersfield, California. He is also involved in Warbird restoration and flies a beautifully restored Curtiss P-40 just for fun. Bill got involved in closed-course racing in 1980 by entering a near stock P-51D called *Mangia Pane*. This racer flew with race number 72 and was piloted by Ron Hevle, the owner and operator of Wheeler Ridge Aviation, a crop dusting operation in Bakersfield. Hevle flew race 72 to first place in the Silver race and sixth in the Gold race at Reno in 1980. In 1981, he flew the same airplane to third place in the Gold or Championship race.

The good showing of *Mangia Pane* prompted Destefani to consider building a dedicated racing machine to compete with the likes of *Sumthin' Else* and *Jeannie*. With his interest in Warbird restoration, Destefani certainly had the resources with respect to airframe components. At this point in time, Bill combined with Frank Taylor of Chino, California. Taylor was also interested in getting into racing and had money to finance an unlimited racer. Destefani and

Taylor formed a partnership, with Bill providing the airplane and crew and Frank providing the finances. Work began at Destefani's hanger at Minter Field, located in Shafter, California, just a few miles north of Bakersfield. Minter Field is an old World War II training base located in the middle of a vast farm area. Destefani's Minter Field crew farmed out some of the rework to rebuilders in Sun Valley and Chino, California. The racer was assembled in Taylor's hanger at Chino and test flown from this airport.

The modifications were extensive and employed the engineering talents of Bruce Boland and Pete Law for aerodynamic refinements and engine systems. The upper portion of the forward fuselage was removed and replaced by a new structure, incorporating a small windshield and canopy. The canopy profile faired aft to the vertical fin dorsal. The canopy was hinged aft, similar to John Crocker's *Sumthin' Else*. Coolant radiators were modified to eliminate any fittings on the bottom of the assembly to permit installation of a shallow profile belly scoop. The P-51 oil cooler was eliminated so the belly scoop housed only the coolant radiator. A P-51H heat exchanger was located in the fuselage to provide oil cooling. Coolant for the supercharger aftercooler provides the cooling medium for the engine oil.

To improve handling characteristics during pylon racing, the trim on the entire empennage of *Dago Red* was modified. The vertical fin is normally set at one degree to the left. *Dago Red* is offset one-quarter degree to the right. The horizontal stabilizer is set at one-half degree positive incidence, instead of the usual two degrees on many P-51s.[1] Australian-built *Mustangs* apparently had two sets of fittings, so the stabilizer could be set at either a positive one-half or a positive two degrees. Destefani used fittings from an Australian P-51 to setup his new racer. Along with the change in stabilizer setting, the elevator trim tab travel was changed from the stock ten degrees up and down to ten degrees up and 25 degrees downward travel. According to Bill Destefani, these new trim settings reduce the control stick loads during pylon turns.[2]

The completed *Dago Red* weighed in at 6250 pounds. The fuel bays in the wing were modified to carry 150 gallons of fuel and 108 gallons of water. Water is fed through spray bars ahead of the coolant radiator to assist in lowering the temperature of the engine and aftercooler coolant liquids. There is also 45 gallons of water-methonal mixture (antidetonant fluid) for injection into the engine during a race.

Dago Red made its debut at the 1982 Reno National Championship Air Races, with Ron Hevle as pilot. Ron was top qualifier at 440 miles per hour and won the championship race at 405 miles an hour. After the Reno race, *Dago Red* returned to Fank Taylor's hanger in Chino, California.

Ron Hevle (third from the left) with the rest of a happy crew after winning the Championship Gold Race at Reno. Photo Credit: Birch Matthews

Destefani sold his interest to Taylor, and Frank proceeded to prepare the racer for an attempt to beat an old record of 465.37 miles per hour set in 1951 by Jacqueline Cochran in a P-51C. In July, 1983, Frank Taylor flew *Dago Red* over a fifteen kilometer course established at Mojave, California. Flying at a high altitude, Taylor successfully set a new record of 517.02 miles an hour, some 52 miles an hour faster than Jackie's old speed mark.

In 1983, *Dago Red* arrived at Reno with a new pilot, Rick Brickert of Sandy, Utah, who would fly the racer through the 1985 race season. That first year, Brickert was the number two qualifier at 439 miles per hour, but failed to finish the championship race due to a broken spinner that failed during the sixth lap. A year later, Brickert qualified in fifth spot at 430 miles per hour, but during the final race the *Merlin* threw a connecting rod in the third lap. Rick was

Race 4 is on the course at Reno. The spray bar cooling augmentation allows the pilot to fly with the belly scoop exit door in the full up position, thus reducing a bit of drag on the airframe. Photo Credit: Chuck Aro

Bill Destefani campaigned two racers at Reno for several years. In the foreground is "Mangia Pane" and in the background sits "Dago Red" at the 1982 races. Photo Credit: Birch Matthews

"Dago Red" was a thoroughbred champion. The revised belly scoop and low profile canopy can be seen as the racer sits on the ramp at Reno in 1982. Photo Credit: Birch Matthews

running in second place at the time. The broken rod resulted in an engine oil fire. Smoke covered the front of the airplane and Brickert headed for the north-south diagonal runway at Reno. He opened the canopy and it blew off, causing fire to fill the cockpit about the time Rick got the wheels on the ground.[3] Although the cockpit got scorched, Rick emerged unhurt. In 1985, with Rick Brickert again aboard, *Dago Red* qualified third at 442 miles per hour and placed third in the championship race with a speed of 426 miles an hour.

After the 1985 race, Frank Taylor and Alan Preston, owner of Stil*leto*, reportedly had a personal bet with *Dago Red* as the prize. Rumor had it that this was how Alan Preston became the new owner of *Dago Red*. Before the 1986 race season, Preston took *Dago Red* back to Bill Destefani to have a new sliding canopy installed. Preston raced the airplane at Reno in 1986, taking fourth in the championship race at 413 miles an hour. In 1986, Alan Preston entered an airplane in each of the four racing classes at Reno and proceeded to fly in each one. It was a strenuous test for Preston and certainly a first in all of air racing history. This racer is still in competition and is a formidable contender each time out.

Strega. With cash on hand from the sale of *Dago Red* to partner Frank Taylor, together with prize money earned with *Dago Red*, Bill Destefani started construction of a new racer. Beginning with a *Mustang* airframe that was about seventy percent intact, a new machine emerged that was in the mold of *Dago Red*, but incorporated some changes in detail. The most recognizable change was the cockpit canopy. The new racer, dubbed *Strega*, had a windshield and sliding canopy similar to that used on the RB-51 *Red Baron*.[4] Indeed, tooling was borrowed from the Red Baron project to make parts for *Strega*. A design change was made to allow the canopy on the new racer to be opened during flight, something that could not be done with the original canopy on *Dago Red*.

The P-51 tail assembly trim was essentially that employed on *Dago Red*, except the vertical fin was repositioned one-half degree to the right. Horizontal tail trim was the same as *Dago Red*. The engine coolant and oil cooling system is also the same, except that no supercharger aftercooler is used with this *Merlin* engine, thus saving airframe weight.

A P-51H heat exchanger is used on Stre*ga* to cool the engine oil. When the aftercooler is eliminated, a large tube is installed between the supercharger exit flange and the engine intake manifold. Antidetonant fluid is injected into the heated, compressed air-fuel mixture in the tube. Although the engine installation is lighter without the aftercooler, more antidetonant fluid is used to offset the higher induction temperatures which result. When the racer was completed, it weighed 6275 pounds, twenty-five pounds more than *Dago Red*.

Strega's introduction to racing was not dramatic. Assigned race number 7, Ron Hevle flew the new racer to Reno in 1983, and qualified in third spot at 436 miles per hour. However, he failed to finish in the final event, completing less than one lap. The next year was virtually a repeat of the disappointing 1983 racing season. Hevle again qualified in third place at 441 miles an hour, but dropped out of the championship race during the seventh lap with a burned piston. The third racing season, 1985, got off to a better start. A race for unlimiteds was held at Minter Field (Bakersfield, California) in June. Ron Hevle and *Strega* were the top qualifiers at 431 miles per hour. The gold race was a real thriller, with *Stilleto* and *Strega* exchanging the lead several times. Finally, *Stilleto* pulled out of the race near the end with very high coolant temperatures. Hevle booted *Strega* home with a winning speed of 425 miles per hour. The potential of the new racer was finally beginning to show. Fate, however, was not kind to Bill Destefani and Ron Hevle at Reno that fall. A rough running engine prevented Hevle from starting the championship race.

Bill Destefani decided to race *Strega* in the 1986 Reno classic. He had acquired the sponsorship of a large tobacco company and now hoped to put *Strega* into the winners circle at Reno. Unfortunately, the process of qualifying and competing in the heat races was not very productive. *Strega* only qualified in seventh position and did not do especially well in the heat races. The sponsorship dried up and things just were not going well. In spite of this, Bill Destefani kept his sense of humor. Late in the race week at Reno, two small zeros were added to the race number, making it read "007." When asked why, Destefani replied, ". . . well race number seven was not bringing us much luck, maybe double "0" seven will turn that around." In the championship race "007" placed third at a speed of 417 miles per hour.

Bill Destefani goes by the nickname of "Tiger" and it was apparent that this tiger was really going after the 1987 race with all the tenacity of a large, hungry cat. Although he had a top crew chief in Bill Kerchenfaut, Destefani engaged one of the best *Merlin* engine rebuilders in the business to build up the 1987 *Merlin* engine; this was Dwight Thorn. On arriving at the pits in Reno it was obvious that "Tiger's" team was ready to race. The large, well-equipped support trailer was set up with a bright red canopy that completely covered their pit area. Late summer in Reno can make working on an airplane in the sun very difficult. At least the crew was to be afforded some protection from the unmerciful sun.

The effectiveness of the Kerchnfaut/Thorn team was

When Bill Destefani sold "Dago Red," he immediately set about building a second champion Mustang racer named "Strega." Race 7 is shown running up on the ramp at Reno. Photo Credit: Birch Matthews

apparent very early in race week. "Tiger" Destefani in *Strega*, and Steve Hinton in *Tsunami*, led the racers onto the course for the opening day of qualifications. *Strega* was on the course ahead of *Tsunami*, with a sound that only a *Merlin* can make when it is running at very high power settings. When *Strega* completed the timing lap, Kerchanfaut radioed Destefani and told him, ". . . They got you at something over 460 miles per hour!" "Tiger" said "Bullshit, I don't have it at full power." Hinton's crew called him on the radio to alert him to Destefani's speed, since *Tsunami* had been programmed to qualify at 465 miles per hour. When Hinton was told that *Strega* had done 466 plus miles per hour he thought his crew was taunting him. He flew his qualifying lap as planned. The old qualifying record was set in 1986 by Rick Brickert flying Frank Sanders' Sea Fury at 452.737

miles per hour. That record fell to Bill Destefani when *Strega* ran the course at 466.674 miles per hour. Steve Hinton in *Tsunami* was two miles an hour slower. He had missed a chance to own the new record. Brickert, in the Sea Fury *Dreadnaught*, was fourth at 448.698 miles per hour, enough to get him in the gold race. The big Sea Fury had never been pushed very hard by any of the racers, particularly a *Merlin*-powered *Mustang*. So a waiting game was played with the Sea Fury pushing *Strega* a bit more in each heat race. Heat 2A run on Friday had *Strega* winning at 441.498 miles per hour, with *Dreadnaught* close at 441.293 miles an hour. Brickert was content to run second so he could push Destefani and his *Merlin* engine. The next race that paired these two strong competitors was Heat 3A on Saturday. Again *Strega* was the victor and *Dreadnaught*

Bill Destefani put on a race at Bakersfield, California in 1985. "Strega" taxies out for time trials at this race. Photo Credit: Neal Nurmi

In 1985, "Strega" was sponsored by Skoal Chewing Tobacco. The racer is seen here at Bakersfield before the competition began. Photo Credit: Neal Nurmi

Neal Nurmi captured the lower surfaces of "Strega" during the 1986 Reno races. Photo Credit: Neal Nurmi

was second, less than a mile per hour slower at a torid pace similar to the first heat race. The situation seemed perfect for *Dreadnaught*. Destefani's *Merlin* had been pushed hard on Friday and again on Saturday. Brickert and the Sanders racing team felt this strategy would pay off on Sunday during the championship race.

If *Strega* jumped into the lead from the pole position, Brickert was to really push the big Sea Fury to make *Strega* go all out. After a couple of laps around the nine mile course, Brickert pulled ahead of Destefani with the intention of improving his new found lead by the end of the lap. After leaving pylon two, "Tiger" Destefani opened the power setting on *Strega* and shot by *Dreadnaught* before they reached the next turn. It was all over. *Strega* went on to set a new race record of 452.559 miles per hour. Rick Brickert in *Dreadnaught* was second at 449.747 miles per hour. After the race Brickert was heard to comment, "I didn't think his *Merlin* would stay together at those speeds but when *Strega* passed me, I knew I could not catch him if the engine held together."

All in all, the week-long battle between Destefani and Brickert – inline engine versus radial – was one of the most hotly contested racing series ever to be witnessed at Reno or any other pylon race. Bill continues to campaign Stre*ga* with success, but his record at Reno during 1987 was surely the pinnacle of Mustang pylon racing. It was absolutely a flawless performance by the pilot, the airplane, and the crew that made it happen.

Bill Destefani continues to vigorously campaign Stre*ga*. His chief competitor is Lyle Shelton's F8F *Bearcat*. Although the Grumman has thus far been just a tad faster, Bill is never far behind in the championship race. In the 1991 gold championship race, *Strega* was pushed to an average speed of just under 479 miles an hour into second place, some two miles an hour slower than Lyle's speed in first place. These phenomenal speeds around a nine mile course demonstrate the caliber of competition which exists. *Strega* is without doubt the fastest *Mustang* in the world today.

Notes

1. P-51Ds, after serial number 44-73827, and 44-12853 and P-51Ks, after serial number 44-12753, had one-half degree positive stabilizer settings as well as all-metal elevators.
2. Race pilot Charles Walling flew a *Mustang* during the late 1940s and commented on pylon turns with this aircraft. In 1948, Walling flew a P-51D owned by J.D. Reed. Walling's comments during an interview were, ". . . the P-38 was a better airplane to fly a pylon with, you just simply eased the stick back, but the P-51 was a much harder airplane to fly in the turns. It took all of your strength to keep the stick back in a turn."
3. Fire retardant "Nomex" flight suits are worn by most pilots. Many also utilize helmets with full face plates as further protection.
4. Strega means "witch" in Italian.

Chapter Twelve
Mustang - THE PROGENITOR

For years, the only participants in post-war Thompson Trophy and contemporary unlimited class air racing have been ex-military "War Birds." Periodically, there were rumors of custom-built racers under construction to compete with the big high-powered fighters. One year, a high performance business aircraft was entered at Reno but was unable to qualify, much less race. In 1982, an amateur-built aircraft, the D'Alessandris JT-SP, was entered in the Reno unlimited class by Howard Goddard of Seal Beach, California. The airplane was powered by a Lycoming TS10-540 engine that gave the little home-built good performance.

Apparently Goddard had hoped to gain publicity to enhance the possibility of selling the craft to small third-world air forces. It qualified at 274 miles per hour. The race committee deemed this too slow to be competitive and it, too, did not race.

A few years later, a second custom-built aircraft appeared at Reno. It was a newly designed, high-speed aircraft powered by a Rolls-Royce *Merlin* engine. The year was 1986. The racer was designed and built by Bruce Boland and crew, for owner John Sandberg. The aircraft was named *"Tsunami,"* pronounced "sue-na-mee," which is Japanese

This rear view of Sandberg's racer, named "Tsunami," was caught in the low level light of the late afternoon sun during the 1986 Reno races. Photo Credit: Neal Nurmi

for "tidal wave." It may well be the wave of the future for unlimited class air racing. At last it appeared that here was an aircraft that could and would compete very favorably with the best of the unlimiteds. To some spectators in the pit area, the silver and blue racer appeared to be yet another modified *Mustang*. Closer inspection told skeptics this was a truly new machine. Why discuss a custom-built racer in a book about *Mustangs*? Because the remarkable P-51 had a definite influence on the general arrangement of the *Tsunami* design. In particular, selection of a *Merlin*, liquid-cooled engine resulted in placement of the cooling radiators in a belly scoop, still the most efficient aerodynamic location for these components on a craft of this type. In this context, the *Mustang* was truly a progenitor.

To better understand the genesis of this new custom-built racer, let us look into the background of its designer, Bruce Boland. Bruce is an affable, outgoing personality with a wonderful sense of humor. He is a graduate aeronautical engineer with a masters degree in aerodynamics. His work at Lockheed Aircraft Corporation centered on stress analysis and aerodynamic loads. More recently, he became division senior engineer for the Lockheed's famous "Skunk Works." Since the late 1960s, Bruce and fellow Lockheed engineer, Pete Law, have been involved in engineering racing modifications for most of the top air racers in the country. Their credits include Darryl Greenamyer's Grumman *Bearcat*, Steve Hinton's RB-51 *Red Baron*, Frank Taylor's *Dago Red*, Cliff Cummins' *Miss Candace*, and Mac McClain's *Jeannie*. All have been top performers and most were record setting aircraft. With the exception of Greenamyer's F8F *Bearcat*, all the others were highly modified *Mustangs*, giving both men an intimacy with the P-51 airplane afforded few other engineers in this profession.

According to Bruce Boland, his original concept for a custom-built racing airplane began some sixteen years earlier in 1970, when he and Ray Poe, another Lockheed technician, talked about a concept for a machine much smaller than the P-51 with the capability to compete in the 1,000 mile air races that were then popular. The dream proceeded to a preliminary design around an Allison V-1710 engine. Engineering trade studies were made, resulting in a requirement for a 1,500 horsepower powerplant to make the design competitive for the Reno races. To put the original design study in context, the winning speed for the championship unlimited race at Reno in 1972 was 416 miles per hour, a record at the time. The design study project continued for about a year. During that time the two men purchased a couple of Allison engines, and made some ribs, bulkheads, a firewall, and main longerons for the proposed racer. Ray Poe subsequently moved out of the local area and

Bruce Boland gave up the project due to cost and other commitments.

Boland says *Tsuanmi's* manger was a hanger in Tonapah, Nevada, during August, 1979. At that time, the *Red Baron* RB-51 *Mustang* with a Rolls-Royce Griffon engine was being prepared for an assault on the world three kilometer speed record. Bruce was one of the technical staff supporting this effort. Because there were inevitable delays getting the racer ready for official timing runs, Bruce had an opportunity to discuss some of his ideas concerning a custom-built racer with John Sandberg, a businessman from Minneapolis. John had an intense interest in air racing, having campaigned a highly modified Bell P-63 *Kingcobra* for several years. He was also involved in rebuilding Allisons and *Merlins* for racing. During these conversations with John, various concepts were discussed, including very small racers similar to the Formula One class but using high powered engines. Design trade studies made by Bruce during the early 1970s were reviewed. The two men recognized that speeds were increasing and therefore design requirements would have to be changed for the proposed racer to remain competitive during the 1980s.

John Sandberg leaned toward building a relatively small racer equipped with a large engine. Both aerodynamic drag and weight would be kept to a minimum. This philosophy, it was reasoned, would permit operating a *Merlin* engine at more conservative power levels, thus achieving greater reliability and durability. It was an attractive prospect, considering all of the blown *Merlins* over the years of pylon racing. John was enthusiastic about Bruce Boland's concepts and asked for a proposal covering the design and construction of such a racer. Once interested, John was anxious to get started. He wanted a proposal developed and available at the coming Reno races, about a month away. Bruce Boland was ready and Sandberg was impressed. He asked Boland to design and build the racer. A month later the deal was made and the *Tsunami* Project began November 1, 1979.

Boland states that, "... *Tsunami* is a totally new concept over the 1970-1972 project, although there was some reference to the earlier data." A year was consumed doing performance calculations, loads analyses, structural arrangement, control surface sizing, and stress analyses, all done by Bruce Boland! Lockheed engineer Mike Wright developed a computer model to back up the designer's stress analysis. Pete Law developed a specification for the cooling system radiators. These were designed and built by Niagara Engineering and Development. Law also prepared conceptual designs for the fuel, oil, antidetonant injection and spray bar systems. Ray Poe and Steve Hinton turned these designs into metal. Most of the airframe construction was

John Sandberg commissioned Bruce Boland to design and build the first truly competitive, original, unlimited racer since the pre-war races in Cleveland. The diminutive Merlin- powered racer traces some lineage to the venerable Mustang. Captured in full flight profile, the clean lines of this custom design are self evident. Photo Credit: Neal Nurmi

done by Boland, Poe, and Tom Emery, with assistance from Don Jansen and Greg Benson. A *Merlin* racing engine was prepared by John Sandberg and Sam Torvik. Hydraulic, fuel, and electrical systems were fabricated by Steve Hinton's shop at Chino, California, where the racer was finally completed and then test flown.

Tsunami was not only influenced by the design of the *Mustang*, some P-51 parts found their way into this new era racer. The engine section forward of the firewall was influenced by the design of the Allison-powered P-51J, although the racer does use a Rolls-Royce *Merlin* engine. This particular engine is the product of JRS Enterprises, a Sandberg-owned engine overhaul and repair facility that specializes in World War II era engines. Sandberg developed this racing engine over a couple of years by flying prototypes in a *Mustang*. The *Tsunami* engine is made up of a number of Rolls-Royce *Merlin* components based upon a V-1650-7 crankcase and supercharger. The crankshaft is from a *Merlin* 114 that was used on the D.H. Mosquito. Head and bank assemblies come from the 624 and 724 series *Merlins* that powered the Canadian North Star transport, a modified Douglas DC-4. The propeller reduction gear as-

sembly is .42 to 1 and obtained from a 500 series *Merlin*. Propeller reduction gearing prevents the propeller tips from reaching supersonic speed at the design speed and power setting of the racer.

The *Tsunami* engine mount is a modified P-51 design. The propeller assembly consists of a P-51 Aeroproducts hub with North American T-28 blades and a P-51H spinner. The retractable tail wheel gear is from a P-51H with a Grumman S2F tail wheel. The radiator coolant door is actuated with a P-51 actuator. The control stick is from the aft cockpit of a North American T-6 trainer. The landing gear is from a Piper Aerostar with Learjet seventeen inch diameter wheels.

The wing airfoil is a modified NACA 63-212 section. It has a 12 percent thickness ratio from root to tip. The dihedral is 5 degrees measured along the lower surface and the wing is installed with positive one degree of incidence. There is no wash out at the wing tips. The NACA 63 series airfoil was chosen to provide volume forward of the main spar for landing gear stowage, much the same as the *Mustang*.

The airplane has been licensed in the amateur-built category. Taxi tests were first run on August 13, 1986. *Tsunami* first flew during the late afternoon of August 17.

This photograph was taken early in the Gold Championship Race at Reno in 1990. Skip Holm, in "Tsunami," trails Lyle Shelton in the "Rare Bear" F8F. Lyle won the race. At full throttle, Skip was unable to catch the "Bear." Photo Credit: Neal Nurmi

Three weeks later it was at Reno with a little over 40 hours flight testing completed. Although the airplane was qualified at a respectable 435 miles an hour, it was plagued with generator problems throughout race week. In the Championship race the generator failed just as race power was applied and an enormous backfire occurred. No cowling parts were blown off the racer due to the backfire, but the structure and cowl panels were badly distorted. Steve Hinton made a safe emergency landing. The airplane remained at Reno for several months while the engine was returned to JRS Enterprises in Minneapolis. The 1987 race season started on a good note with a qualifying speed of nearly 465 miles per hour. Steve Hinton was on the race course to qualify behind Bill Destefani in *Strega*. He flew *Tsunami* according to a plan which should have been sufficient to set a new qualifying record, one of the team goals. It was not to be. Destefani urged *Strega* around the course during qualification, reaching just under 467 miles per hour.

Tsunami suffered engine problems during the championship race and was forced to make an emergency landing. When the racer had nearly rolled to a stop, Hinton turned off the runway. At that moment the side brace on one of the landing gears broke. The brace was unknowingly misaligned, and therefore unstable. The airplane ground looped, causing one gear to break and damaged the right rear spar. The next day Sandberg commented, "We've only got twelve production parts on the airplane and one of them broke." The racer was disassembled and shipped to Steve Hinton's Fighter Rebuilders shop at the Chino, California, airport for repairs. Later, the airplane was returned to John Sandberg's facility in Minneapolis for further modification.

In the intervening years, the racer has met with mixed fortunes. Always a top contender, accidents and engine problems seemed destined to keep the diminutive *Tsunami* out of the winners circle. Finally in June, 1990, Steve Hinton guided *Tsunami* into the winners circle during the unlimited championship race of the Texas Air Races. His winning speed approached 421 miles per hour. It was a milestone for the *Tsunami* project team. Bruce Boland's urge to create a unique unlimited racer, together with John Sandberg's adventurous willingness to sponsor such a project, represents a landmark in contemporary unlimited class competition. And part of *Tsunami's* heritage was the North American Aviation P-51 *Mustang*!

Afterword

Sadly, as this manuscript was going to press, news arrived that John Sandberg, owner of *Tsunami*, was killed 25 September 1991, while flying the racer back to his home base in Minnesota. John was on a straight in final approach to the Pierre, South Dakota airport for a planned refueling stop. Landing a little fast due to a known defect with the pitot tube which gave a higher than actual forward velocity reading, John lowered the split flaps to full open. The left flap actuator failed. Only the right flap deployed rolling the racer inverted. There was insufficient altitude to recover control and *Tsunami* crashed short of the airport.

John will be missed in racing circles because of his enthusiasm and commitment to the sport. He was an innovator willing to try different ideas and technologies to obtain the ultimate unlimited racing aircraft. John will be remembered for, among other things, his experiments with alcohol fuels, turbo chargers and propellers in a never ending quest for greater speed. At one point, he was considering development of a two-stroke racing engine for unlimited class racing. He will perhaps be best remembered for the sponsorship and development of *Tsunami*, the first truly custom-designed unlimited class racer since before World War II. John Sandberg's contributions to air racing engendered a great deal of interest and enjoyment to thousands of fans who saw his airplanes race.

Appendix

Appendix A
SUPERCHARGING THE MERLIN

Among various *Merlin* marks and Packard dash numbers one will find both single-stage and two-stage blowers, or superchargers, terms which in this instance are synonymous. *Merlin* superchargers are driven by the engine crankshaft through a step-up gear drive. Whether single- or two-stage, the supercharger may be operated at either of two speeds called low blower and high blower, respectively.[1] In their original application, the two-stage blower was used to enhance high-altitude engine performance. Single-stage blowers served to increase engine power for specific low-altitude military missions.

The supercharger is an integral and all-important device in unlimited air racing. It is this device which provides over-boosted manifold pressures applied to racing *Merlins*. Fundamentally, the centrifugal blower consists of a wheel or disc incorporating vanes extending over the radius of the disc. This is called a rotor. In turn, the rotor is enshrouded in a close-fitting housing, or blower case. In a two-stage blower, the second rotor is positioned in series with the first. A fuel-air mixture enters the center of the rotor, turns 90 degrees and flows radially outward between vanes. Because the rotor turns at very high speeds, a large centrifugal force is imparted to the fuel-air charge. As the charge leaves the rotor passages it then flows through fixed diffuser vanes allowing the fluid to expand and decelerate, trading velocity for pressure buildup. Properly designed blowers achieve efficiencies as high as 75 percent. It was mathematician Sir Stanley Hooker who refined the *Merlin* supercharger to reach this efficiency level. As noted previously, supercharger rotors run at high speed. The two-stage *Merlin* dash 7 blower is typically used for Reno competitions. At maximum race power settings a *Merlin* will turn 3,800 revolutions per minute. Step-up gears in low blower at this crankshaft speed drive the rotor at 22,000 revolutions with corresponding rotor tip speeds of more than 1,100 feet each second.

Air processed by the blower undergoes compression heating, a decided detriment. As charge temperatures increase, weight density decreases and engine power diminishes. To counteract compression heating, the charge is passed through a heat exchanger called an aftercooler (also referred to as an intercooler) before entering the engine induction passageway. The aftercooler is liquid-cooled and sensible heat in the charge is transferred to the liquid. Depending upon outside air temperature, charge temperatures entering the induction system will vary between say 150 to perhaps 250 degrees F.

Manifold pressure is a function of engine speed because the supercharger is gear driven by the crankshaft. At constant engine speed, manifold pressure realized is dependent upon ambient air conditions of barometric pressure, temperature, and moisture content (humidity). In Reno, where the unlimited course is at an altitude of about 5000 feet, standard altitude pressure is perhaps 13 to 14 percent less than that experienced at sea level. Standard atmospheric values are further modified by prevailing local weather. For instance, if a low-pressure weather front moves through the Reno area, the barometer will drop accordingly. In this situation, the supercharger is pumping from an ambient air pressure lower than standard and the resulting manifold pressure will be correspondingly reduced. In other words, the supercharger must work with whatever ambient air pressure exists. At low barometric pressures, the loss in manifold pressure after supercharging can amount to as much as five percent relative to standard conditions.

The second weather parameter influencing manifold pressure delivered to the engine is air temperature. Weight density (pounds of air per cubic foot) varies directly with temperature. At high ambient temperatures, weight density decreases and less air mass is available for the engine to process. Similarly, charge cooling after supercharging is somewhat reduced when the ambient air stream is hot. In other words, the charge temperatures can never be reduced to a point below the existing ambient air temperature even if the heat transfer process were 100 percent efficient, which it certainly is not.

Humidity also affects engine performance. High moisture content tends to reduce engine power output because chemical energy introduced into the cylinders is diluted. The converse is also true. Climatic conditions in Reno can vary dramatically during race week in September. Frequently, however, weather conditions approximate that of a semi-arid climate, producing pleasantly warm days with low humidity. Under these conditions the *Merlin* blower performs at near ideal capacity, to the delight of race crews.

Much of the preceding discussion centers on race operations in Reno where the altitude of Stead Airfield is about 5,000 feet. Atmospheric conditions often found during the September classic typically result in the following operating conditions and supercharger power consumption for a dash 7 blower in low speed:

Rev/Min	Manifold Press. In.-Hg	Horsepower Consumed
3400	100	620
3600	110	820
3800	120	1050

Thus for each 200 revolutions per minute increase in engine speed, an additional 10 inches of manifold pressure is realized. It is further obvious that high manifold pressure operation consumes a sizable fraction of the engine power output.

Manifold pressures greater than 120 inches have been obtained in *Merlin* racing engines but at lower altitudes than Reno. In 1985, Skip Holm reportedly achieved around 140 inches flying Stilleto during the Bakersfield, California, air race. And Don Wittington ran Precious Metal at a sustained 4,000 revolutions at about 140 inches during a 90 mile test in Florida after the 1979 International Air Race. Engine tear down following Wittington's flight revealed slight cracking around two or three valve keepers. The engine was otherwise apparently undamaged. Six year later at Bakersfield, Skip Holm wasn't so fortunate. At such speeds and manifold pressures, the *Merlin* is, without doubt, stressed to the limit.

It should be noted in passing that not all engine builders use an aftercooler downstream of the supercharger. In the absence of an aftercooler, charge air temperature is reduced by injection of greater quantities of antidetonant fluid. Evaporation of this liquid cools the charge, as would the aftercooler. This approach eliminates the weight of an aftercooler and associated plumbing; however, it requires almost twice as much antidetonant fluid flow, around 0.8 to 1.0 pounds per pound of fuel consumed.

Charge mass flow, predominantly air, provided to an engine by the supercharger is measured in terms of pressure. In the United States, this is commonly referred to as manifold pressure and units of measure are inches of mercury. This relates to a column of mercury in a tube which rises to a height equal to that required to balance a corresponding column of air extending from the surface of the earth to the outermost reaches of our atmosphere. At sea level in a standard atmosphere, the mercury column will measure 29.92 inches. The British refer to manifold pressure as "boost" which is a measure of pressure above or below atmospheric pressure. This is called gage pressure and does not include atmospheric pressure. Units of measure for boost pressure are in pounds per square inch. Conversion

from one system to the other is readily done. One pound of boost (pressure) plus 14.7 pounds per square inch multiplied by 2.04 is equivalent to manifold pressure in inches of mercury. Conversely, inches of mercury divided by 2.04 less 14.7 pounds per square inch gives boost pressure in pounds per square inch. Following is a comparison of some common *Merlin* operating manifold pressures in both inches of mercury and corresponding values in boost or pounds per square inch:

M.P. In.-Hg	Boost lb/in^2	Remarks
30	0	Atmospheric pressure
61	15	Military power, dash 7 engine
67	18	War emergency power, dash 7
80	25	
100	34	
110	39	Race power setting
120	44	Race power setting
130	49	Race power setting
140	54	Race power setting

Some appreciation of pressure force magnitudes on engine components at high boost pressure is seen by considering what happens when 130 inches of mercury manifold pressure is reached during a race. Remembering that air inducted into the supercharger has an ambient pressure of about 30 inches of mercury, one realizes that the supercharger raises this pressure by a factor of 4.3 or about 64 pounds per square inch. When the charge enters the engine cylinder it is further pressurized by the piston. The *Merlin* compression ratio is 6:1 and at the top of the piston stroke the charge pressure is now about 383 pounds per square inch before ignition. The *Merlin* piston has 22.89 square inches of surface area which when multiplied by 383 pounds for each square inch equals 8,770 pounds of force. In other words, at this point in time, some 4.4 tons of pressure force is acting against the piston, cylinder walls, and cylinder head. When the fuel-air charge is ignited, expanding combustion gases result in even greater forces with pressures reaching some 1,100 to 1,200 pounds per square inch. This is almost 14 tons of force acting against the piston and therefore the connecting rod, bearings, and crankshaft. From this exercise, it is seen that the loads acting on various components of the engine are quite severe under racing conditions.

Notes

1. The desirability of supercharging aircraft was recognized in the earliest days of powered flight, certainly prior to 1914. Centrifugal blower development profited from steam turbine technology.

Appendix B
ASSESSMENT OF THE BEGUINE CRASH

Few fatal accidents in the history of high-speed flight and air racing have resulted in as much speculation about a pilot and his airplane as the crash of Bill Odom in the *Beguine* racer. One other comes to mind and that was the demise of Lowell Bayles in the Granville Brothers' Gee Bee Model Z racer. Lowell Bayles was killed during a record speed attempt in Detroit, Michigan, on December 5, 1931. His accident gained wide publicity and notoriety because the record flight attempt was captured on film by a newsreel movie cameraman. Stills appeared in newspapers and footage of the crash was shown in motion picture theaters around the country. Like the *Beguine* racer, the Gee Bee was a controversial design. Both pilots enjoyed a high degree of public acclaim, Bayles for winning the 1931 Thompson Trophy Race and Odom for his globe girdling and long distance record flights. A degree of mystery still shrouds both accidents.

Bill Odom's crash into a Berea, Ohio, home killing a mother and her small child was infinitely more tragic. In spite of a post-crash investigation, the cause of Odom's accident was never specifically identified. Rumors, myths, and a plethora of opinions developed in the days and weeks following the accident. What follows is a more in-depth look at the pilot, the aircraft and the accident.

The Pilot

Bill Odom was a tall, slim, balding young man of 29 when he was killed in the explosion and fiery crash of the *Mustang* named *Beguine*. He was a type "A" personality, always active and seemingly engaged in an unending series of aviation projects. He seemed to enjoy public as well as peer recognition. Raised in Kansas City, Bill attended a local high school and junior college. He learned to fly at the Kansas City Municipal Airport before the war. During the war, he ferried aircraft and simultaneously sharpened his skills at long distance flight and navigation. He made thirty-six crossings of the Atlantic delivering aircraft to England.[1] Most of his flying experience consisted of long distance missions in large multi-engine aircraft.

In 1946, Bill entered a Republic P-47M-1-RE in the Bendix Trophy Race. He arrived at Van Nuys airport for the race but failed to start because of a rough running engine. In his book about the Bendix, author Don Dwiggins relates that later a steel needle was found imbedded in the engine ignition cabling.[2]

At some point in time, probably early 1947, Bill Odom became associated with Milton J. Reynolds of Chicago. Milton Reynolds was chairman of the Reynolds Pen Company. He had become well known and wealthy with the invention of the ball point pen which his company manufactured. Reynolds could afford to indulge himself. He was a private pilot and veteran airline traveler. Why did he become fascinated with a trip around the globe? Franklin Lamb, president of the Reynolds company quoted Milton Reynolds as saying: "Some people collect stamps, some buttons. I want to break the 'round-the-world record."[3] He found a willing accomplice in Bill Odom. As a young boy of thirteen, Odom met world flyer Wiley Post and received an autographed fragment of Post's record setting "Winnie May." Moved by the gift and the famous pilot, Bill Odom promised Wiley that he too would someday fly around the world. With Reynold's backing, he seized the opportunity to keep a childhood promise. Together, the two men planned to secure the record which at that time was owned by Howard Hughes and established in 1938.

The gestation period for this was rather brief. It was conceived on Friday, 17 March and three days later Reynolds bought A Douglas A-26B from Harold Talbot of Connecticut, who in turn had purchased the aircraft from the War Assets Administration.[4] About the same time, Reynolds signed Bill Odom to a contract to fly the airplane. The aircraft was flown to New York's Roosevelt Field, stripped of non-essential equipment and stuffed with fuel tanks. It was christened the *Reynolds Bombshell*. Plans for the globe-circling flight were announced publicly on March 29. The flight was to be launched from La Guardia Airport the following Saturday. Difficulties, reported in the press as mechanical, delayed takeoff. Departure was switched to Newark Airport across the river. Airport management denied permission for the takeoff three days later. Finally, on Saturday, April 13, the flight was underway having departed from La Guardia after all.

A new world record was established when 78 hours, 55 minutes later, Odom touched down once again at La Guardia. The feat brought Bill Odom into immediate prominence within the aviation community and the American public. Quite literally, he was front page news. When the flight ended on April 16, Odom, together with Reynolds and flight engineer Carroll "Tex" Sallee, had surpassed Howard Hughes' around-the-world flight by more than 12 hours. Two days later, the entire crew was congratulated by President Harry Truman during a visit to the White House.

Bill Odom would make a second global flight in the *Bombshell* just four months later. This time he would do it solo. His second flight covered over 19,000 miles and he completed it in three days, one hour, and five minutes. On top of this herculean schedule, Odom again entered his P-47M in the 1947 Bendix Trophy Race. Milton Reynolds provided at least some sponsorship for the Bendix entry. This World War II fighter also carried the name *Reynolds Bombshell*. Odom arrived on the West Coast but again was unable to start. This time the cause was a fuel leakage problem.[5]

Odom appears to have plunged into these various record breaking projects always with enthusiasm, however, frequently with minimal lead time. He was a skilled pilot with multi-engine aircraft on flights over long distances. No one denied his skills in this area. One of his goals was to circumnavigate the globe flying over both poles. He visited Douglas Aircraft regarding the use of wing tip tanks to improve the range of the Douglas A-26B Invader. Chief Engineer Ed Heinemann responded to Odom's visit with a lengthy letter providing results of engineering calculations made to determine acceptable fuel load conditions and corresponding ranges for various configurations of the Douglas airplane.[6] One suggestion made by Heinemann was possible use of Jet Assisted Takeoff (JATO) rockets manufactured by Aerojet Corporation for takeoffs with extreme loads.

During 1948, Odom's married life was deteriorating. He was romantically linked to a nineteen-year-old beauty named Evelyn Thompson of Plandome, New York. His wife, Dorothy Odom, traveled across country to Reno, Nevada, which was known at that time for relaxed requirements in matters of divorce. On September 28, she sued for divorce.[7] It was granted and she won a court settlement giving her custody of their two children. Dorothy Odom returned to New York and settled in Ithaca. A few months later, Bill was engaged to Evelyn Thompson of Manhasset, Long Island; he kept this romance very private. Even with this turmoil, Bill Odom remained preoccupied with flying during 1948. He made the newspapers again with a forced landing in Chesapeake Bay while piloting a four engine flying boat with 92 passengers on a trip from Puerto Rico to New York. Undaunted, he made a trip to China in search of a mountain peak supposedly higher than Mount Everest.

With his personal life reshaped, Odom once again set out to capture new records. At some point in this period, Odom connected with Walter H. Beech, founder of Beech Aircraft Corporation. Bill's objective was to fly non-stop from Hawaii to Teterboro, New Jersey, in a light plane. Walter Beech provided the airplane and financing toward this objective. Odom departed Honolulu in a new Beechcraft Bonanza named the "Waikiki Beech" and headed for the mainland in the middle of January, 1949. He made it as far as Oakland, California. In spite of not reaching his goal, he nonetheless established a light aircraft distance record of 2,406 miles.[8] On Odom's next attempt in March, he successfully flew the Bonanza non-stop from the Islands to Teterboro, New Jersey, setting yet another light plane record. Walter Beech and Bill Odom became well acquainted. Somehow, Bill learned of the *Beguine* project, possibly from Walter Beech. Odom wanted to add the Thompson Trophy to his laurels.

Bill Odom's adventures limited him frequently to personal service contracts with his sponsors. Perhaps sensing a need for something more permanent, he decided to open a business. By June of 1949, he was forming a new enterprise, the Odom Aviation Corporation. On 7 July, he opened for business at Teterboro Airport.[9] This was a flying center for pilot instruction, charter flights and aircraft maintenance. One of the twenty people working for him was his old flight engineer, Carroll Sallee, from his first round-the-world record flight.

Bill was also writing a series of articles concerning flight safety for "Skyways" magazine. He continued to plan a world flight via the North and South Poles. Bill Odom was popular and he was busy. He was guest speaker at the Corporate Aircraft Owners Association meeting in August of 1949, just weeks before the race.[10] With all of these interests and ongoing activities, Bill, Jackie Cochran, and Walter Beech were focusing on the acquisition of J.D. Reed's *Beguine* racer for a shot at the Thompson Trophy Race. Walter Beech prevailed and Reed sold the airplane on Monday, 22 August 1949.[11] This was fifteen days before the fatal crash. When the racer was turned over to Bill and Jackie Cochran, pilot Ken Cooley briefed Odom and gave him a checkout prior to his first flight in the P-51 at Houston. This had to of occured on or after 22 August. Ken recalls that Odom may have made two flights around or near the field at the time. He subsequently flew the aircraft to Cleveland, spent some time familiarizing himself with the race course, and then qualified. Aside from this, Odom flew one race, the Sohio Trophy event on 3 September, which offered only modest competition. He won the race handily. Two days later, he crashed.

The Airplane

Wing Geometry. *Beguine* was the product of Walter Beech's innovative thinking. It was Beech who approached J.D. Reed with the concept for a radically modified Mustang to compete in the National Air Races. At some point in their discussions, Walter proposed that one wing of the racer should be shortened more than the other, about six inches Reed recalled years later. The aerodynamic reasoning remains a mystery. Reed remembers Beech discoursing on the subject, ". . . for an hour." J.D. readily admitted he was not an engineer, so the reasons for making one wing shorter than the other, ". . . were beyond my understanding." Clevelander Mike Kusenda relates that the *Beguine* racer became controversial even before the races.[12] Mike recalled rumors about the *Beguine* wing panels being of different lengths. Various numbers were bandied about. Earl Ortman told Mike that "eighteen inches" had been removed from the left wing. This figure became persistent during race week and, seemingly, forever after. Even J.D. Reed quoted that number years later during an interview. More conclusive, however, are wing panel measurements made from enlarged photographs showing a full front view of the aircraft after it was completed in 1948. Absolutely no difference can be measured between the left and right wing panels in the original as-built configuration. An interview with Virgil Thompson, who was instrumental in the original modification program for *Beguine*, failed to add any validity to the asymmetric wing idea. Thompson's recollection was that oil and glycol heat exchangers (radiators) were attached directly to the ends of the wing spars. This was the only way to take out structural loads imposed by these components. J.D. Reed said in another telephone interview that no structural changes were made to the wings while the airplane was in Houston, in 1949. Another bit of evidence on the subject is found in the entry form for the *Beguine* racer submitted by J.D. Reed for the 1949 races. The wing span is listed at just slightly over 36 feet (36.046) This is precisely the value one would obtain by removing the production tip panels and installing FJ-1 tip tanks.[13]

The final and most conclusive piece of evidence relative to the *Beguine* wing panels was obtained in 1991 from Ed Horkey who provided technical consultation to the project during 1948. Ed stated emphatically that the wing panels were identical in length. What about the modifications made during 1949? J.D. Reed said no changes to the wing were made in Houston. This was confirmed by Ken Cooley who conducted all the tests during the summer of that year. Was one wing shorter than the other? No! How this idea was started shall perhaps always be a mystery.

Drag and Weight Reduction. Was removal of the *Mustang* belly scoop beneficial to overall drag reduction on the racer? And did this change result in reduced airframe empty weight? The answer to both questions would seem to be no.

A North American engineering report summarizes aerodynamic characteristics for the P-51B and C models including frontal area and surface area in specific detail.[14] Comparison of these data with calculations made of the modified *Beguine* show the racer had more frontal area (5.3 percent), increased overall surface area (3.9 percent), and a wing plan form greater (4.7 percent) than the stock C model.[15] The impact of these figures is a drag penalty. This is a penalty which rises exponentially with increasing aircraft speed. On the positive side, addition of the tip pods increased the effective aspect ratio of the wing which was beneficial. With regard to weight, the 1949 National Air Race entry form for *Beguine* indicates 6773 pounds empty. The military P-51C has an empty weight around 7010 pounds.[16] Net weight reduction on the *Beguine* racer was thus less than 240 pounds or about 3.3 percent. J.D. Reed's bronze race number 37 P-51D was basically the same weight as *Beguine*.

There were several factors contributing to limited weight reduction during conversion of the aircraft into a racing machine. Each wing tip pod, including fittings, B-50 radiators, liquid and the external shell or housing weighed about 200 pounds. Coupled with this weight were 70 to 80 feet of lines (plumbing) with tie down fittings delivering oil and coolant to the radiators and then returning these fluids to the engine and supercharger. These lines were filled with fluid at all times. The weight of both fluid and lines increased before the 1949 race when larger diameter lines were installed. The amount of coolant plumbing in *Beguine* far exceeds that required for a stock P-51 *Mustang*.

Another factor contributing to the weight of *Beguine* was the engine. Odom ran with a dash 9 *Merlin*. Anson Johnson and two other racing *Mustangs* from that era used dash 225 *Merlins* with single stage superchargers. These engines were about 240 pounds lighter than the *Merlin* in Odom's airplane.[17] The dash 225 was a low altitude engine and a good choice for the Cleveland race course situated at near sea level. By comparison, todays ultra-fast *Mustangs* have empty weights ranging from about 5900 to 6500 pounds. *Beguine* was a relatively heavy racer based upon empty weight. Gross weight at takeoff for the Thompson is estimated to have been between 9750 and 9800 pounds. The racer would have carried about 260 gallons of fuel (1560 pounds), at least 100 gallons of water-alcohol injection fluid (875 pounds), 21 gallons of oil (157 pounds) and perhaps 25 gallons of ethylene glycol (218 pounds). Allowing another 200 pounds for the pilot and a parachute, gross weight at takeoff was estimated at 9770 pounds. At the time of the crash, Odom would have consumed something like 180 to 200 pounds of fuel and another 90 pounds water, making the aircraft weight at impact something less than 9500 pounds.

Performance. Maximum speed of the *Beguine* racer can only be estimated. No documentation exits. Jackie Cochran told the press that she had flown the racer, ". . . in a tryout at an indicated speed of 515 miles an hour."[18] Claims of 500 plus mile per hour speeds must be taken with a grain of salt, to use an old expression. Consider that the Red Baron RB-51 *Mustang* set a three kilometer piston engine speed record of just under 500 miles per hour in August, 1979. This airplane was powered by a Roll-Royce Griffon engine of considerably more displacement and horsepower than the *Beguine* dash 9 *Merlin*. Anson Johnson's *Mustang*, which unsuccessfully attempted to capture this record in 1952, reached "something in excess of 450 miles per hour."[19] Odom qualified his racer at just over 405 miles per hour. Both Cook Cleland and Dick Becker qualified faster at 414 and 407 miles an hour, respectively.[20]

Odom's qualification speed around the seven pylon course suggests he probably reached 410 to 415 miles an hour on the relatively short, straight segments. This is estimated to be within fifteen miles per hour of the maximum speed the aircraft was capable of achieving. By deduction, Anson Johnson's *Mustang* was somewhat faster. It was also aerodynamically cleaner and probably had a lower empty weight. Neither airplane in their 1949 configurations could match the all-out straight-away speeds of contemporary championship *Mustangs*.

The Accident

The race course in 1949 was defined by seven pylons and was run counter-clockwise. Available information does not reveal where Bill Odom was during the chaotic race horse start of the Thompson. He was probably not in the lead at takeoff. Odom completed the first lap of the race. At that point, he was in third place behind Ben McKillen in first and Cook Cleland in second, both flying Goodyear F2G *Corsairs*.[21] Steve Beville was trailing Odom in another P-51 *Mustang*. Ron Puckett, also flying an F2G, was in fifth just behind Beville. Flying at an altitude of about 200 feet, Bill Odom overturned home pylon moving inside the race course. Civil Aeronautics Administration investigators reported that Odom turned through maybe 60 degrees going around the pylon instead of the 35 to 40 degrees necessary to line up on pylon two.[22] Realizing his error, he rolled out of the left bank into a right turn to regain the course. Instead of leveling off, the racer continued to roll right becoming inverted. The nose of the P-51 dropped 30 degrees and the airplane plunged inverted into a Berea, Ohio, home belonging to Mr. and Mrs. Bradley C. Laird. The accident happened at 4:48 p.m.

There were many conflicting stories related in newspaper accounts of the accident. However, there were at least three excellent witnesses to the fatal accident, one on the ground in proximity to the event and the other two flying the race course just behind Odom. One of the witnesses was Mike Kusenda, who at the time was working with the Columbia Broadcasting System people in a mobile radio broadcasting truck heading for pylon two when *Beguine* crashed. Mike was located south of the home pylon and east of pylon two, inside the course. He saw Odom sharply overturn home pylon, correct and continue rolling right into the inverted position. The second eye witness was Steve Beville, flying the *Galloping Ghost* right behind *Beguine* when the accident happened.

Beville recalls that Odom was flying in close proximity during most of the first lap. Odom would close the gap between *Beguine* and the *Galloping Ghost* on the straight-away segments of the course, but lose ground on the turns. Beville momentarily lost sight of *Beguine* at one point during lap one, only to discover that Bill Odom had irrationally (and dangerously) passed underneath to gain third position.

Beville trailed Odom around home pylon at the beginning of the second lap. He observed Odom overturn the pylon as if heading straight for pylon three, then roll right to a point where the plane went on its back, then crash.[23] Ron Puckett was trailing in third and saw the maneuver Bill Odom went through; however, he didn't see the impact.

Cause of the Accident?

Part of the answer to this question is that Odom momentarily lost sight of his heading landmarks and overturned home pylon. He made a human error. This started a fast moving chain of events leading to the crash. What occurred next – the corrective right bank and continued roll to the inverted position – has been called a high-speed stall by some contemporary reporters as well as later historians. A stall is simply a condition where the wing no longer generates sufficient lift to support the weight of the airplane. This condition can exist in level flight as well as in a turn. When a turn is initiated, centrifugal force adds to the load on the airplane and on the pilot as well. This is called "g" load or force. If the banking aircraft is subjected to a high enough g load, it can stall even when moving at high speed. Odom was running *Beguine* at close to 400 miles an hour in an aircraft weighing 9500 pounds. If during his corrective right roll he experienced as much as a 6 g force (which is high), the racer should not normally have stalled.[24] Under these assumed conditions, stall speed would have been about 280 miles per hour, leaving a comfortable positive margin.

A number of other aerodynamic factors could have adversely played a part in Odom's maneuver, thus increasing the effective g load. For instance, the *Beguine* center of gravity early in the race may have been near the aft limit. If this were true, the (control) stick force gradient may have been very light. In sensing his incorrect flight path, Odom may have reacted with some violence on the control stick, loading up the aircraft far more rapidly than normal. At race altitude, recovery in a *Mustang* entering a stall would have been impossible for Bill Odom or any other pilot. It is also quite possible that his vision became impaired or that his head hit the cockpit canopy structure. Because the seat was elevated to accept the new water-methanol tank, Odom had little if any clearance.

Ed Horkey relates that in 1948 when the racer was modified, addition of the wing tip pods had the aerodynamic effect of increasing the wing span and aspect ratio which decreased the longitudinal stability and control characteristics to some extent. To counteract the possibility of a pilot applying excessive force to the control stick during a maneuver, a bob weight was added to the bottom of the control stick. As the control stick was displaced through a greater distance and during increased g loads caused by the maneuver, more force was required on the part of the pilot. What Ed does not know is whether the bob weight was still in place during the 1949 Thompson Trophy Race when the accident occured.

Ken Cooley was asked about the flying qualities of *Beguine* based upon his experiences performing the test flights prior to the 1949 races. Ken's response was that *Beguine* flying characteristics were essentially the same as a military *Mustang*. He was flying Texas Air National Guard P-51s weekly at the same time he flew the racer and this offered a good opportunity for comparison. Ken realized that one pod was heavier; however, the difference was slight with respect to controlling the airplane. It was just something that the pilot sensed and automatically compensated for during a maneuver.

What really happened? No one will ever know for sure. What can be said, however, is that Bill Odom was much more familiar with high altitude, multi-engine aircraft operation. The entire *Beguine* project was hastily put together. He did not have much time in the racer. Ground hugging pylon flying in a modified fighter aircraft was a new experience for him. His judgement was flawed when he illegally passed Steve Beville during the first lap. These factors, coupled with stress due to a multitude of activities, the race, and a drive to win brought *Beguine* and Bill Odom to a fatal ending.

Notes

1. *New York Times*. September 6, 1949.
2. Dwiggins, Don, *They Flew the Bendix Race*, J.B. Lippincott Company, Philadelphia, 1965, page 127.
3. *New York Times*, Wednesday, 16 April 1949, page 3.
4. *New York Times*, 16 April 1947, page 3. The aircraft was licensed N67834 and carried AAF serial 44-34759.
5. Ibid., page 127. Interestingly, the same P-47 appears to have been entered in the Bendix race a third time in 1948. Jane Page was ferrying the craft from Dallas, Texas to Burbank, California. En route, she landed at Amarillo and blew out one of the tires. Once again, the jinxed airplane failed to start. The episode was reported by the Los Angeles Times, 15 August 1948.
6. Letter from E.H. Heinemann to William P. Odom, undated.
7. *New York Times*, 29 September 1948, page 12.
8. Ironically, Walter Beech received a copy of the "Certificate of Record" confirming the Honolulu, Hawaii to Oakland, California, flight as an "International Straight Line Distance Record," from the Federation Aeronautique Internationale via C.S. Logsdon, a director of the National Aeronautic Association. The certificate was dated 17 December 1949, and was to have been presented to Odom in Washington, D.C. This was a little more than two months after Bill Odom died. Source is correspondence with attachments to C.S. Logsdon from Walter H. Beech, dated 22 December 1949.
9. *New York Times*, Friday, 8 July 1949, page 37.
10. See Editor's Note, *Skyways Magazine*, November 1949, page 57.
11. Reed canceled the sporting license (necessary for entry into the races) by Western Union telegraph, addressed to C.S. Logsdon, Director of Contests Division, National Auronautics Association, dated 22 August 1949.
12. Written correspondence from Mike Kusenda to Dustin Carter dated 22 October 1985.
13. General arrangement drawing, FJ-1 Fury, North American Aviation, Inc., May 1950.
14. Waite, L.L., "Aerodynamic Dimensional Data on P-51B and P-51C Airplanes," North American Aviation, Inc., Report No. NA 5822, 6 August 1943.
15. The radiator pods are included in the wing plan form for the Beguine racer.
16. Gruenhagen, Robert W., *Mustang*, revised edition, Arco Publishing, Inc., New York, 1980. Page 176.
17. One of these racers was J.D. Reed's P-51, race 37.
18. *New York Times*, Tuesday, 6 September 1949, page 1. Jackie Cochran went on to say that she planned to attack several more speed records with Beguine.
19. O'Keefe, Phillip C., "The Saga of N13Y," *Journal of the American Aviation Historical Society*, Vol. 19, No. 4, 1974. Page 292.
20. "Official Standing of Contestants," 1949 National Air Races, Qualification and Race Results published by the contest committee, Cleveland, Ohio, September 1949.
21. National Air and Space Museum (Washington, D.C.) archive data provided courtesy of Walter Boyne, Director, circa 1988.
22. *New York Times*, Tuesday, 6 September 1949. Page 2.
23. Video tape recording courtesy of Oliver Aldrich of a talk given by Steve Beville before the Seventh Annual Air Racing History Symposium, 4 May 1991. See also contemporary press reports.
24. One would anticipate at least momentary visual impairment of the pilot as a minimum physiological condition when subjected to a six g force. This, if it indeed happened, would have added to his loss of orientation on the race course.

SELECTED BIBLIOGRAPHY
BIBLIOGRAPHICAL COMMENTS

The subject of air racing is a difficult field to research. There is a decided lack of documentation specifically treating technical aspects of this subject. Unlike routine engineering or business projects, there is frequently no requirement to generate reports. Calculations are made and the answers then translated into metal. Some modifications are made intuitively and are devoid of any record.

Another reason, one suspects, is a desire on the part of participants to keep at least some of the information to themselves. This is not unreasonable in that air racing, like any sport, is competitive and certainly expensive. This is especially true in context with contemporary air racers. A competitive advantage is a fragile and often fleeting thing. In spite of these factors, research on this project was surprisingly rewarding with respect to the degree of cooperation from those individuals associated with air racing, past and present. For this reason, emphasis was placed upon the many interviews conducted and transcribed for input to the story.

Three areas basic to unlimited air racing are well documented. In fact there is a rich body of literature to be mined in each. These are: Aerodynamics, piston engine development and the chemistry of fuels. In this context, heavy reliance was placed upon the many engineering and scientific texts and documents available on these subjects.

Wherever possible, background and detail information was verified through more than one source. The following primary sources are grouped according to category.

BOOKS

Banks, F.R., *I Kept No Diary*, Airlife Publishing Ltd., Shrewsbury, England. Revised 1983.

Burge, C.G., Editor, *Air Annual of the British Empire*, 1931-1932 and 1936-1937 editions, Gale & Polden Ltd., London.

Birch, David, *Rolls-Royce and the Mustang,* Rolls-Royce Heritage Trust, Derby, England. 1987.

Byttenbier, Hugo T., *The Curtiss D-12 Aero Engine*, Smithsonian Institution Press, Washington, D.C. 1972.

Domonoske, Arthur B. and Volney C. Finch, *Aircraft Engines*, John Wiley & Sons, Inc., New York. 1936.

Fraas, Arthur P., *Aircraft Power Plants*, McGraw-Hill Book Company, Inc., New York. 1943.

Gruenhagen, Robert, *Mustang*, Arco Publishing Co., New York. Revised 1976.

Gruse, William A., *Chemical Technology of Petroleum*, John Wiley & Sons, New York. 1960.

Gunston, Bill, *Rolls-Royce Aero Engines*, Patrick Stephens Limited, Thorsons Publishing Group, Northamptonshire, England. 1989.

Gunston, Bill, *World Encyclopaedia of Aero Engines*, Second Edition, Patrick Stephens Limited, Thorsons Publishing Group, Northamptonshire, England. 1989.

Harvey-Bailey, Alec, *The Merlin in Perspective - The Combat Years*, Rolls-Royce Heritage Trust, Derby, England. 1983.

Hawley, Gessner G., *The Condensed Chemical Dictionary*, 10th Edition, Van Nostrand Reinhold Company, New York. 1981.

Hobson, G.D., *Modern Petroleum Technology*, John Wiley & Sons, New York. 1973.

Hooker, Sir Stanley, *Not Much of an Engineer*, Airlife Publishing Ltd., Shrewsbury, England. 1984.

Hull, Robert, *A Season of Eagles*, Robert Hull Books, Bay Village, Ohio. 1984.

Hull, Robert, *September Champions*, Stackpole Books, Harrisburg, Pennsylvania. 1979.

Huntington, Roger, *Thompson Trophy Racers*, Motorbooks International, Osceola, Wisconsin. 1989.

James, Derek N., *Schneider Trophy Aircraft*, Putnam & Co., Ltd., London. 1981.

Larsen, Jim, *Air Racers*, American Air Museum, Inc., Kirkland, Washington. 1971.

Moss, Sanford A., *Superchargers for Aviation*, National Aeronautics Council, Inc., New York. 1941.

Perry, Robert H., et al., Editors, *Perry's Chemical Engineer's Handbook*, Fourth Edition, McGraw-Hill Book Company, Inc., New York. 1963.

Rogowski, A.R., *Elements of Internal Combustion Engines*, McGraw-Hill Book Company, Inc., New York. 1953

Sloan, Alfred P. Jr., *My Years With General Motors*, Doubleday & Company, Inc., New York. 1964.

Taylor, C.F. and E.S. Taylor, *The Internal Combustion Engine*, International Textbook Co., New York. 1948.

Schlaifer, Robert and S.D. Heron, *Development of Aircraft Engines and Development of Aviation Fuels*, Graduate School of Business Administration, Harvard University, Andover Press, Andover, MA. 1950.

Setwright, L.T.J., *The Power to Fly*, George Allen & Unwin Ltd., London. 1971.

Smith, Herschel, *A History of Aircraft Piston Engines*, Sunflower University Press, Manhattan, Kansas. 1981.

Sweetman, Bill, *High Speed Flight*, Janes Publishing Co., Ltd., London. 1984.

Tegler, John, *Gentlemen, You Have A Race*, Wings Publishing Company, Severna Park, Maryland. 1984.

Wagner, Ray, *Mustang Designer*, Orion Books, New York. 1990.

Weast, Robert C., Editor, *Handbook of Chemistry and Physics*, 67th Edition, CRC Press, Boca Raton, Florida. 1986.

PERIODICALS

Anon., "Thompson Trophy Symbolizes Speed Supremacy in Skies", *The Friendly Forum*, (Thompson Products company newspaper), January 1951.

Anon., "Odom to Race," *Aviation Week*, 29 August 1949.

Anon., "Dot Lemon Enters Houston Speedrun," *Western Flying*, 7 April 1949.

Anon., "Cooley Test-Pilots 'The Beguine,'" *Pipeliner* (Shell Oil Company Magazine), circa summer 1949.

Berliner, Don, "Unlimited!," *Air Britain Digest*, Vol. 36, No. 4, July-August, 1984.

Cox, Jack, "Tsunami," *Sport Aviation*, December 1986.

Evernden, Evan, "Sir Henry Royce," (The First Sir Henry Royce Memorial Lecture), *The Royal Aeronautical Society Journal*, Vol. 60, No. 552, December 1956. See in particular, the discussion section regarding the comments of Major G. P. Bulman.

Kettering, Charles F., "Fuels and Engines for Higher Power and Greater Efficiency," *Journal of the Society of Automotive Engineers*, Vol. 53, No. 6, 1945.

Larsen, Jim, "The Making of a Champion," *National Aeronautics Magazine*, Summer Issue, 1973.

Liming, Roy A. and Carter M. Hartley, "Lofting Problems of Streamline Bodies," *Aero Digest*, 1 April 1945 and 1 July 1945.

Lovesey, A.C., "Development of the Rolls-Royce Merlin from 1939 to 1945," *Aircraft Engineering*, July 1946.

Matthews, Birch, "Cobra," *Journal of the American Aviation Historical Society*, Vol. 8, No. 3, 1963.

McCarthy, Mike, "Merlin - The Wizard of the War," *Old Motor*, September, 1981.

McLarren, Robert, "More Original Designs Would Help National Air Races," *Automotive Industries*, 1 October 1948.

McLarren, Robert, "Technical Interest Seen in Racers," *Aviation Week*, 13 September 1948.

McLarren, Robert, "Workmanship Pays Off in the Races," *Aviation Week*, 13 September 1949.

Nelson, William R., "The North American P-51 Mustang," *Aviation*, July 1944.

O'Keefe, Phillip C, "The Saga of N13Y," *Journal of the American Aviation Historical Society*, Vol. 19, No. 4, 1974.

Overstreet, Robert, "Ken Cooley Puts Reed Beguine Through Tough, Testing Dive," *Houston Press*, circa 1 July 1949.

Phelps, Mark, "The Oldest Mustang," *Sport Aviation*, May 1989.

Reeder, Jack, "The Mustang Story," *Sport Aviation*, September,1983.

Sherman, Scott and Kent Sherman, "Racing Stiletto," *Air Classics*, Vol. 25, No. 4, April 1989.

Tegler, John, "RB-51 Red Baron," *Western Flyer*, March 1975.

ORAL HISTORY

Steve Beville: Video tape recording made of speech to the Society of Air Race Historians, 4 May 1991. Beville discusses modifications made to the "Galloping Ghost" as well as his recollections of seeing Bill Odom crash. Recorded by Oliver Aldrich.

Bruce Boland, Pete Law and Ray Poe: Audio recording of an interview by Birch Matthews and Dusty Carter, 23 November 1985. Documents aerodynamic, engine and support system modifications made to unlimited class racers.

Ken Cooley: Audio/video recordings of an interview made by Oliver Aldrich, 2 October 1991. Cooley describes his flight testing of the Beguine racer prior to the sale of the airplane to Floyd Odlum. This interview documented that there was no difference in the left and right wing span in 1949.

Bill DeStefani: Transcribed notes of an interview conducted by Dustin Carter, circa 1987. Interview covered modifications made to "Strega," Bill's highly modified P-51 championship racer.

Al Heinike: Notes transcribed of interviews by Birch Matthews circa July 1988. Subject of interview was the dual fuel system installed on the Maytag Mustang.

Ed Horkey: Interview conducted by Oliver Aldrich and Birch Matthews on audio and video tape, 14 September 1991. This tape discusses the initial aerodynamic modifications to the Beguine racer in 1948. Ed Horkey states emphatically that there was no difference in the span of the left and right wing panels.

Ed Horkey: A second interview of Ed Horkey was made by Jeff Compton on 25 October 1991. The subject again was the Beguine racer.

Jimmie Leeward: Telephone interview concerning Merlin engine operating parameters and limits of reliability, later transcribed to audio tape by Birch Matthews, 17 February 1986.

P.J. "Sep" Mighton: Correspondence and notes of (various) interviews by Jerry Skinner circa 1963. Discussed the innovations and history of Earl Ortman's P-51 entrant in the 1946 races at Cleveland.

Wilson Newhall: Audio recording of speech presented to Chicago historians, 2 May 1964. Recorded by John Andrews and provided courtesy of Tony Yusken. Speech documents his participation in the Cleveland races.

Mike Nixon: Audio recording of an interview by Birch Matthews, 1 July 1986. Mike Nixon explained the various modifications made to Merlin engines to make them competitive.

Maryette Ortman: Various letters of correspondence from wife of the late Earl Ortman to Birch Matthews circa 1963-1964. Describes her remembrances of the 1946 races with her husband.

J.D. Reed: Audio recording of an interview by Oliver Aldrich, 19 February 1986. This tape documents the memories of Reed with respect to the Beguine racer.

J.D. Reed: Audio recording of an interview by Kurt Voss on 10 August 1989. Tape recounts Reed's recollections of the Beguine racer.

Russ Schleeh: Transcribed notes from a telephone interview by Birch Matthews, circa July 1988. Recounts his memories of flying the Maytag Mustang with the dual fuel system as well as the pre-race accident that eliminated the airplane from the Reno races.

Lyle Shelton: Transcribed notes of a telephone interview by Birch Matthews, circa 1986. Lyle recounted his experience flying a Mustang at Reno in the early years.

Virgil Thompson: Audio recording of an interview by Dustin Carter, 18 September 1985. This oral history describes Virgil's work on the construction of Beguine in 1948.

Charles Walling: Audio recording of an interview by Oliver Aldrich, 19 February 1986. Tape includes some memories of Beguine during the 1948-1949 era.

Dave Zueschel: Transcribed notes of an interview by Dustin Carter, circa 1986. Reveals some of the methods used by Zueschel to modify Merlins for air racing. Interview also included modifications made to racing Mustangs.

DOCUMENTS

Abbott, Ira H., Albert E. von Doenhoff and Louis S. Stivers, Jr., "Summary of Airfoil Data," NACA Report No. 824, 5 March 1945.

Anon., "P-51D Maintenance Manual," North American Aviation, Inc., Report No. NA-8248, 1 December 1944.

Anon., "Mark Number Chart for Rolls-Royce Piston Engines," Production Drawing Office, Rolls-Royce Ltd. Derby, England, February 1953

Anon., Letter dated 26 November 1957, to Civil Aeronautics Administration from District Director of Internal Revenue, documenting the sale of P-51D Mustang license N79111 on 28 October 1954, by Jack B. Hardwick to one I. S. Schwartz, believed to have been a purchasing agent for the Israeli government. Document originally obtained by Dick Phillips.

Department of Commerce, Civil Aeronautics Administration file on North American P-51D, NX4845N (Beguine racer). Various documents covering the existence of this racer when purchased by Paul Mantz until Jacqueline Cochran applied to have the aircraft removed from the CAA records on 16 September 1949. File provided courtesy of Kevin Grantham via Oliver Aldrich.

Hoerner, Sighard F., "Aerodynamic Shape of the Wing Tips," U.S. Air Force, Wright-Patterson Air Force Base, Technical Report No. 5752, 1949.

Hoerner, Sighard F., "Fluid-Dynamic Drag," published by the author, Brick Town, N.J., revised edition, 1965.

Jacobs, Eastman N., "Preliminary Report on Laminar Flow Airfoils and New Methods Adopted for Airfoil and Boundary Layer Investigations," NACA Report, 25 April 1939.

Liming, Roy A., "Master Wing Ordinate Chart," North American Aviation, Inc., 5 June 1942.

Lippincott, Harvey H., "Blade Assembly," Drawing SK-12853, Hamilton-Standard Propellers via United Technologies, correspondence dated 17 July 1986.

Meixner, Bill, "Race Plane Crashes in Berea," undated. Bill Meixner researched and prepared an unpublished manuscript covering the details of Bill Odom's crash into a Berea, Ohio home.

Phillips, Dick, Letter dated 10 June 1991, to Birch Matthews describing sale of N79111 to Israeli agents and the use of this license number for other aircraft circa 1952-1954. These details were uncovered by Dick Phillips by employing the "Freedom of Information Act."

Reed, J.D., "National Air Race Entry Form," for P51C, N4845N, (Beguine) and pilot Kenneth C. Cooley, dated 8 August 1949.

Reed, J.D., "National Air Race Entry Form," for P-51D, N37492, and pilot James P. Hagerstrom, dated 8 August 1949.

Sweeney, Jack, "Water Injection Servo, Model WI-1," UHU Corporation, 12 February 1979. Describes water injection system installed in John Crocker's racing Mustang.

Voglewede, T.J. and E.C.B. Danforth, "Flight Tests of the High-Speed Performance of a P-51B Airplane," NACA Memorandum Report No. L4L18, 18 December 1944.

Wait, Louis S., "Briefing for P-51 Pilot Instructors," North American Aviation, Inc., Report No. 8679, 8 August 1945.

Waite, L.L., "Aerodynamic Dimensional Data on P-51B-l-NA, P-51B-5-NA and P-51C-1-NT," North American Aviation, Inc., Report No. NA 5822, 6 August 1943.

NEWSPAPERS

Anthony (Kansas) Republican: September 9, 1948. This source provided an account of the forced landing of Beguine in 1948, while enroute to Cleveland.

Cleveland News: Various editions, 1946-1949. One of two evening newspapers in Cleveland which covered the National Air Races all four post-war years.

Cleveland Plain Dealer: Various editions, 1946 -1949. Cleveland morning newspaper covered the races all four years. Background source material on the races.

Cleveland Press: Various editions, 1946-1949. Cleveland's other evening newspaper provided coverage each year of the races. Paper featured Charles Tracy as aviation editor. Excellent background source of information.

Fresno Bee: Various editions in 1948. General information on the races via wire reports.

New York Times: Various editions, 1946-1949. Feature articles on the air races.

Index

About the authors:

The late **Dusty Carter** was a retired North American Rockwell aerospace engineer with more than forty years experience as a designer of aircraft systems and space vehicles. He was supervisor of the conceptual design group that evolved the Space Shuttle Orbiter design. At retirement he was in charge of advanced design concepts for the Space Shuttle program.

Dusty's interest and fascination with air racing began in 1936 when he attended his first National Air Race at Mines Field, later to become Los Angeles International Airport. From that point forward, he avidly followed the sport and attended many of the national racing events. A product of his interest was a previous book, *Race Planes and Air Races*, Volume XIII, by Aero Publishers, Fallbrook, California. In addition, Dusty wrote articles on contemporary air racing as well as air race history for foreign publications, notably *le fanatique de L'AVIATION* published in Paris, France. He wrote a number of articles for the *Journal of the American Aviation Historical Society* on a variety of historical subjects. He was an avid photographer and his photographs were published in a variety books, journals and magazines.

Dustin Carter was a founding member of the American Aviation Historical Society which began operations in 1956. He served on the Society's Board of Directors for approximately fifteen years, ten years as elected President.

He was born and raised in Los Angeles, California. Dusty attended trade school as an aeronautical engineering student and went directly into the aircraft industry as an engineer. During his long career, he worked for many of the aircraft manufacturers in Southern California.

Birch Matthews, a senior engineer with TRW Space and Defense Sector in Redondo Beach, California, has had a life-long interest in aviation history with emphasis on aircraft technical development. His enthusiasm for air racing began when he attended the National Air Races in Cleveland, Ohio, in 1946. A past president and ten year member of the Board of Directors for the American Aviation Historical Society, Birch has written eleven historical articles on racing, Bell Aircraft fighters, the Merlin engine, and aviation fuels which were published in the Society's Journal. In addition, he published a monograph on the Bell P-39 Airacobra which was presented at the Los Angeles symposium on "Fifty Years of Fighter Aircraft Development."

For a period of two years, Birch regularly wrote columns about contemporary air racing and the subject of photography for the American Aviation Historical Society's quarterly Newsletter. He has also published articles in two other aviation related newsletters. His photographs of racing aircraft have appeared in several aviation books and magazines as well as in official race programs for the Reno National Championship Air Races. During his career with TRW, Birch authored or co-authored a dozen technical papers on liquid propellant rocket engine development and pulsed laser holography and photography. This work resulted in his contributing chapters to three technical books on rocket engine combustion and pollution control instrumentation.

Born and raised in Cleveland, Ohio, Birch graduated from Case Institute of Technology. He was an infantry officer with the 505th Airborne Infantry Regiment of the 82nd Airborne Division during the Korean War. He worked for Bell Aerospace Corporation in New York, before moving to the West Coast in 1965 to join TRW.